CLOSURE IN *THE CANTERBURY TALES*

CLOSURE IN *THE CANTERBURY TALES*: THE ROLE OF THE PARSON'S TALE

Edited by
DAVID RAYBIN
and
LINDA TARTE HOLLEY

2000
Studies in Medieval Culture XLI
Medieval Institute Publications

WESTERN MICHIGAN UNIVERSITY

Kalamazoo, Michigan, USA 49008-3801

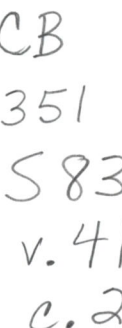

© Copyright 2000 by the Board of the Medieval Institute
Kalamazoo, Michigan, USA 49008-3801

Library of Congress Cataloging-in-Publication Data

Closure in the Canterbury tales : the role of The parson's tale / edited by David Raybin
and Linda Tarte Holley.
    p. cm. -- (Studies in medieval culture ; 41)
  Includes bibliographical references and index.
  ISBN 1-58044-011-8 (casebound : alk. paper) -- ISBN 1-58044-012-6 (paperbound :
alk. paper)
    1. Chaucer, Geoffrey, d. 1400. Parson's tale. 2. Repentance--Christianity--History of
doctrines--Middle Ages, 600-1500. 3. Christianity and literature--England--History--To
1500. 4. Chaucer, Geoffrey, d. 1400--Technique. 5. Chaucer, Geoffrey, d.
1400--Religion. 6. Repentance in literature. 7. Clergy in literature. 8. Rhetoric, Medieval.
9. Closure (Rhetoric) 10. Sin in literature. I. Raybin, David. II. Holley, Linda Tarte,
1940- III. Series.

PR1868.P43 C57 2000
821'.1--dc21

                                           99-046313

Cover design by Linda K. Judy

Printed in the United States of America

For my parents

David Raybin

For Louise Barton Holley,
who showed "the goode wey"

Linda Tarte Holley

CONTENTS

ACKNOWLEDGMENTS

This book developed out of a session on The Parson's Tale organized by Linda Tarte Holley for the International Meeting of the New Chaucer Society at Canterbury in 1994. The stimulating discussion that extended the session beyond its time frame and into the hallways led Prof. Holley and her co-presider, David Raybin, to recognize that there was substantial interest in pursuing the project further, and a call for contributions was put out. Judith Ferster, Peggy Knapp, Richard Newhauser, Daniel Ransom, and Gregory Roper responded to the editors' call, while Charlotte Gross and Siegfried Wenzel engaged to revise and expand their Canterbury presentations. Prof. Holley's Epilogue and Index, Prof. Raybin's essay and Annotated Bibliography, and the editors' Introduction complete the volume.

We wish to thank our students for their ideas, insights, tolerance, and sometimes pleasure in hearing us expound on The Parson's Tale, on closure and open-endedness, and on Chaucer's spirituality. We think especially of the young Carolinian who said, "OK, I've read The Parson's Tale; now what do I *do*?" and the young Illini who proclaimed that The Parson's Tale was the *only* part of *The Canterbury Tales* worth reading.

Prof. Raybin notes with gratitude that the Council for Faculty Research at Eastern Illinois University awarded him a Presidential Summer Research Grant to foster this project and that the EIU English Department offered generous material support.

We are much indebted to Thomas H. Seiler and the editorial staff of Medieval Institute Publications, especially Candace Porath and

Leslie La Corte, for their sharp eyes and unfailingly superb work in seeing the book through production.

For Susanna Fein and Lester Holley, for the children—Elizabeth, Carolyn, and Jonathan—who endured, accepted, and even appreciated our many hours at work on this volume, and for two grown sons, now friends, who might read this book, our abundant thanks.

INTRODUCTION

Oure sweete Lord God of hevene, that no man wole perisse but wole that
we comen alle to the knoweleche of hym and to the blisful lif that is
perdurable,/ amonesteth us by the prophete Jeremie, that seith in thys
wyse:/ "Stondeth upon the weyes, and seeth and axeth of olde pathes (that
is to seyn, of olde sentences) which is the goode wey,/ and walketh in that
wey, and ye shal fynde refresshynge for youre soules, etc." (X.75–78)[1]

The opening lines of The Parson's Tale reflect the cleric's
proposal that he close the Canterbury feast with "a myrie tale in
prose" (line 46). The tale he recounts is *myrie* in much the same way
as the *comedye* Chaucer announces towards the close of *Troilus and
Criseyde* (V.1788). Like the book that is *The Canterbury Tales*, The
Parson's Tale ends with a hopeful vision of salvation; in each case
the speaker looks forward to "the endelees blisse of hevene" (X.1076)
obtained through "the benigne grace of hym that is kyng of kynges
and preest over alle preestes" (line 1091). Harry Bailly has asked the
Parson to "knytte up wel a greet mateere" (line 28); he is to be
fructuous (line 71) and, in a term ascribed to the Parson and the narrator, *vertuous* (lines 38, 63). In joyful response, the Parson offers a
meditation on Penitence, "the tree of lyf to hem that it receyven" (line

---

[1]Except as otherwise noted, all citations from Chaucer's works in this volume are
drawn from *The Riverside Chaucer*, 3rd ed., gen. ed. Larry D. Benson (Boston,
1987). For the abbreviations, see ibid., at p. 779.

127), that pulls together many of the various images and strands of thought that occupy *The Canterbury Tales*.[2]

For all its spiritual cheerfulness, however, and all its obvious importance as a tale to conclude tales, a final voice to subsume all the other voices headed to Canterbury, a last word from a notable maker of words, the tale which Chaucer assigns to his righteous cleric seems to have inspired *sentence* and *solaas* in remarkably few critics. Studies of Chaucer's spirituality often refer to the Parson and the Parson's Prologue, but only occasional and generally cursory analysis has been given to the language of The Parson's Tale. It is a rare reader of *The Canterbury Tales* who imagines him- or herself to have taken seriously Chaucer's suggestion that a reader who does not wish to hear a particular tale should "Turne over the leef and chese another" (I.3177). Nonetheless, the critical history of The Parson's Tale (and, indeed, of much of Chaucer's overtly spiritual writing) leads one to suspect that many a modern scholar eager to consume The Miller's Tale is inclined to turn over the leaf upon encountering the Parson's.

The bibliography that closes this volume attests to the small number of critical studies that focus on the Parson's Prologue and Tale, and, of those, how many treat the Parson's Prologue only. It is further distressing that even scholars who do consider seriously the matter of The Parson's Tale almost uniformly open their accounts by apologizing for Chaucer's composition of this tale, as in this example drawn from an influential article by Lee W. Patterson:

[2]On ParsT as "meditacioun" as well as penitential handbook or treatise, see Thomas H. Bestul, "Chaucer's Parson's Tale and the Late-Medieval Tradition of Religious Meditation," *Speculum* 64 (1989): 600–19.

> For most of Chaucer's readers the *Parson's Tale* provides a conclusion to
> *The Canterbury Tales* that is at best drab, at worst a betrayal of all that is
> thought to be most Chaucerian. Even sympathetic readers find it something
> to argue away rather than interpret. . . .[3]

In asking readers to turn the pages *of* The Parson's Tale, and not to turn *from* it, this volume rejects the tradition that assumes the tale to be of questionable literary value. The studies included here span the range of Parson's Tale criticism from the textual, to the philological, to the hermeneutical. What they share is the assumption that if one is to understand the role of The Parson's Tale, one must begin by accepting the language and method by which Chaucer fashioned it. Such is the example of Chaucer's earliest editors, who judged the tale interesting and worthy of being copied with care. A tale which, more than any other of *The Canterbury Tales*, directs a reader to a life of good works, good thoughts, and happy ending deserves no less.

To read The Parson's Tale affirmatively does not require that one accept its value system as authoritative. In a movement that seems to hearken back to arguments propounded by Frederick Tupper and Ralph Baldwin,[4] some critics have assigned The Parson's Tale a privileged position because of what they see as the retrospective governing power of its orthodox spiritual message. One must be wary here. The implicit eagerness to affirm Chaucer's spiritual orthodoxy has inspired powerful critiques from Charles Muscatine and E. Talbot

---

[3]Lee W. Patterson, "The 'Parson's Tale' and the Quitting of the 'Canterbury Tales'," *Traditio* 34 (1978): 331.

[4]For Charles Muscatine ("Chaucer's Religion and the Chaucer Religion," in *Chaucer Traditions: Studies in Honour of Derek Brewer*, ed. Ruth Morse and Barry Windeatt [Cambridge, 1990], p. 251), the "ur-text" for the "revisionist" movement is Baldwin's "remarkable Johns Hopkins dissertation, *The Unity of the Canterbury Tales*, published in 150 copies in 1955."

Donaldson that might give pause even to an enthusiast's fervor. For Muscatine, "the *Parson's Tale* doesn't sound as if it belongs to the end of the *Canterbury Tales*." Echoing the manual's tendency towards encyclopedic enumeration, he labels the tale an "endless, narrow, small-minded, inveterately enumerative, circumstantially punitive list of sinful acts," and even goes on to question its textual status, postulating a dead or dying Chaucer and a text that "found its way into the *Canterbury Tales* under unusual circumstances . . . unrelated to the literary and artistic making of the rest of the work." Donaldson's evaluation is more humorous but no less devastating: "in literary terms it is ill-tempered, bad-mannered, pedantic, and joyless, and when it is used as a gloss to the other tales it distempers them, fills them with ill-humour, coats them with dust, and deprives them of joy."[5]

The witty disparagements of Muscatine and Donaldson notwithstanding, we cheerfully offer a volume of essays on The Parson's Tale. In doing so, we do not intend to affirm that the beliefs expounded in the tale are incontestably orthodox (this orthodoxy has been contested) nor that they are necessarily admirable (that has been contested, too), but, in opposition to Muscatine, we do grant the tale its textual validity. We hold, moreover, that the book that is *The Canterbury Tales* offers a complex and pervasive view of spiritual matters that cannot properly be understood without a thorough consideration of its closing entry. And finally, in direct contradiction to the view that only "specialists read it, and that under a species of compulsion,"[6] we contend that it is actually possible to *like* The Parson's Tale, that is, to enjoy the sense of play to be found in it, the clarity of its method, and the rhythm of its prose. To skeptics, we

---

[5]Muscatine, "Chaucer's Religion," pp. 256–58; E. Talbot Donaldson, *Speaking of Chaucer* (New York, 1970), p. 173.

[6]Muscatine, "Chaucer's Religion," p. 255.

answer: Read The Parson's Tale aloud and permit yourself to be caught up in the reverberations of its iterative voice.

Our pleasure, we might add, is historically grounded. As long as religion has been, religious-minded people have flocked to hear the sermons and lectures of eloquent speakers, and as long as writing has been, such people have been drawn to the *summae*, tracts, glosses, and manuals of persuasive authors. Chaucer's own contemporaries surely were interested in and derived a significant measure of satisfaction from a leading writer's serious tales of *gentilesse, moralitee,* and *hoolynesse.* Surviving manuscripts indicate that the tales of the spiritual Chaucer—the prose tales and the rhyme royal tales—were sufficiently attractive to his fifteenth-century audience to be copied independently of *The Canterbury Tales* at least as often as any of the other tales and generally more often.[7] The Parson's Tale was copied apart from the collection twice (once with The Tale of Melibee) and enjoys a general manuscript history every bit as reliable and extensive as that of the bawdy tales so popular today. Charles A. Owen, Jr., has raised especially fierce objections to The Parson's Tale's authenticity as Chaucer's intended conclusion to the tales, but even Owen acknowledges that "For a large majority of mediaeval readers the Parson's Tale and the Retraction belonged at the end of *The*

---

[7]Figures offered by Helen Cooper, *Oxford Guides to Chaucer: The Canterbury Tales* (Oxford, 1989), report two surviving manuscripts independent of *CT* for MLT, SNT, and ParsT (pp. 126, 359, 400); five for PrT and Mel (pp. 287–88, 313); six and possibly seven for ClT (p. 186). Most of the tales do not survive independently of *CT*, and no other tale survives in more than two independent manuscripts. See also the complete listing of *CT* manuscripts in Derek Pearsall, *The Canterbury Tales* (London, 1985), pp. 321–25.

Canterbury Tales."[8] One who hopes to appreciate the place of Chaucer's faith in his overall outlook must consider this tale.

As a closing section, the Parson's Prologue and Tale and Retraction complete the framing of *The Canterbury Tales* begun by the General Prologue. David Lawton, in an substantial article that considers what led poet or compiler to construct such a frame, argues that the textual history of The Parson's Tale "shows that it [wa]s conceived—either by Chaucer himself or . . . by [h]is [fifteenth-century] editors[—] . . . as a decorous gesture, a suitable ending to the Canterbury pilgrimage."[9] Lawton's careful choice of the words *decorous* and *suitable* is suggestive; these are wide-ranging terms that do not quite specify the implicit meanings that Chaucer (or his editors) would have thought appropriate, or why he would have judged them so. The common motivation behind the essays appearing in this volume is to determine the responses to the broad question of Chaucerian decorum and suitability that arise from close examination of the tale's language, construction, and textual history.

The volume opens with Siegfried Wenzel's evaluation of the current state of Parson's Tale scholarship. Wenzel notes that recent studies have tended to be more interpretative than philological, though source, genre, and rhetorical study remains important and helpful. Among interpretative studies, he sees two principal tendencies: a *perspectivist* approach, apparently waning in popularity, which reads the tale as coequal to the other tales, and an increasingly dominant *teleological* approach which sees the tale as somehow set

---

[8]Charles A. Owen, Jr., "What the Manuscripts Tell Us about the Parson's Tale," *Medium Aevum* 63 (1994): 240.

[9]David Lawton, "Chaucer's Two Ways: The Pilgrimage Frame of *The Canterbury Tales*," *Studies in the Age of Chaucer* 9 (1987): 12.

apart and expressive of Chaucer's intention. The Parson's Tale, as viewed from this latter perspective, acknowledges the themes, images, and patterns of the earlier tales, but transcends them, presenting a "higher stage in a progression . . . of tale-telling." Wenzel concludes that such an ending is appropriate to *The Canterbury Tales*, and that "Chaucer, at least from the moment he wrote the General Prologue, intended to close this poem with something like The Parson's Tale."

The two studies which follow model Wenzel's distinction of textual and interpretative scholarship, and further suggest how conclusions obtained by the two approaches may coincide. David Raybin's analytic essay treats The Parson's Tale as it reflects the spiritual Chaucer's strong interest in the practicalities of life in the world. Raybin finds in the tale's structure and imagery a dual focus on the complex minutiae of sin and the radical simplicity of penitence and grace which, he suggests, indicates that Chaucer does not abandon, at the close of *The Canterbury Tales*, the appreciation of human diversity that marks the book generally. Noting that Chaucer carefully distinguishes the various and distinctively human paths of Penitence from the single "righte wey of Jerusalem celestial" that most people cannot follow, Raybin contends that the emphasis in The Parson's Tale on the details of the present life provides spiritual grounding for the acceptance of human failing that appears throughout *The Canterbury Tales*.

Richard Newhauser's philological investigation of late-medieval vernacular penitential manuals moves from a general exploration of the genre to confront The Parson's Tale for the first time with its "closest equivalent," the Middle High German *Erchantnuzz der Sund* of Chaucer's almost exact contemporary, Heinrich of Langenstein. Newhauser's precise textual analysis shows that Langenstein's ultimate sources, like Chaucer's, are the *summae* of Raymond of Pennaforte and Guillelmus Peraldus, and that the manual which

Langenstein abstracts from these sources, like The Parson's Tale, is "bare of catechetical elaboration" and is "doctrinally focused." Recognition of this closely defined generic affiliation, Newhauser proposes, refocuses one's understanding of the self-conscious literariness of The Parson's Tale and of how this literariness figures in the tale's position as the closing element of the Canterbury collection. Rather than the simple assertion of "religious orthodoxy" that some critics have seen, The Parson's Tale "may be part of the same careful steps in developing a literary subjectivity with which the journey first began."

Daniel Ransom's essay turns the volume to an alternate kind of philology as the author of the forthcoming Variorum edition of the Parson's Prologue and Tale evaluates evidence of the early reception of The Parson's Tale. Wynkyn de Worde's printed text of The Parson's Tale (1498) was the copytext for William Thynne's 1532 edition and a major influence on all editions well into the nineteenth century, when editing from manuscripts became standard. Ransom shows that de Worde's Parson's Tale text, unlike much of his *Canterbury Tales* text, "is clearly derived from a manuscript of considerable quality" that the editor would have taken some pains to consult. This early editor's judgment that it was worth special effort to ensure that this particular text be accurate indicates that one of Chaucer's fifteenth-century readers viewed The Parson's Tale as especially important. No less notably, de Worde's editorial decision promoted an appreciation of Chaucer's presumed orthodox spirituality among centuries of readers of the *Tales*.

The next two essays examine The Parson's Tale's authorial and narrative voices. The significance of Chaucer's hypothesized association with Lollardy has much engaged students of Chaucer's religion. Peggy Knapp investigates the poet's religious conviction by examining his use of a cluster of words associated with Lollard texts. Indicating which words Chaucer does and does not use, Knapp argues that the tale's linguistic choices square with the Parson's General

Prologue portrait and thus establish the teller "as an uncompromising reformer and yet a preacher of familiar doctrine," a hybrid speaker whose words mingle orthodoxy and heterodoxy much as Chaucer himself does throughout *The Canterbury Tales*. Knapp postulates that in creating such a voice Chaucer's text functions "to neutralize the demonization of Lollardy," thus showing the poet himself to have been playing an active role in contemporary spiritual/political debate.

In contrast, Judith Ferster argues for reading the voice of The Parson's Tale not as Chaucer's but strictly as the Parson's own, with the tale offering not "Truth, but truth-according-to-the Parson." Incorporating five distinct models for the interaction of self and society, the Parson edits the language of his sources to emphasize his own ideas regarding subjects as diverse as, for example, the potential sinfulness of marital sex, the social injustices that have led to popular discontent and insurrection, and the primacy of penitence in offering a path to salvation. Ferster finds that the Parson's rhetoric reflects this one speaker's selections from among a variety of current beliefs and that his choice of subject matter is tied to his own ambivalent position vis-à-vis the pilgrimage. The narrator is "not a transparent medium of truth, but an advocate"; the tale's conclusions express not the poet's rejection of the views expressed by earlier narrators but a final example of the "idosyncracies of fiction" that distinguish each of *The Canterbury Tales*' voices.

The following two essays look directly to the role of The Parson's Tale in the closing of *The Canterbury Tales*. Gregory Roper examines the late-medieval function of penitential handbooks as aids in "construct[ing] the penitent as a particular kind of self" who through recognition of his/her sinful condition is enabled to discard it. The handbooks map penance as a process that restores wholeness to the divided self even as it restores the *Imago Dei* to the sinful human soul. Roper argues that Chaucer's practice in The Parson's Tale is similar, as the tale shows readers how to identify and transcend the "limitations and depredations of the rhetorical self," the fashioning of which the poet has explored throughout *The Canterbury Tales*. For Chaucer himself, this transcendence leads directly to the self-aware theological, psychological, and rhetorical confession that is the Retraction.

Charlotte Gross acknowledges that The Parson's Tale provides an *ending* to *The Canterbury Tales* that asks a reader to conduct "a practical scrutiny of self" distanced from the fictional world of pilgrims and tales, but she denies that this request embodies the resolution of tensions that would constitute *closure*. Drawing on Augustine's distinction between *expectatio futurorum* ("expectation of future things") and *intentio ad superiora* ("orientation . . . towards the eternal"), Gross examines Chaucer's changes and additions to "the temporal structure and texture" of his sources for The Parson's Tale. The poet's many modifications (temporal images and references, changed verb forms, the inserted discussion of sins and remedies) have the effect that, far from directing a reader toward some "transcendent reality," the "goode wey" of The Parson's Tale leads to the prosaic "here and now" of contemporary English life.

Linda Tarte Holley's epilogue "closes," as she says, "the eschatological account." Having many traditions from which he might have selected a study of the sins and their remedies, Chaucer chose for The Parson's Tale a text that lays out a "modern" rationalism lying "in that uneasy space, narrow but fruitful, where the spiritual and intellectual aspects of reason . . . gain energy from each other." The Parson's Tale offers a measuring of sin, an intellectual bookkeeper's reckoning, a reasoned moral accounting. Problems are defined, management plans are offered, the books balance, and a reader of *The Canterbury Tales* is left to wonder: "What comes next?"

The volume concludes with a full annotated bibliography of scholarly writing on The Parson's Tale. Professor Wenzel's comments in his opening essay offer his authoritative evaluations of recent scholarly contributions. The descriptive annotations in the bibliography are intended simply to facilitate further thoughtful study of this important tale. Perhaps critical appreciation of Chaucer's accomplishment can be extended to comprehend all of *The Canterbury Tales.*[10]

CHARLESTON, ILLINOIS   DAVID RAYBIN
RALEIGH, NORTH CAROLINA   LINDA TARTE HOLLEY

---

[10]As their authors often refer to works not included in the annotated bibliography, the citations in each individual essay are given in full in the notes to that essay. While references to ParsT criticism conform to those in the bibliography, they are not keyed to the bibliography.

THE PARSON'S TALE IN CURRENT LITERARY STUDIES

SIEGFRIED WENZEL

As in earlier years, interest in The Parson's Tale during the last decade has been primarily critical and interpretative rather than textual or philological. To be sure, the question of the tale's authenticity continues to occupy a small number of scholars who attempt to explain the enormous differences found in the surviving manuscripts with respect to the inclusion and order of the tales. But whether one holds that the order of the tales in the earliest manuscripts was established by the poet himself, or, conversely, was worked out by different literary executors and scribes who gained possession of Chaucer's work after his death, there is little room for questioning that the text now called "The Parson's Tale" was written by Chaucer; and since it appears in the surviving manuscripts from the very beginning on, any attempt to deny that Chaucer intended it for his *Canterbury Tales* and for the final position it occupies there will have to rest on arguments that are not strictly textual. Thus, Charles Owen continues to defend his view that the ending as we have it is not Chaucer's because it goes against the announced plan of a journey to Canterbury and a return to London, and he does so by a detailed study of the manuscript tradition through the fifteenth century.[1] The other

---

[1] Charles A. Owen, Jr., "Pre-1450 Manuscripts of the *Canterbury Tales*: Relationships and Significance," *Chaucer Review* 23 (1988): 1–29, 95–116; *The Manuscripts of the Canterbury Tales* (Cambridge, 1991).

major study of the manuscript tradition published in this decade courteously acknowledges this view as possible but then sets it aside as not pertinent to a strictly textual analysis of the manuscript tradition.[2]

Yet the texture of the tale, and by implication Chaucer's compositional work and intention for it, continue to pose questions that remain unaddressed. After a Latin source text for the sections on the virtues had been found and led to identifying two related Latin treatises (rather than Peraldus) as sources for the sections on the vices, it became logical to ask whether Chaucer's section on penitence might not also derive from a shorter treatise than Pennaforte's *Summa* that co-existed with these treatises on the vices and virtues in a single manuscript or collection of pastoral works, or perhaps even formed with them a single work on which the poet relied for the entire tale. Large treatises on penitence and on the vices and virtues were indeed combined several times in the late fourteenth and early fifteenth centuries.[3] That such a combination into a single and shorter handbook may have existed and may have been known to Chaucer remains an intriguing possibility, and a chance discovery of such a text cannot be ruled out. Another question that remains open concerns the language of Chaucer's source text. Some scholars remain convinced that Chaucer's source for The Parson's Tale was in

---

[2]Norman F. Blake, *The Textual Tradition of the Canterbury Tales* (London, 1985).

[3]William C. McDonald, "The Nobility of Soul: Uncharted Echoes of the Peraldean Tradition in Late Medieval German Literature," *Deutsche Vierteljahrsschrift für Literaturwissenschaft und Geistesgeschichte* 60 (1986): 543–71; Siegfried Wenzel, "The Continuing Life of William Peraldus's *Summa Vitiorum*," in *Ad Litteram: Authoritative Texts and Their Medieval Readers*, ed. Mark D. Jordan and Kent Emery, Jr. (Notre Dame, Ind., 1992), p. 139.

French, not Latin.[4] This issue could, I think, be reasonably settled even without further source hunting by a sensitive and comparative syntactic and semantic analysis of late fourteenth-century translations of religious texts from Latin and French into Middle English.

Besides its authenticity and sources, The Parson's Tale continues to invite a modest amount of interest in its genre. By now, heavy argumentation from both pens and word processors should convince Chaucerians that technically The Parson's Tale is a treatise or manual, not a sermon, even if the fictional setting in which it is delivered is that of an oral discourse on a religious subject before a larger audience committed to hearing it out. Still, it might pay to examine Chaucer's, or the Parson's, own generic term *meditacioun* more closely, as Thomas Bestul has done in what I consider a fresh contribution to the genre question.[5] His attempt to show that formal aspects of The Parson's Tale agree with late-medieval meditations may not convince everyone that the tale in fact is generically a meditation; but his discussion of medieval reflections on the act of meditating, backed by a fascinating definition given by Richard of St. Victor, allows him to derive further insights into the function of the tale as *meditatio* that place his study alongside the most thoughtful critical essays on the tale's function and give it an importance that both philologists and critics will have to ponder.

Examination of rhetorical and stylistic aspects of the tale also appears in some other studies, though much of what these say about the tale's style does not break new ground. That Chaucer makes his Parson look like a Lollard in the General Prologue, and further makes him speak like one in the link after The Man of Law's Tale, will not

---

[4]For example, John Norton-Smith, *Geoffrey Chaucer* (London, 1974), p. 155.

[5]Thomas H. Bestul, "Chaucer's Parson's Tale and the Late-Medieval Tradition of Religious Meditation," *Speculum* 64 (1989): 600–19.

raise any eyebrows, and we may take it as fairly well established that, while the fictional Parson could hardly be a Lollard, Chaucer apparently uses him to express his sympathy with the moral concerns of this movement.[6] That his tale itself "shares some notable congruences with Lollard discourse,"[7] however, is questionable since the same congruences exist between the tale and orthodox treatises and sermons, whereas terms that have been identified as characteristic of the Lollard vocabulary are notably absent from the tale.[8] More thought-provoking is the argument that on stylistic grounds the tale seems to address two different audiences—parish priests as well as their actual congregations.[9] This view, however, seems to lose some force when one realizes that the same mixture can be found in Chaucer's sources, especially *Quoniam*.[10] To further derive socio-historical inferences from such stylistic features remains a questionable enterprise, as scholars who have explored this possibility themselves

---

[6] Anne Hudson, *The Premature Reformation: Wycliffite Texts and Lollard History* (Oxford, 1988), pp. 391–92.

[7] Peggy Knapp, *Chaucer and the Social Contest* (New York, 1990), p. 92.

[8] Anne Hudson, "A Lollard Set Vocabulary?" in *"So meny people longages and tonges": Philological Essays in Scots and Mediaeval English Presented to Angus McIntosh*, ed. Michael Benskin and M. L. Samuels (Edinburgh, 1981), pp. 15–30, repr. in Anne Hudson, *Lollards and Their Books* (London, 1985), pp. 165–80; Christina von Nolcken, "A 'Certain Sameness' and Our Response to It in English Wycliffite Texts," in *Literature and Religion in the Later Middle Ages: Philological Studies in Honor of Siegfried Wenzel*, ed. Richard G. Newhauser and John A. Alford (Binghamton, N.Y., 1995), pp. 191–207.

[9] Beryl Rowland, "Sermon and Penitential in *The Parson's Tale* and Their Effect on Style," *Florilegium* 9 (1987): 125–45.

[10] See Wenzel, "The Continuing Life," pp. 150–51.

come to admit;[11] and a similar focus on Chaucer's style from a gender-oriented base leads to results that can hardly be said to make more than fairly obvious comments about the tale.[12]

Another article that deals with the Parson's rhetoric leads us from textual studies to attempts at critical interpretation. Laurie Finke focuses on the "contrasting attitudes towards language" that Chaucer's Parson and the Host presumably have, and then goes on to speak of the "dialectic of solemnity and play that Chaucer establishes in the *General Prologue* and reiterates throughout the *Tales*."[13] *Dialectic, disjunction, dichotomy*, or, as the most recent paper of this kind has it, "the disturbing jolt . . . disruption and disappointment,"[14] are all terms that highlight the malaise Chaucer's readers experience at the difference between The Parson's Tale and the rest of the work. To explain the difference, to find a way that would place The Parson's Tale in a meaningful relation to *The Canterbury Tales* as a whole, has been a major task of Chaucer criticism over the last century, and all indications are that it will remain so. In the attempt to relate The Parson's Tale to the other tales and the pilgrimage framework and to reconcile its obvious differences in tone, style, and subject matter, the reader has, I think, two basic options: one is to read The Parson's Tale as one among twenty-four tales in which Chaucer has a wide variety of characters tell tales that, to say the least, fit their narrators'

---

[11]See Knapp, *Chaucer and the Social Contest*, p. 94.

[12]Jane Cowgill, "Patterns of Feminine and Masculine Persuasion in the *Melibee* and the *Parson's Tale*," in *Chaucer's Religious Tales*, ed. C. David Benson and Elizabeth Robertson (Cambridge, 1990), pp. 171–83.

[13]Laurie A. Finke, "'To Knytte Up Al this Feeste': The Parson's Rhetoric and the Ending of the *Canterbury Tales*," *Leeds Studies in English*, n.s., 15 (1984): 97.

[14]Phyllis Portnoy, "Beyond the Gothic Cathedral: Post-Modern Reflections on the *Canterbury Tales*," *Chaucer Review* 28 (1994): 280.

professions and personal characteristics, and may do so in an ironic vein; the other is to read The Parson's Tale as in some fashion set apart. I will call the former view *perspectivist* and the latter *teleological*, that is, having an orientation toward a goal.

The perspectivist view continues to be held by a number of critics,[15] but by and large it seems to have lost the popularity it once had and has given way to readings that are willing to privilege The Parson's Tale in some fashion. These readings also shift their critical focus from what the fictional Parson says to what Chaucer the poet is doing here. The latter embraces two closely related aspects of literary technique: one is the act of closure, the other a possible movement or progression from the General Prologue and the individual tales to The Parson's Tale and the Retraction. That The Parson's Tale is intended to close the work we call *The Canterbury Tales* hardly needs comment, since its prologue says so several times. That it carries out its intention by proposing values that contrast sharply with what nearly every reader has experienced as the appealing world of the preceding tales, full of artistic delight and insight into the human condition, is similarly obvious. While critics who see in this change a positive turn towards looking at life's business from a higher perspective still use terms that hold predominantly negative connotations—such as claiming that in this "Not-a-Tale" Chaucer "dismantle[s]," "cancels out," "destroys," "rejects," or "abandons" what he had constructed so far—they yet accept this turn as meaningful and designed, whose germs can be found in the work from its very opening lines.[16] The flat assertion that "the

---

[15]Finke, "'To Knytte Up Al this Feeste'"; Helen Cooper, *The Structure of the Canterbury Tales* (Athens, Ga., 1984), passim; Jill Mann, *Geoffrey Chaucer* (Atlantic Highlands, N.J., 1991), p. 121.

[16]Derek Pearsall, "Chaucer's Religious Tales: A Question of Genre," in *Chaucer's Religious Tales,* ed. Benson and Robertson, p. 16; James Dean, "Dismantling the

Parson's Tale . . . has often been seen as an appropriate conclusion to the Canterbury collection"[17] now yields to more probing efforts to ask: appropriate—how?

In answer, these critics do not simply point to verbal echoes from the tales in The Parson's Tale (surveyed by Patterson[18]); much less do they read the tales and the fictional pilgrims as exempla or types of the vices that are defined and condemned by the Parson. Instead, they find that, through specific themes, images, structural patterns—and verbal echoes, too—*The Canterbury Tales*, from the General Prologue on and through its "large, distributed middle," expresses wider concerns that are eventually transcended in The Parson's Tale. Traugott Lawler, for instance, sees a movement from multiciplicity in many aspects to oneness,[19] and two other book-length studies, while following a narrower historicist approach and tracing in *The Canterbury Tales* a concern with social organization, come to very

---

Canterbury Book," *PMLA* 100 (1985): 746–62; Lee W. Patterson, "The 'Parson's Tale' and the Quitting of the 'Canterbury Tales'," *Traditio* 34 (1978): 379, and *Chaucer and the Subject of History* (Madison, 1991), pp. 20, 246; Patterson, "The 'Parson's Tale'," p. 376; Patterson, *Chaucer*, pp. 316–17, and Stephen Knight, "Chaucer's Religious Canterbury Tales," in *Medieval English Religious and Ethical Literature: Essays in Honour of G. H. Russell*, ed. Gregory Kratzmann and James Simpson (Cambridge, 1986), p. 158; Robert M. Jordan, *Chaucer's Poetics and the Modern Reader* (Berkeley, 1987), p. 164.

[17] C. David Benson, *Chaucer's Drama of Style: Poetic Variety and Contrast in the Canterbury Tales* (Chapel Hill, 1986), p. 38.

[18] Patterson, "The 'Parson's Tale'."

[19] Traugott Lawler, *The One and the Many in the Canterbury Tales* (Hamden, Conn., 1980). The (Aristotelian) notion of the "distributed middle" underlies Paul G. Ruggiers, *The Art of "The Canterbury Tales"* (Madison, 1965), passim.

similar conclusions.[20] Somewhat differently, Paul Taylor notices the occurrence of nature images at the beginning of the General Prologue and of The Parson's Tale and traces the theme of speech through the tales, whereby he finds a movement from emptiness to fulfillment.[21] David Lawton similarly discusses the thematic conflict between poverty/discretion/virtue on one hand and avarice/easy speech/vice on the other implicit in the portrayal of several pilgrims in the General Prologue and in their tales, a conflict that at last is brought into the open by The Parson's Tale.[22] The increasing concern with speech and the value of fiction in some of the tales that lead up to The Parson's Tale (primarily The Manciple's Tale but also The Nun's Priest's Tale and, earlier, The Pardoner's Tale) has been observed before. But its possible function of linking The Parson's Tale thematically to other concerns of the poet that emerge gradually as the existing tales progress, at least in the Ellesmere order, is now receiving fuller attention.[23] How far these studies themselves transcend the perspectivist reading of earlier critics can perhaps best be measured by the fact that the essays I have mentioned are willing to attribute this movement not to the fictional Parson but to the poet's own intention and insight; even a Marxist critic such as Stephen Knight finds in *The Canterbury Tales* a succession of sequences through which Chaucer

---

[20]Paul A. Olson, *The* Canterbury Tales *and the Good Society* (Princeton, 1986); Paul Strohm, *Social Chaucer* (Cambridge, Mass., 1989).

[21]Paul Beekman Taylor, "The Parson's Amyable Tongue," *English Studies* 64 (1983): 401–09.

[22]David Lawton, "Chaucer's Two Ways: The Pilgrimage Frame of *The Canterbury Tales*," *Studies in the Age of Chaucer* 9 (1987): 3–40.

[23]Most recently in a monograph devoted to the medieval "sins of the tongue" or deviant speech: Edwin D. Craun, *Lies, Slander, and Obscenity in Medieval English Narrative: Pastoral Rhetoric and the Deviant Speaker* (Cambridge, 1997), chap. 6.

eventually, in The Parson's Tale, returns to religious and social orthodoxy—a view of Chaucer's position or mentality that also seems to emerge from Lee Patterson's recent study.[24]

The central notion that underlies these critical readings—that The Parson's Tale forms a different and higher stage in a progression or forward movement of tale-telling—naturally has to make assumptions that return us to the textual matters I discussed earlier, specifically the order of the tales in the various manuscripts and the question of whether any of the existing orders can be ascribed to Chaucer himself. Lawton faces this objection squarely. In an analysis which I find remarkably sensible as well as comprehensive (because it includes a number of issues which contemporary writers on The Parson's Tale would agree must be faced, such as the pilgrimage theme and the Wycliffite tones), he shrewdly assumes that *The Canterbury Tales* might have been ordered and put together by an editor and then asks what this person would have found in Chaucer's genuine work, primarily the General Prologue and the Parson's Prologue, that could have determined him to put The Parson's Tale where it is and in the form we have it. Lawton finds this to be the medieval literary practice of deferment and the thematic conflict implicit in several portraits and tales. This critical strategy defuses the power the textual problem of tale order has to explode any progressive reading, and it puts its finger on what many readers have always felt: that The Parson's Tale can indeed be read as the fulfillment of things hinted at in the General Prologue. With this much affirmed, Lawton then concludes that the existing structure of *The Canterbury Tales* might just as well be accepted as intended by Chaucer himself.

This view, that Chaucer, at least from the moment he wrote the General Prologue, intended to close this poem with something like

---

[24]Knight, "Chaucer's Religious Canterbury Tales"; Patterson, *Chaucer*.

The Parson's Tale, will of course not please all readers. Quite apart from those who are unwilling to look at him as anything other than a cherished precursor of modern or post-modern sensibilities, some readers will find it stupid to think that such an intelligent, sensitive, sympathetic artist as Chaucer would "labor over fool's gold"[25] and create characters and tales full of life, realism, and pleasing artistry, only to revoke them at the end. One could reply to this objection that perhaps, as he did in *Troilus*, Chaucer deliberately involves his readers (and even more his Narrator, of course) emotionally in the storytelling and in the world he creates in the tales, but that at the end of the poem he as deliberately leads them to a higher plane and thus effects in them a catharsis of mind and will. Fool's gold is what looks like gold in the eyes of fools, and I would maintain that, for alert medieval readers or listeners, the poet embedded enough hints in the early parts of the work to remind them that there is a higher reality behind the phenomena that strike our senses. Isn't this artistic process and structural progression, which plays with the reader's sense of appearance and reality, just like what happens in *Paradise Lost*, where Satan with his gigantic sense of freedom and self-determination eventually turns into a snake with ashes in his mouth—even if some readers may continue to feel that he is the real hero of the poem?

---

[25]John M. Hill, *Chaucerian Belief: The Poetics of Reverence and Delight* (New Haven, Conn., 1991), p. 160 n. 5.

"Manye been the weyes": The Flower, Its Roots, and the Ending of *The Canterbury Tales*

David Raybin

The General Prologue of *The Canterbury Tales* opens with one of Chaucer's most memorable images, a desiccated plant that flowers in the April rain:

> Whan that Aprill with his shoures soote
> The droghte of March hath perced to the roote,
> And bathed every veyne in swich licour
> Of which vertu engendred is the flour. . . . (I.1–4)

What readers normally—and quite properly—see in the image are the sweet showers of line one and the flowering plant of line four, its stalk rising from the ground to support the single flower that is a favorite symbol of beauty, faith, perfection of all kinds, and, at the opposing extreme, the transience of all such earthly excellence. The implied metaphor extends smoothly into visions of springtime renewal, paschal rebirth, nascent love, wondrous adventure. As central to the image as the rain and flower, though, are the *droghte* and *roote* of line two, so penetrated by the fragrant showers of April that "every veyne" now has been watered. The stress in this metaphor is on the strength that lies in multiplicity.[1] A myriad of tiny veins, innumerable individually insignificant fibers rendered collectively fecund when all are bathed in the life-giving springtime "licour," is the necessary source for the engendering of the admirable single flower.

The description of pilgrimage which closes the famous opening sentence mirrors the image of the vibrant flower and its once-stricken roots:

> Thanne longen folk to goon on pilgrimages,
> And palmeres for to seken straunge strondes,
> To ferne halwes, kowthe in sondry londes;
> And specially from every shires ende
> Of Engelond to Caunterbury they wende,
> The hooly blisful martir for to seke,
> That hem hath holpen whan that they were seeke. (lines 12–18)

The spiritual flower, too, is single, even as its roots, stretching across England as an alternative to "straunge strondes" and "ferne halwes," are many. The many pilgrimages, the many palmers, the many faraway shrines and "sondry londes," the multiplicity of "every shires ende / Of Engelond," join to lead to the single "hooly blisful martir"

---

[1]Traugott Lawler, *The One and the Many in the Canterbury Tales* (Hamden, Conn., 1980), also discusses what he calls "the one and the many in *The Canterbury Tales*," but with an emphasis on the tales' ultimate singularity of vision at odds with Chaucer's intense interest in the varieties of experience. With Robert M. Jordan, *Chaucer's Poetics and the Modern Reader* (Berkeley, 1987), p. 170, I believe that "[t]he heterogeneity of the *Canterbury Tales* cannot be persuasively interpreted away or subsumed by a theory of unity, for the *Tales* expresses Chaucer's fascination with multiplicity, his lifelong devotion to—or continuing experimentation with—the diverse modes of human discourse." It is the contention of this essay that ParsT offers an ending to *CT* that focuses attention on the poet's "fascination with multiplicity."

of Canterbury, who had helped each of the suddenly emergent springtime travelers in a sadder time of sickness.

To this reader of Chaucer's spirituality, these memorable images suggest that the religiosity of *The Canterbury Tales* is not one that presents a simple single ideal for human behavior. The images in the opening sentence are of multiple roots needed to produce a new flower, a host of small birds required to form a new melody, a collection of far-wandering pilgrims joined to acknowledge one martyr. Moreover, the sense which I see offered here of an inclusive, hence tolerant, spirituality is supported when one looks to the structure and imagery of the more didactic closing Canterbury tale that is the subject of the present essay. Not only do the broadly encyclopedic scope and more narrow penitential focus of The Parson's Tale highlight the juxtaposition of myriad human behaviors and a common spiritual goal, but modified versions of the roots-flower and pilgrimage images appear in the opening passages of the tale, joining with the opening of the General Prologue to provide a frame of imagery within which Chaucer's book may be read.[2] As the roots-flower and pilgrimage metaphors are developed in The Parson's Tale, they are used to articulate an inclusive spiritual behavioral model that champions variety.

Noting the human propensity to fall into a variety of sins, Chaucer counters these failings with a rather typical fourteenth-century vision of "Penitence, that may be likned unto a tree" (X.112):[3]

---

[2]See Linda Georgianna, "Love So Dearly Bought: The Terms of Redemption in *The Canterbury Tales*," *Studies in the Age of Chaucer* 12 (1990): 114; also Paul Beekman Taylor, "The Parson's Amyable Tongue," *English Studies* 64 (1983): 401.

[3]The extended metaphor is not in Chaucer's principle source, Pennaforte; see Siegfried Wenzel, "Notes on the *Parson's Tale*," *Chaucer Review* 16 (1982): 240–43; and Wenzel's notes to lines 112–27 in *The Riverside Chaucer*, p. 957.

> The roote of this tree is Contricioun, that hideth hym in the herte of hym
> that is verray repentaunt, right as the roote of a tree hydeth hym in the
> erthe./ Of the roote of Contricioun spryngeth a stalke that bereth braunches
> and leves of Confessioun, and fruyt of Satisfaccioun. (lines 113–14)

Like the illnesses and prayers that motivate the individual Canterbury
pilgrims, like a plant's tiny veins covered and protected by the earth, the
root of contrition is conglomerate (the tale will shortly show it to be
classifiable under four heavily subdivided principal understandings) and
is nurtured in a secret and private place, "hyd in the herte of man" (line
115). Nourished by the water of tears, this root supports the stalk,
spreading branches, and countless leaves that parallel the many possible
acts of confession (to be discussed in the tale in an extended examination
of the Seven Deadly Sins and their remedies) and are comparable also,
as has been noted frequently, to the pilgrims' many stories. Finally, atop
the plant sits the most admirable fruit of satisfaction (subject of the tale's
brief concluding section), the redolent springtime flower, pious image of
devotion, prayer, bodily pain, and the perfection they produce, image
also of the shrine which is the pilgrims' goal.

Let us reflect for a moment on Chaucer's presentation of that
flower. In the Middle Ages, perfection of all kinds might be portrayed
in the image of the flower, and most particularly the perfection of pilgrimage: as Donald Howard notes, "A pilgrimage, though a linear
journey, was made by many pilgrims to a central shrine; all roads led
to Jerusalem in a wheel-like pattern."[4] The wheel image, however,
common as it was, does not conform exactly to Chaucer's evocation of
pilgrims traveling to suburban London by way of many paths/roots,
then funneling into the single road/stalk on which they join together for
a communal journey to the shrine/flower at Canterbury. Chaucer's
framing image for pilgrimage stresses not the untainted flower alone—

---

[4]Donald R. Howard, *The Idea of the Canterbury Tales* (Berkeley, 1976), p. 203.

the hub at the center of a wheel—but the entire plant of Penitence, a plant which in its organic growth toward perfection stands as "the tree of lyf to hem that it receyven" (line 127). It is thus more accurate to Chaucer's portrayal to see in the extended metaphor of pilgrimage not a transcendent circle of godly/angelic/saintly perfection existing outside of earthly time and space, but something of a fan leading into a more linear (albeit, as the morally various tales suggest, braided, twisted, and winding) human movement toward such perfection, yet itself remaining in the world. This vision of perfection, as the present discussion will show, acknowledges the human condition of wayward sinfulness;[5] that is to say, to return to the terms of the collection's opening metaphor, its achievement requires that a preexistent drought be broken by rain. As in many of Chaucer's texts, the authorial focus is on process, on movement from an unsatisfactory initial condition toward a vaguely defined something better, with a relative disregard for any sense of conclusion or closure.[6]

Anticipating the reintroduction of the roots-flower image, the opening lines of The Parson's Tale mirror the pilgrimage image in just such terms, glossing Jeremiah 6.16 to indicate a focus as much on paths as on destination:[7]

---

[5]See Lee W. Patterson, "The 'Parson's Tale' and the Quitting of the 'Canterbury Tales'," *Traditio* 34 (1978): 342.

[6]See Karla Taylor, *Chaucer Reads "The Divine Comedy"* (Stanford, 1989), pp. 2–3, for a similar view, comparing ParsT and Dante.

[7]The passage and initial gloss are not in Chaucer's principal source, Pennaforte; see Wenzel's introductory note in *The Riverside Chaucer*, p. 956. On the originality in Chaucer's use of this passage, see Judson Boyce Allen, "The Old Way and the Parson's Way: An Ironic Reading of the Parson's Tale," *Journal of Medieval and Renaissance Studies* 3 (1973): 256–59; Chauncey Wood, "Artistic Intention and Chaucer's Uses of Scriptural Allusion," in *Chaucer and Scriptural Tradition*, ed. David Lyle Jeffrey (Ottawa, 1984), p. 36.

> Manye been the weyes espirituels that leden folk to oure Lord Jhesu Crist
> and to the regne of glorie./ Of whiche weyes ther is a ful noble wey and a
> ful covenable, which may nat fayle to man ne to womman that thurgh
> synne hath mysgoon fro the righte wey of Jerusalem celestial;/ and this wey
> is cleped Penitence. . . . (lines 79–81)

Since the publication in 1955 of Ralph Baldwin's influential study of
the "unity" of the Canterbury book, interpreters commonly have
emphasized the single spiritual path they see suggested by The
Parson's Tale's lengthy discussion of penitence as it relates to the
Seven Deadly Sins.[8] This scholarly emphasis on what has been
perceived as a single path and its goal ought not obscure the poet's
own assertion that "Manye been the weyes espirituels that leden folk
to oure Lord Jhesu Crist." Chaucer does not say here that the way of
penitence is a better path; he calls the path "ful noble" and "ful
covenable," yes, but not better and certainly not "righte."[9] To the contrary, penitence, in Chaucer's terms, is a second-best solution, or,
more accurately, as the tale's minute exploration of the many aspects
of penitence will most abundantly show, a collection of second-best
solutions, offering a remedial course for all those who "thurgh synne
hath mysgoon fro the righte wey."[10]

Indeed, like the pilgrims modeled in the General Prologue, penitents travel not one common road, but many distinct ones. Howard
notes that the "complexities of this flower or 'rose' design are

---

[8]Ralph Baldwin, *The Unity of the Canterbury Tales*, Anglistica, vol. 5 (Copenhagen,
1955), esp. pp. 95–105.

[9]Penitence has been called the "righte wey" by Rodney Delasanta, "Penance and
Poetry in the *Canterbury Tales*," *PMLA* 93 (1978): 241; and Trevor Whittock,
A Reading of the Canterbury Tales (Cambridge, 1968), p. 286.

[10]See Allen, "The Old Way," p. 267.

infinite."[11] This infinite complexity, the many and various shapes which transform a point into an expansive circle or fan, is crucial to understanding the open-ended vision of human need and capacity that informs *The Canterbury Tales* generally and is pointed to directly in its ending preacher's tale. It is instructive in this regard that, whereas the discussion of contrition in the first major section of The Parson's Tale is substantive and dense (expanded from Chaucer's apparent source), and the exploration of sins and their remedies in the middle of the tale is still longer and more intricate (apparently involving an intertwining of sources), Chaucer's examination of satisfaction in the tale's final major section is short and pointedly simple, following closely a single source. The resultant overwhelmingly dispropor-tionate focusing on root and especially stalk and branches at the expense of flower mirrors the poet's strategy in the Parson's Prologue of hinting that the pilgrims have approached Canterbury (or is it London?[12]) but choosing not to go on to offer any description of or even direct allusion to the shrine that is the object of their pilgrimage. A goal is acknowledged but barely discussed, thereby allowing the process involved in journeying toward the goal—the movement through life that has been the collective concern of the earlier Canter-bury tales and is now to be the subject of The Parson's Tale—to receive largely undivided attention.

A self-consciously philosophical passage in The Knight's Tale furnishes something of a rationale for Chaucer's emphasis on the in-dividualized problematics of present action, clarifying the distinction between the straight and closed "righte wey of Jerusalem celestial"

---

[11]Howard, *The Idea*, p. 202.

[12]See Charles A. Owen, Jr., *Pilgrimage and Storytelling in the Canterbury Tales: The Dialectic of "Earnest" and "Game"* (Norman, Okla., 1977); John Matthews Manly, "Tales of the Homeward Journey," *Studies in Philology* 28 (1931): 613–17.

that The Parson's Tale sees as having been abandoned and the more winding and open "ful covenable" paths of penitence that the tale points to as offering "ful noble" remediation. Arcite is in despair. He has been freed from prison and restored to wealth and status but has been banished from Athens and, as he imagines, has lost Emelye, whom he may not see, to Palamon. In his sorrow Arcite realizes that, victimized by his humanity, he has mistaken the way of the world:

> We witen nat what thing we preyen heere;
> We faren as he that dronke is as a mous.
> A dronke man woot wel he hath an hous,
> But he noot which the righte wey is thider,
> And to a dronke man the wey is slider.
> And certes, in this world so faren we;
> We seken faste after felicitee,
> But we goon wrong ful often, trewely.
> Thus may we seyen alle. . . . (I.1260–68)

Arcite's understanding conforms with the Parson's. There is a "righte wey," but that path is hard to find. In fact, people cannot find it. One notes a telling insistence on the first-person plural: "we" appears seven times in these lines. In our pursuit of perfection, in our pilgrimage through the world, the best we can do is follow what The Parson's Tale calls the "ful noble wey" of penitence, a path which, because it involves sin, is both difficult and crooked, in Egeus's terms, "a thurghfare ful of wo" (line 2847). Our path is the "slider" path of the drunken man once the drunken Miller interrupts the Host to insist—hierarchies notwithstanding—that he and not the Monk will respond to The Knight's Tale.

As this metaphorical slipperiness implies, a life lived within the world necessarily encompasses open-endedness, variety, diverse ways of approaching the world. A single path, however winding, would be the "righte wey," Christ's path, perhaps the extraworldly journey of a saint's life but certainly not that of an ordinary human striving to be virtuous. To recognize that a path is not "righte," to acknowledge its divergence, is to assert its characteristically human uniqueness, and indeed its interest as a subject for poetic study. To paraphrase Tolstoy, all straight paths are alike; each crooked path is crooked in its own way. In the world Chaucer presents, diversity— and thus sin and confusion—is an essential, if not always pleasant, part of the human experience.

Indeed, a key message of The Parson's Tale is that penitence offers "ful noble" paths, appropriate paths, precisely because it adapts so well to the abundant variety of sinful behaviors that characterizes human experience. Over and over again, The Parson's Tale uses the word *diverse* in suggesting the multitude of options by which a person may commit just one of a subcategory of one of the Seven Deadly Sins, yet these negative references to variety do not indicate that Chaucer considers the human condition beyond help. "For certes," The Parson's Tale insists,[13] "after the diverse [disordinaunces] of oure wikkednesses was the passioun of Jhesu Crist ordeyned in diverse thynges" (X.275). Sins are not without recourse. Perhaps Chaucer repeats the negative references to get at the Boethian notion that misfortune, in all its open-ended variety, serves a necessary role in enabling people to understand the full range of the good (an idea I will pursue below). What is essential as regards redemption, what provides many alternatives to the "righte wey" and as penitence a most noble and proper alternative, is that penitential remediation is founded in the universality of the Passion. Readers who confront The Parson's Tale empathetically will remark many

---

[13]The passage is without parallel in Pennaforte; see Thomas H. Bestul, "Chaucer's Parson's Tale and the Late-Medieval Tradition of Religious Meditation," *Speculum* 64 (1989): 607.

references to their own deleterious character and behavior but will note also that they are encouraged to respond to these failings in the forgiving context established in the tale's opening line: "Oure sweete Lord God of hevene" wishes "that no man wole perisse but wole that we comen alle to the knoweleche of hym and to the blisful lif that is perdurable . . ." (line 75). It is so that this hope may be achieved that it has been granted that "Manye been the weyes espirituels that leden folk to oure Lord Jhesu Crist" (line 79).

At the end of the Parson's Prologue the general narrator reports the company's inclination "To enden in som vertuous sentence" (line 63) and closes the poetry of *The Canterbury Tales* with the Host's articulation of the shared desire:[14]

> Beth fructuous, and that in litel space,
> And to do wel God sende yow his grace! (lines 71–72)

The Host's words, expressing the view of "us alle" (line 67), mix admonition and request, suggesting a correspondence between the grace the Parson will receive and the grace God may offer through his words. They also link the poet's readers (complicit in our shared desire for the closure implied in the Host's demand that the Parson "knytte up wel a greet mateere" [line 28] and the Parson's promise "To knytte up al this feeste and make an ende" [line 47]) with the Host's and Parson's fellow travelers. The stress imposed on the second-person "yow" by its strong position in *The Canterbury Tales*' final line of verse is powerful and inclusive, so that while the Host's direct address is to the Parson, asking that his speech be short and

---

[14]Though Manly's rearrangement has been adopted by almost all subsequent editors, these are the prologue's final lines in all known manuscripts. See Emerson Brown, Jr., "The Poet's Last Words: Text and Meaning at the End of the *Parson's Pro-logue*," *Chaucer Review* 10 (1976): 236–42.

sweet, the spiritual sense underlying the message applies to all who hear it. After a long journey and much tale-telling, little time remains. If the pilgrimage on which we have embarked (be it the collective pilgrimage of *The Canterbury Tales* or the self-defined pilgrimages of our individual lives) is to be profitable, if the pilgrims, readers included, are, like the Parson, "to do wel," then we are enjoined to turn our attention to moral issues quickly, insofar as divine grace shall allow.

Here again, the call to be fructuous predicated on divine acceptance of human fallibility incorporates not just recognition or tolerance but also an endorsement of the variousness of human behavior and experience. Rejecting "fables and swich wrecchednesse" (line 34), the principal matter of the pilgrimage and book up until this point, the Parson consents—should Jesus "for his grace" grant him the capacity—to "shewe" us the "wey" of the pilgrimage to the celestial Jerusalem (lines 48–51) precisely because, in his terms, the pilgrims are not presently on that route, precisely because we need to be shown the proper path. So framed, the appeal for virtuous behavior predicates that we/the pilgrims have not heretofore been virtuous, indeed that without God's assistance we/the pilgrims are unable to be virtuous. The spiritual and literary paradoxes cry out. One's belief in the divine offering of grace indicates not simply the deity's response to the human need for grace but also one's own acceptance of that need.[15] The Parson's Tale offers not only the moral preacher's response to the wayward tales that have come before but

---

[15]See Paul G. Ruggiers, "Serious Chaucer: The *Tale of Melibeus* and the Parson's Tale," in *Chaucerian Problems and Perspectives: Essays Presented to Paul E. Beichner, C.S.C.*, ed. Edward Vasta, Zacharias P. Thundy, and Theodore M. Hesburgh (Notre Dame, Ind., 1979), p. 92.

also the poet's own acceptance of those tales.[16] Grace would have no place in the striving for perfection were human behavior naturally proper. The Parson's Tale would have no place in the world of poetic fiction were it not preceded by *The Canterbury Tales*' other less "noble" voices.

In sum, The Parson's Tale opens in the context of an acceptance of human limitation and variety that is strikingly reminiscent of the acknowledgment of diverse individual sickness which closes the opening sentence of the General Prologue, therein completing the circle of the tales' benevolent imagery of grace and understanding: first quoting, translating, and glossing Jeremiah, then evoking the tree of Penitence, the tale reminds us that the essential meaning in our wildly variant lives (the subject and body of the spiritual matter that is to follow) is to be found in the desiccated root and branches of March as well as in the flourishing flower of April. Removed from its position as the concluding Canterbury tale, The Parson's Tale undoubtedly would be taken (and ignored) by most readers of Chaucer simply as the poet's unpoetic translation/edition of a standard handbook on penitence, much as his *Treatise on the Astrolabe* has been received. It is the contention of this essay that the Parson's Prologue and the opening and closing sections of The Parson's Tale, recalling the opening lines of the General Prologue and reflecting a spiritual ideology that permeates the entire *Canterbury Tales*, ask that the tale be read in a different light, as a penitential handbook to be sure, but a handbook for those who have enjoyed the life and vitality of the predominantly worldly tales and are curious as to how that vision of the human condition might be integrated into an overtly

---

[16]As Baldwin puts it, Chaucer "recognizes all too clearly the humanity, the aberrancy, the rendings of passion and evil, but he never discusses them heavy-handedly" (*The Unity*, p. 39).

spiritual frame. To this end, the second section of the essay will examine the structure and language of The Parson's Tale to demonstrate the extent to which the variety of divinely acceptable paths to salvation emerges as a central tenet of Chaucer's most self-conscious evocation of his spirituality. The closing section will draw upon related passages from other spiritually concerned tales to suggest how Chaucer's returning to his opening theme at the end of his book does—and does not—enable the poet "To knytte up al this feeste and make an ende."

STRUCTURE AND LANGUAGE OF THE PARSON'S TALE

Contemporary readers of The Parson's Tale invariably are struck by the excursus on the Seven Deadly Sins and their remedies that occupies more than half the narrative. Notwithstanding Lee Patterson's sturdy defense of the combination of an extensive discussion of penitence and a lengthy discourse on the sins as typical in a fourteenth-century penitential manual and in this instance admirably restrained, many readers have found the treatment of the sins "excessively schematic and obtrusive," "confused and disproportioned," or, in Lounsbury's killing phrase, "one long level of tediousness."[17] The

---

[17]See Patterson, "The 'Parson's Tale'," pp. 338–39. The criticisms of the tale come from Norman E. Eliason, *The Language of Chaucer's Poetry: An Appraisal of the Verse, Style, and Structure*, Anglistica, vol. 17 (Copenhagen, 1972), p. 79; Mark H. Liddell, "A New Source of *The Parson's Tale*," in *An English Miscellany Presented to Dr. Furnivall in Honour of His Seventy-Fifth Birthday* (Oxford, 1901; repr. 1969), p. 257; and Thomas R. Lounsbury, *Studies in Chaucer: His Life and Writings*, 3 vols. (1892; repr. New York, 1962), 1:206. Wenzel's comment in *The Riverside Chaucer*, p. 956, praises the tale's logic while acknowledging its lack of proportion: "the linking of the treatment of the deadly sins to the discussion of penance is logical

present discussion contends that Chaucer's integration of the sins into his elaboration of penitence is designed to form a structurally balanced whole[18] and that the ideological thrust of the tale generally and of the treatment of sins and remedies in particular is consistent with the general embracing of variety that the opening of The Parson's Tale establishes as its theme.[19] My method will be first to offer a brief overview of the tale's structure, then to explore how structure informs meaning. I acknowledge with regret that this initially skeptical reader's feeling that The Parson's Tale is fascinating and sensitively written—a feeling I have found no reason to challenge since first reading the tale aloud some years ago and finding myself smitten by its smooth, lucid prose and careful design—is, like faith, a position that cannot be argued.

Notwithstanding manuscript rubrics in Ellesmere that indicate only three main subdivisions, The Parson's Tale has five principal parts:

I.   An introductory section (lines 75–127; 53 lines) defines penitence and indicates its three causes, three types, and three stages.

---

and paralleled in other handbooks. Likewise, the startling disproportion of Chaucer's section on the sins and their remedies to the remainder of the tale is neither unique nor a good argument against his authorship." A large number of scholars and teachers express their dissatisfaction with the discussion of the sins by ignoring it.

[18] For an illuminating discussion of the ParsT as displaying "the principles of inorganic structure" characteristic of Gothic art and of the *CT* generally, see Robert M. Jordan, *Chaucer and the Shape of Creation: The Aesthetic Possibilities of Inorganic Structure* (Cambridge, Mass., 1967), esp. pp. 230–38.

[19] On Chaucer's active role in composing ParsT, see Wenzel's comment in *The Riverside Chaucer*, p. 956, endorsing the "probability that instead of mechanically combining two Latin treatises The Parson's Tale embodies material [chosen] intelligently from a larger number of sources."

II. A discussion of contrition (lines 128–315; 188 lines) delineates six reasons for contrition, explains how to be contrite, and asserts the ultimate value of contrition.[20]

III. A discussion of confession (lines 316–1028; 713 lines) describes the general source of sin and two principal categories of sin (71 lines), offers an extended analysis of the Seven Deadly Sins and their remedies—the seven cardinal virtues—(571 lines), and explores seven circumstances that aggravate sin and four conditions for a true confession (71 lines).

IV. A discussion of satisfaction (lines 1029–75; 47 lines) describes the three manners of alms-giving and four manners of bodily pain, then explains and counters four ways penitence may be disturbed.

V. A general summary (lines 1076–80; 5 lines) offers a lyrical evocation of the boundless bliss of heaven that is the fruit of penitence.[21]

Though the surface texture of the narrative rambles, especially in the discussion of sins and remedies, the general unity of design suggested by this outline is extremely effective in binding the tale together. Indeed, a most interesting feature in Chaucer's structuring of The Parson's Tale is the way suggestions of symmetry join with boldly asymmetrical elements to articulate a common spiritual theme.

---

[20]The division between the first two sections is hidden in Ellesmere by the absence of an extratextual rubric announcing Contrition, but the sections are clearly distinguished by the logic and wording of the discussion.

[21]In Ellesmere sections IV and V appear together under the rubric of Satisfaction without any extratextual distinction, but once again the parts are clearly distinguished by the logic and wording of the discussion.

The tale's structure provides four main indications that Chaucer was moving toward symmetry: (a) the discussion of sins and remedies appears in the middle section of the tale's middle part; (b) the discussion of confession in section III is surrounded by the sections on contrition and satisfaction, which are in turn framed by the introductory and summary sections; (c) section III contains 71 lines on either side of the 571-line elaboration of sins and remedies; (d) the 53 lines of the introductory section I are balanced by the combined 52 lines of sections IV (treating satisfaction) and V (the general summary). This patterning suggests that Chaucer was working from two directions: (1) the more general framing strategies (a) and (b) provide for an overall structural balance obvious even to a casual listener or reader; (2) the more detailed correspondences (c) and (d) indicate an authorial consciousness of the number of lines used that is all the more significant for the sustained effort required in the course of composition/translation and especially revision. Like many a contemporary, Chaucer apparently felt that a devout spiritual text ought to have a numerically satisfying structure.[22]

Still, Chaucer's challenges in fashioning a balanced structure from The Parson's Tale's combination of sources are not fully met and perhaps were not meant to be.[23] The tale's symmetry suffers two

---

[22]Chaucer shows such a concern for numerical balance in PrT, where the song's symmetrical structure points to the ugly central stanzas describing the young *clergeon*'s burial in excrement (VII.565–78).

[23]The same reasoning would apply if Chaucer translated a (hypothetical) single source combining elements on penance drawn from Pennaforte or one of its derivatives and elements on the sins and their remedies drawn from texts similar to *Primo/Quoniam* and *Postquam*. Discounting the extremely unlikely possibility of a source so close to ParsT that Chaucer took no liberties in translation, one can assume that even a single source would have lacked some of the symmetries Chaucer incorporates into his text.

principal disruptions: (1) the discussion of contrition in section II stands outside the tale's schema for balanced line numbering, yet as the match for the discussion of satisfaction in section IV, it plays a necessary part in the tale's overlaid organizational frame; (2) the discussions of the various sins and remedies in the central portion of section III are so vastly different in length as to give the impression of structural imbalance even as they in fact total the requisite x71 lines that mark the section's symmetry. These overt asymmetries suggest either that The Parson's Tale which we read represents work in progress—ingenious Chaucer eventually would have resolved even sticky structural problems—or that Chaucer was satisfied with the mix of symmetry and asymmetry, whether because the combination suited his purposes in concluding *The Canterbury Tales* with this Parson's Tale or because the anomalies simply didn't matter much to him. The present discussion assumes that it is unhelpful to imagine the tale unfinished (regardless of how likely one judges this to be[24]) and therefore treats the combination of symmetry and asymmetry as integral to the articulation of the tale's message.

One repents because one sins; the equation is one-to-one. One repents in accordance with a common pattern because wherever it may begin, the path to righteousness ultimately follows a universal sequence: the numberless roots of contrition that support the metaphorical tree of penitence all nourish the common stalk, myriad branches, and innumerable leaves of confession that are the support and pathway to the flower of satisfaction that stands for the heavenly

---

[24]On ParsT as possibly "unfinished and unrevised," see Siegfried Wenzel, "Chaucer's Parson's Tale: 'Every Tales Strengthe'," in *Europäische Lehrdichtung: Festschrift für Walter Naumann zum 70. Geburtstag*, ed. Hans Gerd Rötzer and Herbert Walz (Darmstadt, 1981), p. 97; also Morton W. Bloomfield, *The Seven Deadly Sins* ([East Lansing, Mich.], 1952; repr. 1967), p. 192.

Jerusalem. Yet even as each penitent must understand the universal as the signifier of the common path all good people ultimately must follow—all confessions take the same form—heartfelt penitence also requires that the individual penitent recognize and accept (for the sake of correction) the defining characteristics of the individual self, that is to say, insofar as it is sin in its infinite variability that distinguishes the self, that each penitent acknowledge the nature of his or her particular sins.

This understanding of each individual as a characteristic sinful product of the postlapsarian species appears in the structure of The Parson's Tale in the mixed symmetry and asymmetry of the design. Let us consider the asymmetrical elements first, beginning with the discussion of contrition. Defined in the tale as the "verray sorwe that a man receyveth in his herte for his synnes" (line 129), contrition is the first emotional/intellectual act for any person who hopes to escape the constraints of worldly behavior, an essential step in the process common to all penitents and thus an independent part of the five-fold structure of the tale. Yet along with this formal universality contrition is meaningful only if, in words Chaucer follows Pennaforte in wrongly attributing to Bernard, it is "hevy and grevous, and ful sharp and poynaunt in herte" (line 130), a suffering that penitents share insofar as the surface structure of pain can be generalized in our common language yet that, like all pain, is experienced as distinctive by each individual sufferer.[25] Intensely personal, private, and painful, in Chaucer's words "wonder sorweful and angwissous" (line 304), the act of contrition triggers God's mercy by signaling one's individual readiness for salvation even as it joins one into the common

---

[25]See Robert M. Correale, "Nicholas of Clairvaux and the Quotation from 'Seint Bernard' in Chaucer's *The Parson's Tale*, 130–132," *American Notes and Queries* 20 (Sept.–Oct., 1981): 2–3.

mass of penitents. Accordingly, the main thrust of Chaucer's lengthy discussion of contrition (159 of the 188 lines) is on the six general causes that move people to contrition, causes which (as the many subcauses suggest) involve distinctive memories, fears, and hopes for each penitent but which are universal in that each penitent is responding to an awareness of the sickness that is sin.

The discussion of the sins in section III extends the focus on classification, examining in drawn-out detail the human being's status as both a typical example among many such examples and a unique being judged entirely on his or her own merits. The framing subject is the Seven Deadly Sins of pride, ire, envy, sloth, avarice, gluttony, and lechery, but, as Chaucer proclaims in noting that each of these "chief synnes hath his braunches and his twigges, as shal be declared in hire chapitres folwynge" (line 389), the sharper focus is on the classification of the sins as they affect the most minute practical details of behavior and thus distinguish the particular human life. The tendency toward sin joins each individual into the common mass of sinners, but the hypnotic recounting of untold numbers of minutely distinguished sinful types and subtypes insists on the distinct attributes of each sin, the apparently random uniqueness of each combination of sins. Be his subject the three shrews of anger, the five fingers of lechery, the typical characteristics and moral consequences of unlawful trade, the five species of backbiting, the ten branches of gluttony, or the various signs of despair, somnolescence, and idleness, Chaucer's uncharacteristically spare listing of subtly distinguished sins[26] (each with its many subvariants) emphasizes the susceptibility of every individual in the face of so diverse a menu, the ultimate insignificance of any particular combination of choices, and the exponential inevitability

---

[26]See Patterson, "The 'Parson's Tale'," pp. 344–47, on the unusually spare quality of Chaucer's prose in ParsT.

that each combination of choices will be as nonreplicable as is the chooser's DNA.[27]

Larry Scanlon has wisely noted of The Parson's Tale's "intricate system of taxonomy" in the discussion of sin that "this very intricacy demonstrates the multiplicity, the endless variety of forms the resistance of sin can take."[28] In significant contrast, the forms of resistance *to* sin, the remedies available to the (repentant) sinner, are described only briefly and in more general terms. The contrast

---

[27]It should be emphasized that the intense focus on the details of sin signifies the typically Chaucerian interest in variety, not a particular interest in perversion peculiar to this tale or its teller. Consider, to take an extreme example, the much-discussed listing of four causes for masturbation that readers searching for irony in the tale have seen as evidence of the Parson's excessive curiosity about sexuality. The condemnatory reading ignores the poet's intense interest in sexuality in order to condemn the speaker's presumed interest in the subject on the basis of a few words taken out of context. But why should not a parson—or a poet—discuss masturbation in the same tone used when discussing adultery, lust, and sex between spouses? The ideologically-inspired mockery of the Parson brings to mind the attacks on then-Surgeon General Jocelyn Elders in that it condemns the *mention* of masturbation without either examining the speaker's language or considering how the discussion of masturbation compares to discussions of other similarly common behaviors. A full discussion of sexuality—the kind of discussion Chaucer undertakes throughout *CT*—will encompass a wide variety of perspectives and behaviors, and it need not exclude the orthodox. In the context of ParsT, where overabundant detail is the norm, the delineation of four motivations is unexceptional and the presentation of these motivations is typically matter-of-fact. See John Leyerle, "Thematic Interlace in 'The Canterbury Tales'," *Essays and Studies* 29 (1976): 110–12, for a view similar to my own.

[28]Larry Scanlon, *Narrative, Authority, and Power: The Medieval Exemplum and the Chaucerian Tradition* (Cambridge, 1994), p. 13.

reflects a fundamental distinction the tale draws between the human and divine. The "fifthe thyng that oghte moeve a man to contricioun," Chaucer notes earlier in the tale, "is remembrance of the passioun that oure Lord Jhesu Crist suffred for oure synnes" (line 255). One who can "understonde that in mannes synne is every manere of ordre or ordinaunce turned up-so-doun" (line 260)—that is to say, that sin is so pervasive and various in its opposition to the simplicity of divinely created order that it distorts the most minute features of every aspect of human life—will see why it is that in "the diverse [disordinaunces] of oure wikkednesses was the passioun of Jhesu Crist ordeyned in diverse thynges" (line 275). When The Parson's Tale remarks that only the Passion, the ultimate manifestation of God's grace, could neutralize the complexities/sinfulness of human behavior and, in its paradoxically universalizing simplicity, permit redemption, it does not so much deny as assert the pull of sin and its dominance in the world. Seen in this light Chaucer's concise presentation of the remedies for sin (anticipating his still briefer discussion of satisfaction) reflects in its very imbalance the relationship between the primal simplicity of truth and the fascinating complexity of sin: unity, as reflected in the simple acts that overwhelm all combinations of sin, is a sign of the deity; number and volume, as reflected in the complex, organic intertwinings of the branches and twigs of sin, are the defining constructs of the world.

The symmetries in The Parson's Tale affirm this identification of diversity with humanity. Most telling in this regard is the relation of structure to content in section III, the tale's most complex rearrangement of a group of sources.[29] In a bold assertion of control over a

---

[29]Likely (transitional) sources for some of the material in section III have been discovered by Wenzel. See especially "The Source for the 'Remedia' of the Parson's Tale," *Traditio* 27 (1971): 433–53, and "The Source of Chaucer's Seven Deadly Sins," *Traditio* 30 (1974): 351–78.

potentially unwieldy mass of material, Chaucer divides in half his Pennafortean-inspired theoretical discussion of the definition and meaning of confession to construct a frame around the lengthy Peraldean-inspired explorations of sins and remedies. The orderly frame discussion grounds the asymmetrical treatment of sin by expressing the speaker's confidence that the truth of confession, the "verray shewynge of synnes" (line 318), will permit any person to connect with divine virtue, regardless of the particular intricacies of that person's human (mis)behavior.

It is interesting to note here that the simple balance of the frame masks the more involved elaboration of the core discussion in much the same way as the common form of the species masks the distinctiveness of the individual: this underlying commonality lies very much at the heart of the message that the frame strives to communicate. After defining confession, the frame's opening portion announces Adam as the source of sin and thus death, placing all readers in a common lineage. A brief retelling of the Fall further establishes the commonality of human experience, as the path of each individual's entry into sin is allegorized by the representation of the serpent as "suggestion of the feend," Eve as "the delit of the flessh," and Adam as "the consentynge of resoun" (line 331). Indeed, not only is the fleshly desire of concupiscence universal in the species, but so is the manner of passage from desire to action: "flesshly concupiscence" leads to "the subjeccioun of the devel," "a flambe of delit," "consentynge of synne," and finally the actual doing of sin (lines 350–54). The form of sin defines the species; the particular combination of sins defines the individual.

Following the carefully arranged enumeration of sins and remedies (lines 387–957), Chaucer closes the confessional frame by first repeating his insistence on the pervasive universality of sin—"Synne is every word and every dede, and al that men coveiten, agayn the lawe of Jhesu Crist" (line 959)—and then balancing this reminder with two brief lists that mediate between the diversity of sin and the singleness of redemption. The first list delineates the qualities that determine the severity of an individual sin. For all the variations on sin that have been articulated in the previous pages, each sinful act may be classified in terms of seven categories: the sinner's personal status, the role of intermediaries, and the act's situation, location, repetition, cause, and circumstances (lines 958–81). The second list indicates the conditions that permit confession to be successful in countering sin. For all the surface distinctions that mark each sub-subcategory of sin, true and profitable confession depends on meeting the four conditions which offer universal redemption: "sorweful bitternesse of herte" (line 983), timeliness, complete confession to a single priest, and nine rules governing confessional form and honesty (lines 982–1028). The two lists share a patterning that both allows for the variety characteristic of the individual and permits that all people be embraced in the simplicity of the divine. It makes sense, in these terms, that even as the categories and conditions have their subunits, the language in which they are articulated is markedly terse. As the discussion of confession closes, as Chaucer moves rapidly toward his even more concise discussion of the fruit of satisfaction, a reader's personal, self-articulating involvement in the study of sin is endorsed by the recognition that human variety is acceptable to God, indeed is accommodated in the divine order.

It was suggested above that Chaucer's interest in the pilgrimage journey rather than the destination shrine is reflected in The Parson's Tale in his focus on the stalk and branches of sins and remedies at the expense of the flower of satisfaction. How rapidly the poet moves to end his text is evidenced structurally as the tale's concluding sections IV and V are together as long as the introductory section I. There is a certain balance to be sure, but it is a balance achieved by a conciseness that insists on how limited is the human role in redemption and how easily expressed the divine. One may offer alms in three manners (contrition of heart, pity for one's neighbors' faults, and the giving of good counsel and comfort to those in need [lines 1030–37]), submit to bodily pain in four (prayers, vigils, fasting, and self-discipline [lines 1038–56]). That's all: sin is the human lot, redemption the offering of God. It is fitting then that even as the penitent must be wary of all four failings that disturb penitence (dread, shame, hope, and despair), wanhope is most worrisome, for despair questions the efficacy of divine love in the face of human behavior. It is in response to this kind of questioning that Chaucer closes his discussion of satisfaction by reiterating the comforting message that is the centerpiece in The Parson's Tale's call for penitence: people cannot avoid either the innumerable daily examples of venial sin or the devastating lapses into deadly sin, but in response to this need, humankind has been granted the Passion that offers redemption for all instances of human failing, however great or frequent they may be:

> The firste wanhope comth of that he demeth that he hath synned so greetly and so ofte, and so longe leyn in synne, that he shal nat be saved./ Certes, agayns that cursed wanhope sholde he thynke that the passion of Jhesu Crist is moore strong for to unbynde than synne is strong for to bynde./ . . . And though he never so longe have leyn in synne, the mercy of Crist is alwey redy to receiven hym to mercy. (lines 1071–73)

The Parson's Tale ends with Chaucer's famous (albeit brief) contrasting of life on earth to "the endelees blisse of hevene . . . *ther alle harmes been passed of this present lyf* " (lines 1076–77; my emphasis). The final phrase keeps a reader pondering how characteristic of human life earthly harms are. Such pains, Chaucer one last time insists, are universal, tied to "the body of man, that whilom was foul and derk, . . . that whilom was syk, freele, and fieble, and mortal," and that was subject to "hunger, thurst [and] coold" (lines 1078–79), and to the mind, that must suffer the "contrarioustee of wo," "grevaunce," and fear of "the peyne of helle" (line 1077). Even those who would be virtuous must suffer: the road to heaven is paved with "poverte espiritueel," "lowenesse," "hunger and thurst," "travaille," and "deeth and mortificacion of synne" (line 1080).[30] In this life one can endure pain, but one cannot escape its many forms. Nor can one escape the infinite varieties of sin, though one repent for one's misdeeds. Indeed, if one judges from the orthodox perspective of The Parson's Tale, suffering and sin, mitigated only by a recognition of the divine grace that redeems all that is characteristic of the species, seem to be the human lot.

SPIRITUALITY AND CLOSURE IN *THE CANTERBURY TALES*

Yet all is not lost. To read The Parson's Tale as predicated upon the inseparability of intrinsically imperfect and various human behavior and immeasurably forgiving divine response is also to see the tale as confirming a basic Chaucerian tolerance for a flawed humanity and justifying the poet's interest throughout *The Canterbury Tales* in exploring (usually in an accepting, even joyful tone) many aspects of human nature and experience that would be deemed unsatisfactory by the spiritually conservative. Indeed, a central theme in *The Canterbury Tales* seems to be that patient endurance in the face of

---

[30]Laurie A. Finke, "'To Knytte Up Al this Feeste': The Parson's Rhetoric and the Ending of the *Canterbury Tales*," *Leeds Studies in English*, n.s., 15 (1984): 104–05, deconstructs the syntax of ParsT's final sentence in ways that parallel my reading of the final paragraph. In particular, Finke notes how the vision of "the endelees blisse of hevene" that the Parson conjures is deeply affective yet strangely "earthbound, tied to the physical image of the body, however transformed, just as his earlier description of the punishments of hell is tied to the body's frailty." In place of transcendence, one finds that "his vision of the resurrection of the body ignores the dissolution of the self essential to the mystical experience."

misfortune and evil is conducive and sometimes even necessary to effecting the transition from sin to salvation. The theme is especially prevalent in the tales told by the clerical pilgrims, taking shape as it is developed from one tale to another. The remainder of this essay will examine four of the more self-conscious articulations of the relationship of evil/sin to salvation to suggest what Chaucer's interest in connections between the diverse forms of wickedness and faith tells us about his spirituality, his more general sense of the place of closure in human life, and the role of The Parson's Tale in closing *The Canterbury Tales.*

The Friar's Tale features a dialogue on the workings of the divine order between a thievish summoner and a disguised devil. The setting for the theoretical exchange is not one in which one would normally expect wisdom to appear. The summoner's principal interest is in the practicalities of financial gain; he wishes to learn how to advance more quickly in his wicked, worldly profession. The devil is on a diabolical mission; he is in search of prey to take back with him to hell. Even the tale's narrator is dubious; the Friar is a rogue whose purpose in telling the story is to mock a professional rival. Yet in still another situation where structure mirrors message, the story's Dantesque setting offering a kind of objective correlative to the *sententia,* the self-proclaimed "feend" argues directly for the divine usefulness of devils, advancing, in tones strikingly similar to what one imagines to be Chaucer's own, the Boethian argument that though a devil's goal will be to subvert—that is what defines a devil—his method occasionally serves a happier purpose:

> For somtyme we been Goddes instrumentz
> And meenes to doon his comandementz,
> Whan that hym list, upon his creatures,
> In divers art and in diverse figures. (III.1483–86)

One should be wary of the error that would imagine God's many "instrumentz" or "comandementz" as promoting evil. As illustrated by the contrasting fates given on the one hand to the thoroughly wicked summoner and on the other to the mildly blasphemous but generally venial carter whom the summoner seeks to subvert, the devil will act only against those who willingly accept his offerings. Those—like the carter and the old woman—who do not give themselves over to evil will not be overcome and, as the devil puts it, will in fact discover that the very act of resistance opens the doorway to grace:

> Whan he withstandeth oure temptacioun,
> It is a cause of his savacioun. . . . (lines 1497–98)

Playing under such rules, a devil—the embodiment of sin—is dangerous only to himself and to those who accept demonic values. Evil, like sin, attacks in various forms: "Somtyme we feyne, and somtyme we aryse / With dede bodyes, in ful sondry wyse" (lines 1507–08). In this variety of tones and disguises it seeks to tempt, to frighten, to confuse whoever may be susceptible. To the virtuous, however, the bluster of threats and blandishments represents but another manifestation of the divine will that we be saved.

A similar line of reasoning appears in The Pardoner's Prologue, where the devil's metaphor is literalized in the person of the Pardoner. This dubious cleric, projected as a villain at least as unsavory as the Friar, closes the self-introduction detailing his vast repertoire of subversive strategies by explaining to his audience that

> . . . though myself be a ful vicious man,
> A moral tale yet I yow telle kan,
> Which I am wont to preche for to wynne. (VI.459–61)

Alongside the Pardoner's sinful nature stands his self-proclaimed ministerial success in persuading his listeners to exchange greed for penitence. He is quite proud of his skill, confident in the hypocrisy that allows him to satisfy his own avarice by successfully preaching against that same sin in others:

> But though myself be gilty in that synne,
> Yet kan I maken oother folk to twynne
> From avarice and soore to repente. (lines 429–31)

Insofar as the Pardoner is correct in his self-assessment—and it is most relevant in the present context that the tale Chaucer assigns to this unscrupulous narrator is an exceptional example of the sermon exemplum, powerful in its spare story line and evocative spiritual imagery—the suggestion here, as in The Friar's Tale, is that what moves people from sin to virtue is not necessarily contact with the virtuous.[31] To the contrary, as human paths are various and winding, as human merit is variable and limited, so God uses devils, and unpleasant pardoners, to offer diverse solutions to overcome the equally diverse varieties of sin.

The morally problematic Friar's Tale and Pardoner's Prologue passages indicate the practice by which the demonic serves the divine. The analysis at the close of The Clerk's Tale, assigned to an idealized and presumably more reliable narrator,[32] articulates the theory behind this practice. Following the disturbing story which dwells on the perverse cruelties a noble husband inflicts on his patient wife, Chaucer steps back to assign a specific divine purpose

---

[31] In the late fourteenth century the debate over the efficacy of an immoral cleric was active and polemical. Chaucer typically obscures the issue, articulating ostensibly sensible opinions in the voices of unreliable narrators and characters.

[32] That it is possible to separate out a narrative voice that is not Chaucer's is dubious. See the discussion in H. Marshall Leicester, Jr., *The Disenchanted Self: Representing the Subject in the Canterbury Tales* (Berkeley, 1990), pp. 1–6.

and appropriate human response to the intensity of suffering that seems to be the human lot. God, we are told,

> . . . suffreth us, as for oure excercise,
> With sharpe scourges of adversitee
> Ful ofte to be bete in sondry wise . . .
> And for oure beste is al his governaunce.
> Lat us thanne lyve in vertuous suffraunce. (IV.1156–62)[33]

The equation is instructive: the "sharpe scourges" God grants as the rights of adversity affect us much as the successive tribulations devised by Walter (playing here a fiendish role analogous to that of the devil in *Job*) affect Grisilde. The divine purpose in thus permitting suffering is not to uncover our weaknesses. Unlike Walter, who "wondred" if his wife's patience were the product of "subtiltee," "malice," or "crueel corage" (lines 687–92), God needs no mechanics to measure the value in his creation, "for certes he, / Er we were born, knew al oure freletee" (lines 1159–60). Neither is it God's purpose to test the will or tempt the virtue of those whom he has already judged worthy of redemption. Walter might need "[t]o tempte his wyf" (line 452), "[t]o tempte his wyf yet ofter" (line 620), and "his wyf to tempte moore" (line 786), but God "ne tempteth no man that he boghte" (line 1153).[34] Rather, much as it is on the weaving path of her husband-imposed trials that God leads Grisilde "[t]o the outtreste preeve of hir corage" (line 787), enabling her to demonstrate through Job-like obedience the full measure of her worth, so too it is in the

---

[33] A similar assertion of the deity's use for diversity appears in The Wife of Bath's Prologue: "God clepeth folk to hym in sondry wyse, / And everich hath of God a propre yifte— / Som this, som that, as hym liketh shifte" (III.102–04).

[34] On the medieval idea of redemption as a divine purchase and Chaucer's treatment of this idea in *CT*, see Georgianna, "Love So Dearly Bought."

"sondry wise" of "sharpe scourges of adversitee" (figured as devils in
The Friar's Tale and as the Pardoner in his Prologue), in the erring
paths of our drunken, difficult, wandering lives, that God "preeveth"
us—that is, tempers us, enables us, strengthens us—". . . al day, it is
no drede" (line 1155). And this "proving" displays justice as it ought
to be, as it must be: "For greet skile is he preeve that he wroghte"
(line 1152).

In such a view, variety, with all its slipperiness, pain, and confusion, is the mark of the wayward human life, as it is the mark of
penitence. An example in The Tale of Melibee—the text closest in
spirit as well as diction to The Parson's Tale—offers an especially
direct insight into how penitence figures in Chaucer's thematic emphasis on divergent responses. Following an assault on Melibee's
house and daughter, the young lord calls together his many counselors to decide on a course of action. As is common for Chaucer, the
proposals are various—"the yonge folk" urging active war while
"thise olde wise" counsel a more thoughtful restraint—and articulated at some length (VII.1008–49). Melibee's self-reflexive response, like that of January in The Merchant's Tale, is indicative of
his own moral limitations: discounting the sycophantic motivations
of the more militant counselors and not even considering the Job-
model that would preach patient acceptance, Melibee welcomes the
cry for a revenge that would assume his untainted innocence and
assert the inherent wrongfulness of the troubles that have been visited
upon him.

In face of this worldly self-assurance, Melibee's wife offers a
moral wisdom more complex than its surface seems. In judging
advice, explains, it is necessary to make "division bitwixe youre
conseillours — this is to seyn, bitwixen youre trewe freendes and
youre feyned conseillours" (line 1255). Melibee, she contends,
foolishly has

cast alle hire wordes in an hochepot, and enclyned youre herte to the
moore part and to the gretter nombre . . . ./ And sith ye woot wel that men
shal alwey fynde a gretter nombre of fooles than of wise men,/ . . . ye se
wel that in swiche conseillynges fooles han the maistrie. (lines 1257–60)

The surface argument—an argument found so frequently in *The
Canterbury Tales* that one must read it as central to Chaucer's
thought—is that the quality of a thought does not equate with the
quantity of its advocates, indeed that there is no correlation between
absolute truths and the majority opinions of a mass of men. One need
recognize, however, that to grant the weakness of mass thought is not
to affirm that there exists a simple absolute truth that a wise person can
find. The universal tendency to sin predicates that all people will—in
their various ways—be mistaken. True wisdom, and with it closure,
lies in Prudence alone and thus outside ordinary human possibility.

Indeed, when one joins with Prudence in "consider[ing] of what
roote is engendred the matiere of thy conseil and what fruyt it may
conceyve and engendre" (line 1209), when one filters out the chaff to
concentrate the words of "thise olde wise" who counsel restraint, one
finds that truths are not as obvious as falsehoods and that the wise,
too, are uncertain in their understanding. Like Arcite in his lamentation over man's drunkenness, the wise speakers in The Tale of
Melibee acknowledge how limited is human vision when it comes to
predicting consequences—as "oon of thise olde wise" (line 1037)
puts it, "but certes what ende that shal therof bifalle, it is nat light to
knowe" (line 1040)—and how correspondingly dependent we are on
divine assistance. They offer not a determinate proactive policy that
would provide worldly closure but a call to just that kind of penitential self-examination that The Parson's Tale will show to be so
diverse in its numberless minutiae.

Among the wise, a surgeon notes that his profession can do no
more than offer "to every wight the beste that we kan, where as we
been withholde, and to oure pacientz that we do no damage" (line

1012). An "advocat that was wys" puts forth as his surest counsel "that right anon thou do thy diligence in kepynge of thy propre persone" (lines 1021–26). Prudence herself, in a lengthy summarizing argument, explains that truth lies not in a defined journey through the world but in penitential self-examination and cleansing: Melibee should "taken conseil in youreself" and "dryve fro youre herte thre thynges that been contrariouse to good conseil . . . ire, coveitise, and hastifnesse" (lines 1120–22). Still, to recognize intrinsic human limitation and acknowledge with Egeus that "[t]his world nys but a thurghfare ful of wo" (I.2847) is neither to imply that one can avoid traveling nor to deny the centrality of the journey. It is through Melibee's encounter with the world—through his suffrance of the wounds inflicted upon him by his enemies and his reasoned consideration of the advice offered by his massed counselors—that the young lord places himself on the path of reconciliation that is earthly penitence as permitted by "the grace of God" (VII.1015, 1034).[35] So, too, to return to the principal subject of this volume, The Parson's Tale may offer what from an orthodox perspective is a necessary coda to *The Canterbury Tales*, but the very necessity that such a perspective be articulated depends on poet and reader having made the journey of those tales.

The opening paragraph of The Parson's Tale conjures the variety of human possibilities to assert that penitence alone offers a sure pathway to God. The tale's final paragraph uses the earthy physicality of the body as the vehicle of the metaphor by which it evokes the eternal bliss of heaven. The aim of this essay has been to show how the assertion in these framing passages of the physical primacy of the world and the incredible diversity of worldly paths informs The

---

[35]On the metaphoric connection of the journey/pilgrimage with penitence, see James Dean, "Chaucer's Repentance: A Likely Story," *Chaucer Review* 24 (1989): 65–73.

Parson's Tale generally, as Chaucer goes far beyond simply implying the universality of human failing to revel in the beauties produced by the variety that defines the human.[36] It is supremely fitting that the imagery of sin and redemption should direct readers back to the roots and flower of the joyful opening sentence of the General Prologue. Chaucer does more than assume the necessity that all people participate in the fallen world; he builds his *œuvre* upon this assumption as he creates the great edifice of human accomplishment that is *The Canterbury Tales*.

---

[36]I have argued elsewhere that CYT proposes a similar authorial delight in the wondrous earthly diversity of the fallen world; see David Raybin, "'And Pave It Al of Silver and of Gold': The Humane Artistry of the Canon's Yeoman's Tale," in *Rebels and Rivals: The Contestive Spirit in* The Canterbury Tales, ed. Susanna Greer Fein, David Raybin, and Peter C. Braeger (Kalamazoo, Mich., 1991), pp. 189–212.

THE PARSON'S TALE AND ITS
GENERIC AFFILIATIONS

RICHARD NEWHAUSER

The more precisely one can define the generic affiliations of the Parson's prose, the better position one is in to describe the nature of its unique achievement. Because the concept of genre itself influences the type and method of production and reception of literary works in general, genres become essential elements in the communication process in which all literature participates.[1] More than mere frameworks for expression or categories of retrospective criticism, genres belong to the determinants of comprehension in the relationship between an author, his/her literary production, and the reader's horizon of expectations at work in the process of the reception of literature.[2] In this relationship, genres, as "literary-social institutions,"[3] act as the medium of negotiation for the necessary consensus between the author and the reader on all matters of instruction, entertainment, morality, and the like. Yet enjoyment, aesthetic purpose, may in one setting become part of the institutional

---

[1] Klaus W. Hempfer, *Gattungstheorie: Information u. Synthese* (Munich, 1973), p. 91.

[2] Hans Robert Jauss, "Theorie der Gattungen und Literatur des Mittelalters," in *Généralités*, ed. Maurice Delbouille (Heidelberg, 1972), p. 110; repr. H. R. Jauss, *Alterität und Modernität der mittelalterlichen Literatur* (Munich, 1977), p. 330.

[3] Wilhelm Vosskamp, "Gattungen als literarisch-soziale Institutionen," in *Textsortenlehre—Gattungsgeschichte*, ed. Walter Hinck (Heidelberg, 1977), pp. 27–42.

intent of a form otherwise devoted to matters more didactic, for no one form fulfills only one function, and no function is reserved for one type of literature alone.[4] How difficult it is to articulate the precise functions of a genre becomes clearest perhaps when one is faced with the confusing variety of religious prose and the system of genres of pastoral literature it incorporates, which proliferated towards the end of the Middle Ages. Scholarship is still very much in an early stage of differentiating the horizon of expectations in the reception of such forms as the treatise on vices and virtues, expositions of the Decalogue, or manuals of instruction of various kinds among what W. A. Pantin has termed a "great mass of anonymous mystical and devotional writings"[5] that flooded the consciousness of medieval readers by the later fourteenth century.

The Parson's Tale belongs to a specific genre among this mass of late-medieval religious prose, that of the penitential manual, a literary form which is well represented in Latin from the thirteenth century onwards and, by the late Middle Ages, in all European vernaculars as well. Though the literary framework of *The Canterbury Tales* demands that the reader imagine a parish priest speaking to the pilgrims, his tale is clearly not a sermon in any technical sense of that term.[6] Penitential manuals took their place among other catechetical and devotional forms, the *pastoralia* of the later Middle Ages, which had the broad function of disseminating a normative theology both throughout the echelons of the clergy and, ultimately, among the laity

---

[4]Richard Newhauser, *The Treatise on Vices and Virtues in Latin and the Vernacular* (Turnhout, Belgium, 1993), p. 14.

[5]W. A. Pantin, *The English Church in the Fourteenth Century* (Cambridge, 1955), p. 247.

[6]Siegfried Wenzel, "Notes on the *Parson's Tale*," *Chaucer Review* 16 (1982): 248–51.

as well, in this case by informing the practice of the *confessarius* and also by preparing the conscience of the penitent for the examination of sins to be confessed.[7] In England, as elsewhere, many types of instructional prose were produced to educate the clergy in matters of hearing confession. These included pastoral *summae* like Thomas Chobham's *Summa confessorum* (ca. 1216), the *Summa 'Qui bene presunt'* by Richard of Leicester (Wetheringsett) (ca. 1215–20), Robert Grosseteste's *Templum Dei* (ca. 1220–30), or William of Pagula's *Oculus sacerdotis* (1319–28), forms which covered the entire syllabus of instruction legislated in the wake of Lateran IV,[8]

---

[7]Dieter Harmening, "Katechismusliteratur. Grundlagen religiöser Laienbildung im Spätmittelalter," in *Wissensorganisierende und wissensvermittelnde Literatur im Mittelalter: Perspektive ihrer Erforschung, Kolloquium 5.–7. Dezember 1985*, ed. Norbert Richard Wolf (Wiesbaden, 1987), pp. 97–98.

[8]*Thomae de Chobham Summa confessorum*, ed. F. Broomfield (Louvain, 1968). The *summa* of Richard Leicester (Wetheringsett) is unedited; see the recent study by Joseph Goering, "The Summa 'Qui bene presunt' and Its Author," in *Literature and Religion in the Later Middle Ages: Philological Studies in Honor of Siegfried Wenzel*, ed. Richard G. Newhauser and John A. Alford (Binghamton, N.Y., 1995), pp. 143–59; Leonard E. Boyle, "Three English Pastoral Summae and a 'Magister Galienus'," *Studia Gratiana* 11 (1967): 134–44. Robert Grosseteste, *Templum Dei*, ed. Joseph Goering and F. A. C. Mantello (Toronto, 1984). William of Pagula's work is unedited; see Joseph Goering, *William de Montibus (ca. 1140–1213): The Schools and the Literature of Pastoral Care* (Toronto, 1992), pp. 95–98; Leonard E. Boyle, "The *Oculus Sacerdotis* and Some Other Works of William of Pagula," *Transactions of the Royal Historical Society*, 5th series, vol. 5 (1955): 81–110, repr. in Leonard Boyle, *Pastoral Care, Clerical Education and Canon Law, 1200–1400* (London, 1981). On the literature of *pastoralia* in England in the thirteenth and fourteenth centuries, see Goering, *William de Montibus*, pp. 58–99; Robert R. Raymo, "Works of Religious and Philosophical Instruction," in *A Manual of the Writings in Middle*

and *summae* specifically on penitence like Robert of Flamborough's *Liber poenitentialis* (ca. 1207–15), which were more emphatically legal texts.[9] In the same way, the examination of the conscience in matters of sin was aided by a number of genres, such as treatises on the vices and virtues like the *Summa iusticie*, probably by John of Wales (d. 1285), or Richard Lavynham's *A Litil Tretys on the Seven Deadly Sins* (later fourteenth century), texts which were limited to a discussion of sin and virtue alone,[10] and more inclusive treatises on a variety of topics of religious instruction like Robert Mannyng of Brunne's *Handlyng Synne* (1303).[11] But the penitential manual was

---

English 1050–1500, ed. A. E. Hartung, vol. 7 (New Haven, 1986), pp. 2255–378, 2467–582; Lee W. Patterson, "The 'Parson's Tale' and the Quitting of the 'Canterbury Tales'," *Traditio* 34 (1978): 334–40; Homer G. Pfander, "Some Medieval Manuals of Religious Instruction in England and Observations on Chaucer's Parson's Tale," *Journal of English and Germanic Philology* 35 (1936): 243–58.

[9]Robert of Flamborough, *Liber poenitentialis: A Critical Edition with Introduction and Notes*, ed. J. J. Francis Firth (Toronto, 1971); see Pierre Michaud-Quantin, *Sommes de casuistique et manuels de confession au Moyen Âge (XII–XVI siècles)* (Louvain, 1962), p. 21.

[10]On the *Summa iusticie*, see Newhauser, *The Treatise*, pp. 132–33; Siegfried Wenzel, "The Continuing Life of William Peraldus's *Summa Vitiorum*," in *Ad Litteram: Authoritative Texts and Their Medieval Readers*, ed. Mark D. Jordan and Kent Emery, Jr. (Notre Dame, Ind., 1992), pp. 142–43, 154–55; Jenny Swanson, *John of Wales: A Study of the Works and Ideas of a Thirteenth-Century Friar* (Cambridge, 1989), pp. 12–14. *A Litil Tretys on the Seven Deadly Sins by Richard Lavynham, O.Carm.*, ed. J. P. W. M. van Zutphen (Rome, 1956).

[11]*Robert of Brunne's "Handlyng Synne," A.D. 1303, with those parts of the Anglo-French treatise on which it is founded, William of Wadington's "Manuel des Pechiez,"* ed. Frederick J. Furnivall, 2 vols., EETS, o.s., vols. 119, 123 (London, 1901, 1903), repr. as 1 vol. (Millwood, N.Y., 1978); see Fritz Kemmler, *'Exempla' in Context:*

designed in particular to address both the sacramental and the psychological/pedagogic functions involved in penance, preparing the confessor to hear confession and instructing the penitent's conscience in what to confess, and it was calculated to do so with some degree of exclusiveness. These dual functions of penitence had begun to emerge in ecclesiastical literature on the topic since the theologians of "contritionism" in the twelfth century had promoted the idea that the confessee's internal shame for committing sin was an integral element in the process of penance. By the thirteenth century, confession and examination of the sinner's conscience in terms of the vices and virtues became essential to the expiation of sin, not a mere assessing of a number of tariffs as had been characteristic of the church's earlier penitential system.[12]

The dual nature of the penitential manual's functions is clearly represented in Chaucer's bipartite amalgamation of two major sources in The Parson's Tale, with a section on penance per se adopted from Raymond of Pennaforte's *Summa de paenitentia*, and a section on the vices and remedial virtues dependent ultimately on Guillelmus Peraldus's *Summa de vitiis et virtutibus*.[13] Raymond

---

A Historical and Critical Study of Robert Mannyng of Brunne's 'Handlyng Synne' (Tübingen, 1984); D. W. Robertson, Jr., "The Cultural Tradition of *Handlyng Synne*," *Speculum* 22 (1947): 162–85.

[12]Jean Delumeau, *Sin and Fear: The Emergence of a Guilt Culture 13th–18th Centuries*, trans. Eric Nicholson (New York, 1990), p. 197.

[13]The source for penitential matters is Raimundus de Pennaforte, *Summa de paenitentia*, 3.34: De paenitentiis et remissionibus (in Raimundus de Pennaforte, *Summa de paenitentia*, ed. Xaverio Ochoa and Aloisio Diez [Rome, 1976], cols. 793–882). I have made use of two important MSS of Peraldus's double *summa* (see below, n. 41) and the following printed editions: *Summa virtutum ac vitiorum Guilhelmi Paraldi Episcopi Lugdunensis de ordine predicatorum*, 2 vols. (Paris:

composed his *summa* on penitence between the years ca. 1225–27, reworking it with an eye to the *Decretals* of Pope Gregory IX between the years ca. 1235–36. Peraldus published his treatment of the vices ca. 1236 and put it in circulation together with his *summa* on the virtues by 1249/50, though they were an influence on Chaucer only through the intermediaries of the *Primo, Quoniam,* and *Postquam* texts identified by Siegfried Wenzel, redactions of Peraldus's *summae* composed very shortly after the publication of the originals.[14] Both Raymond and Peraldus were Dominicans, and their

---

Johannes Petit, Johannes Frellon, Franciscus Regnault, 1512), and *Summa virtutum ac vitiorum*, 2 vols. (Lyon: Pierre Compagnon et Robert Taillandier, 1668). A collaborative critical edition of Peraldus's *Summa vitiorum* has been undertaken by Kent Emery, Jr., Joseph Goering, Richard Newhauser, Catherine Pinchetti, and Siegfried Wenzel as the general director of the project. Though earlier scholars recognized that Peraldus was only an ultimate source for Chaucer, they compared ParsT directly with Peraldus's work; see Germaine Dempster, *"The Parson's Tale,"* in *Sources and Analogues of Chaucer's Canterbury Tales*, ed. W. F. Bryan and Germaine Dempster (Chicago, 1941; repr. New York, 1958), pp. 723–60; Kate Oelzner Petersen, *The Sources of the Parson's Tale* (Boston, 1901; repr. New York, 1973).

[14]On the date of composition of the redactions of Raymond's work, see *Summa*, ed. Ochoa and Diez, pp. lxiii–lxxxi; on Peraldus's double *summa*, see Antoine Dondaine, "Guillaume Peyraut, vie et œuvres," *Archivum Fratrum Praedicatorum* 18 (1948): 162–236. On the wide transmission of both works, see Morton W. Bloomfield, Bertrand-Georges Guyot, Donald R. Howard, and Thyra B. Kabealo, *Incipits of Latin Works on the Virtues and Vices, 1100–1500 A.D.* (Cambridge, Mass., 1979), no. 5054 (Raymond), and nos. 1628 and 5601 (Peraldus); Raymond, *Summa*, ed. Ochoa and Diez, pp. xciii–xciv; and Thomas Kaeppeli, *Scriptores ordinis praedicatorum medii aevi*, vol. 2 (Rome, 1975), pp. 133–42, no. 1622 (Peraldus). For the remedies for the sins, Chaucer used the text referred to by its opening word as *Postquam: Summa virtutum de remediis anime*, ed. Siegfried Wenzel (Athens, Ga., 1984); see Siegfried

immensely popular and influential works are not only responses to the need for penitential literature occasioned by the canons of Lateran IV; they are also very much statements of a Dominican self-consciousness and assertiveness in becoming the agency to propagate the results of that council. Their works achieved such wide transmission because they met the needs of a specifically Dominican education system, designed to train friars for penitential tasks,[15] before they became adopted for more general purposes in the community of Christians at large. The continued currency of the two *summae* at the end of the fourteenth century is testimony to the vitality with which the Dominicans of the early thirteenth century took on their task of carrying their pastoral message to the mass of Christians. The Parson's manual, that is to say, is in effect highly indebted to early Dominican documents, and one should keep in mind that the basis for Chaucer's penitential theology is thus a conservative one, founded on sources which were roughly 150 years old by the time he adopted them for The Parson's Tale.

Wenzel, "The Source for the 'Remedia' of the Parson's Tale," *Traditio* 27 (1971): 433–53, and the introduction in *Summa virtutum*, ed. Wenzel, pp. 2–30. For the material on the sins, Chaucer used redactions of Peraldus's *Summa de vitiis*: *Primo* and *Quoniam*, both unedited; see Siegfried Wenzel, "The Source of Chaucer's Seven Deadly Sins," *Traditio* 30 (1974): 351–78. For MSS of these works, see Bloomfield et al., *Incipits*, no. 4166 (*Primo*) and no. 5059 (*Quoniam*, to which should be added Dublin, Trinity College MS. 306, fols. 1ra–121vb—see *Summa virtutum*, ed. Wenzel, p. 46 n. 25). For the dates of *Primo*, *Quoniam*, and *Postquam*, see *Summa virtutum*, ed. Wenzel, p. 12.

[15]Leonard E. Boyle, "Notes on the Education of the *fratres communes* in the Dominican Order in the Thirteenth Century," in *Xenia medii aevi historiam illustrantia oblata Thomae Kaeppeli O.P.*, ed. Raymund Creytens and Pius Künzle, vol. 1 (Rome, 1978), pp. 249–67.

If the use of the penitential manual for the confessor has been much studied by scholars, the same cannot be said for its second function as a guide for the analysis of the conscience in matters of sin and virtue. Thomas Bestul has recently pointed to the important background of The Parson's Tale in late medieval meditative prose, yet it is clear to him as well that the major objects of the Parson's "meditacioun" are the vices and virtues which form the bulk of the work.[16] Until the late Middle Ages, the treatise on vices and virtues had been the major genre to address this meditative function centered around the object of the vices and virtues, in Latin as well as in the vernacular. This genre fulfilled varied functions in the course of its long history; certainly some of these functions came to include private meditation and public reading in surroundings not under the immediate control of church authorities. Nevertheless, even when the genre of the treatise on vices and virtues was subsumed into the penitential manual and its dominant function became the ecclesiastically regulated preparation of the conscience of the penitent for the sacrament of confession, its meditative functions were never discarded. The penitential manual, in fact, represents the amalgamation of the forms and functions of the genre of the treatise on penance and the genre of the treatise on vices and virtues. As such, it can be understood as one of a number of late-medieval genres composed incrementally of what had developed as standard pieces in a catechetical corpus to form handbooks by accretion, texts amounting to the consolidation of individual tractates into new genres with both instructional and meditative functions. Indeed, Peraldus's treatise on the vices and virtues itself actually served as a source for devotional prose throughout Europe in the late Middle Ages; Domenico Cavalca's

---

[16]Thomas H. Bestul, "Chaucer's Parson's Tale and the Late-Medieval Tradition of Religious Meditation," *Speculum* 64 (1989): 600–19.

Medicina del cuore, for example, depends on the *Summa de vitiis et virtutibus* for its examination of the virtues and the beatitudes.[17] Furthermore, the Pecham constitutions and subsequent ecclesiastical legislation in England which provided more detailed guidance on basic doctrinal questions concerning catechesis and the sacrament of confession as specifications of what had been legislated in Lateran IV supported the development of conditions for transmission in which the majority of English treatises on the vices and virtues came to be found in their most typical codicological setting alongside other works of pastoral and devotional interest. A case in point is the transmission of the Middle English work on the sins beginning "Pride, enuye, & wraþ ben synnes of þe feend," which occurs in five different manuscripts in connection with a variety of catechetical pieces and devotional works such as treatments of the Decalogue or the "meditations of St. Anselm" and the "charter of heaven."[18] Thus, it is not unusual to find Middle English works on sin and virtue added to other catechetical pieces in a codicological environment which amounts to a type of *ad hoc* handbook in which they would have served the purposes of meditation as well as those of preparation for the sacrament of confession. The meditative function of the part of Chaucer's work dealing with the vices and virtues, in other words, is closely related to that of other handbooks in late medieval English culture, just as its overall form is recognizable in the system of *pastoralia* in fourteenth-century England. It should also be noted that in this generic and historical sense The Parson's Tale can be seen as an appropriate conclusion to the entire *Canterbury Tales*, for it

---

[17]Domenico Cavalca, *Medicina del cuore*, ed. A. Bottari (Rome, 1738–64); see R. Lotti, "Alcune osservazioni sulle fonti biografiche del Cavalca," *Lettere Italiane* 35/4 (Oct.–Dec. 1983): 509–16.

[18]Newhauser, *The Treatise*, pp. 168–71.

recapitulates in one literary form, whose principle of construction is accretion, one of the structural principles of the *Tales* as a whole, that of simply adding one tale to another on the road to Canterbury.

Like other forms which had grown by accretion in the later Middle Ages, a great number of vernacular penitential manuals expand their treatment of the two major elements of the genre by adding a certain amount of further catechetical material to the treatment of penitence and the sins—material on the Decalogue, Credo, Gifts of the Holy Ghost, and the like. Such additions in fact became very common as the search for more biblically authentic bases for penance expanded in the later Middle Ages beyond the Seven Deadly Sins, which are mentioned nowhere in Scripture. Jean Columbi's *Confession generale* gives a good view of how the treatment of the sins in confession was supplemented by catechetical material.[19] After a general discussion of the conditions necessary for confession, which is typical of the genre, this work offers chapters on confessing the seven sins, with sections for all the "especes et branches principales" of each sin. The vices are found in the common order of the acronym SALIGIA, formed from the first letters of their Latin designations (*superbia, avaritia, luxuria, ira, gula, invidia, accidia*).[20]

---

[19]Jean Columbi, *Confession generale auec certainez reigles vtiles tant a confesseurs que a penitens. Compose par reuerend Pere maistre es Ars et en Saincte Theologie frere Jehan columbi frere mineur euesque de Troye et penitencier de nostre sainct pere le Pape en Auignon*, 2nd ed. ([Lyon]: Barnabe Chausard, 1548); an earlier edition was printed in Avignon, 1499. See the excellent study by Geneviève Hasenohr, "La Littérature Religieuse," in *La Littérature française aux XIVe et XVe siècles*, ed. Daniel Poirion (Heidelberg, 1988), p. 273.

[20]On SALIGIA (pride, avarice, lust, wrath, gluttony, envy, sloth—though avarice and sloth can change positions in this list) and other acronyms for the vices, see Morton W. Bloomfield, *The Seven Deadly Sins* ([Lansing, Mich.], 1952; repr. 1967), pp.

Yet Columbi then also adds chapters on confession according to the ten commandments, confession according to the seven deeds of mercy (bodily and spiritual), and finally confession according to the seven sacraments. *Le Confessional appelle le directoire des confesseurs*, attributed falsely to Jean Gerson, provides another view of this expansion of material, for one finds here material on the articles of faith, sacraments, ten commandments, spiritual weaknesses, gifts of mercy, and five senses, but only within the framework of the vices and virtues in confession.[21] Both of these texts are directed to the analysis of confession and sin, as is the Parson's manual, but Chaucer's work remains focused on the two core elements in the penitential manual to the exclusion of most extraneous matter. Lee Patterson has emphasized the uniqueness of this trait of The Parson's Tale among Middle English penitential manuals which, like most of their French equivalents, use the occasion provided by a presentation of penitence and sin to inform their readers of more general catechetical materials as well.[22]

Yet Chaucer's work is not without any analogue in comparable vernacular penitential manuals of the later Middle Ages. Perhaps the closest equivalent can be found in Middle High German in Heinrich

---

86–87; Arthur Watson, "Saligia," *Journal of the Warburg and Courtauld Institutes* 10 (1947): 148–50; Giuseppe Rotondi, "'*Saligia*' e '*Chulcama*.' Postilla all'*Anticerberus* di Bongiovanni da Cavriana," *Rendiconti del Reale Istituto Lombardo di Scienze e Lettere,* serie 2, vol. 63 (Milan, 1930): 1110–14; Otto Zöckler, *Das Lehrstück von den sieben Hauptsünden. Beiträge zur Dogmen- und zur Sittengeschichte, insbesondere der vorreformatorischen Zeit,* in Otto Zöckler, *Biblische und kirchenhistorische Studien,* vol. 3 (Munich, 1893), pp. 66–81.

[21] Pseudo-Jean Gerson, *Le Confessional appelle le directoire des confesseurs* ([Poitiers], n.d.); see Hasenohr, "La Littérature," p. 274.

[22] Patterson, "The 'Parson's Tale'," pp. 339–40.

of Langenstein's *Erchantnuzz der Sund*, a manual which is just as bare of catechetical elaboration as Chaucer's and, if anything, even more doctrinally focused than The Parson's Tale. Henricus Heinbuche de Hassia dictus de Langenstein, to use the full form of his name in Latin documents, was born some time in the first half of the four-teenth century, probably in the village of Langenstein in Hessen (Germany); he died in Vienna in 1397. Although both Chaucer and he lived during approximately the same period of time, Langenstein's life was spent more consistently in the pursuits of an advanced scholar of his day: he was educated at the University of Paris, where he achieved the baccalaureate in 1363, taught as a *magister artium* for the next ten years, and lectured in the theology faculty from 1376. His political engagement against Clement VII during the Great Schism forced him to leave Paris ca. 1382, but in 1384 he was offered a position at the university in Vienna by Albert III of Austria, where first as professor, then as dean of the theology faculty, and finally as rector he was decisive in reforming its curriculum of studies and making the university a renowned center of learning.[23] The breadth of his intellectual interests is seen in his preserved works, which encompass natural science, ecclesiastical politics, and, above all, theological and devotional works of various genres. There are thus a number of areas of overlap between Langenstein's writings and those of Chaucer, but clearly differences as well: Langenstein's concern with practical theology is far deeper than Chaucer's; the English writer's poetry has no equivalent in the German professor's *œuvre*.

---

[23] Georg Kreuzer, *Heinrich von Langenstein: Studien zur Biographie und zu den Schismatraktaten unter besonderer Berücksichtigung der Epistola pacis und der Epistola concilii pacis* (Paderborn, 1987); Justin Lang, *Die Christologie bei Heinrich von Langenstein: Eine dogmenhistorische Untersuchung* (Freiburg/Br., 1966), pp. 1–30.

Most of Langenstein's texts were composed in Latin, but the *Erchantnuzz der Sund*, perhaps his most popular treatise and still extant in 77 manuscripts, is found only in Middle High German.[24] Langenstein's work on the German text has been questioned, but his authorship of what one must then posit as the German translation's Latin original, probably no longer extant, is considered beyond doubt.[25] The vernacular text is, in any case, in the Bavarian dialect, not that of Langenstein's native Hessen; if it is not a composition by Langenstein himself, then it was prepared on the basis of Langenstein's work by someone from the region of Bavaria about whom nothing further is known. It is possible to be more precise about the dating of the German manual than it is of the Parson's penitential work, for its dedication to Albert III, its transmission mainly in Austria and Bavaria, and its German dialect make it likely that the *Erchantnuzz der Sund* was composed after Langenstein arrived in Vienna in 1384, while the *terminus ad quem* is provided by

---

[24]Heinrich von Langenstein, *Erchantnuzz der sund*, ed. Rainer Rudolf (Berlin, 1969); see Thomas Hohmann and Georg Kreuzer, "Heinrich von Langenstein," *Die deutsche Literatur des Mittelalters: Verfasserlexikon*, 2nd ed., vol. 3 (Berlin, 1981), cols. 768–69; Thomas Hohmann, "Initienregister der Werke Heinrichs von Langenstein," *Traditio* 32 (1976): 419 no. 232. For the manuscripts, see *Erchantnuzz*, ed. Rudolf, pp. 28–50, and the review of this edition by Peter Wiesinger in *Anzeiger für deutsches Altertum und deutsche Literatur* 86 (1977): 36–37. For Langenstein's works, see Hohmann and Kreuzer, cols. 764–72, and Georg Kreuzer, "Heinrich von Langenstein und seine Wirkung," in *Hugolin von Orvieto: ein spätmittelalterlicher Augustinertheologe in seiner Zeit*, ed. Willigis Eckermann and Bernd Ulrich Hucker (Cloppenburg, 1992), pp. 187–97.

[25]Peter Wiesinger, "Zur Autorschaft und Entstehung des Heinrich von Langenstein zugeschriebenen Traktats 'Erkenntnis der Sünde'," *Zeitschrift für deutsche Philologie* 97 (1978): 42–60.

the earliest manuscript, completed according to its colophon in 1393.[26] The ultimate sources for Langenstein's work are precisely those also represented in The Parson's Tale, though in the portion of the German manual devoted to penance, Langenstein supplemented Raymond of Pennaforte's *Summa de paenitentia*, 3.34, with material adapted from John of Freiburg's *Summa confessorum* (written late in the thirteenth century, and itself a reworking of material in Raymond's *Summa*), and he apparently drew directly on Peraldus's double *summa* for his treatment of the sins without any intermediaries such as Chaucer used.[27]

As in The Parson's Tale, penance and the vices and virtues are the only two areas covered in the *Erchantnuzz der Sund*; none of the catechetical matter so common in other penitential manuals is afforded a place in its focused treatment of penitence and sin. Chaucer organizes his presentation of the six issues dealing with penitence that are announced early in the tale largely into the three major parts of the work which follow the three steps of penitence enumerated by

---

[26]See the dedication, *Erchantnuzz*, chap. 1 (ed. Rudolf, p. 52): "Darvmb hab ich mir gedacht, in eren des durchleuchtigen hochgeporn fursten, meins gnedigen herrn herczog Albrecht ze Osterreich, etleich stukch vrchund vnd chraft des scheffs der puezz zu schreiben. . . ." The earliest codex of the work is Vienna, Schottenstift MS. 213; see *Erchantnuzz*, ed. Rudolf, pp. 28–29.

[27]Rainer Rudolf, "Heinrichs von Langenstein 'Erchantnuzz der sund' und ihre Quellen," in *Fachliteratur des Mittelalters: Festschrift für Gerhard Eis*, ed. Gundolf Keil et al. (Stuttgart, 1968), pp. 53–82. See also William C. McDonald, "The Nobility of the Soul: Uncharted Echoes of the Peraldean Tradition in Late Medieval German Literature," *Deutsche Vierteljahrsschrift für Literaturwissenschaft und Geistesgeschichte* 60 (1986): 543–71.

Raymond: contrition, confession, and satisfaction.[28] The long analysis of the vices and their remedial virtues is included in the midst of the second part of the manual dealing with confession, following the SIIAAGL order of sins (pride, envy, wrath, sloth, avarice, gluttony, lust) represented in Chaucer's sources, the order used most frequently in the pastoral literature of his day. Each article on the sins places that vice in the context of the other seven, defines it, accounts for its detestability, enumerates its species, and analyzes its remedy. Langenstein's work shows less formal integration of his sources, for while his treatment of penitence is also organized around its three parts,[29] it is clearly separated from the analysis of the vices and their remedies which follows the first section on penitence by a second introduction that mentions Albert once more and also expands the conception of the intended audience of the manual's instruction to include those interested in receiving practical education in matters of moral theology:

> Wann ich vor hab geschriben etwas von der peicht vnd daz nicht gar volpracht ist gebesen, hab ich gedacht, ze lob vnd ze sêlden vnd hail der sel, besunder meins genêdigen lieben herren, herczog Albrechts, von den sÿben todsunden ze schreiben all mainung der lerer, daz sich ain yedleich mensch vor den svnden paz hůten můg vnd auch wizz, waz todsvnd sein

---

[28]For Chaucer, see X.82–83: "what is Penitence, and whennes it is cleped Penitence, and in how manye maneres been the acciouns or werkynges of Penitence,/ and how manye speces ther been of Penitence, and whiche thynges apertenen and bihoven to Penitence, and whiche thynges destourben Penitence." For the three parts of penitence in Raymond, see *Summa*, 3.34.7 (ed. Ochoa and Diez, cols. 802–03).

[29]*Erchantnuzz*, chap. 4 (ed. Rudolf, p. 55): "dy erst sach oder tagbaid ist dÿ rew des herczen, dy ander ist dÿ peicht des mundes, dÿ dritt ist dÿ volfůrung der aufgesaczten půzz vber dÿ svnd."

vnd waz nach den gang vnd wÿ man sich davör hůten můg vnd waz wider dÿ svnd gůt sey (*Erchantnuzz*, chap. 24 [ed. Rudolf, p. 79]).[30]

Langenstein's text demonstrates in this way as clearly as The Parson's Tale the growth of the penitential manual through accretion, and its overall form is streamlined to make penitential doctrine and the teachings on the sins immediately accessible to its audience. In Part 1, an introduction announces the topic of the manual using the metaphor of the ship of penitence (chaps. 1–4), and three sections follow dealing with contrition (*rew*, chaps. 5–8), confession (*peichten*, chaps. 9–21), and satisfaction (*werich*, chaps. 22–23), with an emphasis on their interdependence, on the impossibility, for example, of completing penance by contrition without confession or by good works without contrition and confession. Part 2 follows Peraldus closely in presenting the sins in general (chap. 24) and then sections on the individual sins in their Peraldian order (GLAASII), which was unusual in the history of the vices and virtues: gluttony (*frazzheit*, chaps. 25–27), lust (*vncheusch*, chaps. 28–32), avarice (*geittichait*, chaps. 33–36), sloth (*trakait*, chaps. 37–40), pride (*hoffart*, chaps. 41–54), envy (*neÿd*, chaps. 55–57), and wrath (*zorn*, chaps. 58–62). In each case, Langenstein follows the threefold construction of Peraldus's tractates on the sins (detestability of each vice, its species, the remedies against it). Only the treatment of the last sin, and thus

---

[30] All translations, unless otherwise noted, are my own. *Translation:* Since I have written something earlier on confession and it has not been fully completed, I have intended, for the praise and the blessing and salvation of the soul, especially of my gracious dear lord, Duke Albert, to write down all the opinions of the teachers about the Seven Deadly Sins so that each and every person can better protect himself from the sins and also know what deadly sin is and what comes along with them and how one can protect oneself from them and what is beneficial against sin.

the manual as a whole, ends incomplete, without mention of the remedy for wrath.

The closer comparison of Chaucer's and Langenstein's penitential manuals to their sources will demonstrate both their indebtedness to the formal characteristics of the genre which the works represent and the particularity of each one as a work in its own right. There is clearly no question here of the textual dependence of one work on the other, nor does the issue of verbal fidelity lie at the center of any such comparison, that is, the relative degree to which the works remain faithful to the texts of the individual treatises which make up their sources. Rather, a differential analysis of this type may develop a way to characterize the distinctive qualities of these individual works within the context of related representatives of the same genre.[31] One can note to begin with, as the brief description of the contents of the works above has shown, how much both The Parson's Tale and the *Erchantnuzz der Sund* follow the structure of their sources and the careful presentation of the analysis of penitence and the vices as the exterior determinants of their form. Both works cover the same range of topics, and in the same order, as their sources, and, presumably because the *summae* of Raymond, John of Freiburg, Peraldus, and the thirteenth-century Latin derivatives of Peraldus are massive texts, filling generally hundreds of folios in manuscript, both the English and German texts often represent considerable abridgments of their sources.

There are a number of ways in which Chaucer's text represents an abbreviation of what is found, for example, in Raymond and *Quoniam*. Only a minute examination of all parts of Chaucer's text and its sources, including manuscripts which may represent an English redaction of Raymond's *Summa*, will allow a final determination in this

---

[31] For this type of analysis within a genre, see Alastair Fowler, *Kinds of Literature: An Introduction to the Theory of Genres and Modes* (Oxford, 1982).

matter, but in general one can say that Chaucer borrows from his sources those passages which provide him with the generic framework of the penitential manual without drawing on the inner-ecclesiastical and technical discussions intended for the use of the clergy involved in the sacrament of penitence, and in many cases without making use of the expansion of the material through quotations from Scripture and patristic authorities in which his source texts abound. Within this generic framework his text often represents additional material of his own, but his abbreviations generally reflect only the beginnings of major divisions of the matter as they are found in his sources. He supplies transitions where necessary but does not follow the often extended discussions in his sources beyond their initial phase. This method of borrowing may be illustrated by Chaucer's treatment of three sections of the analysis of penitence—the actions and species of penitence and what is necessary for true penance—all of which he adopted from Raymond. I have italicized below those passages which are direct verbal parallels in Chaucer's text and Pennaforte's *Summa,* and I quote the relevant sections from Raymond in full in order to make it more readily apparent how much Chaucer's text represents only the outline of his topic as found in his Latin source:[32]

(Chaucer, ParsT X.95–111)

And now, sith I have declared yow what thyng is Penitence, now shul ye understonde that *ther been three acciouns of Penitence.*/ The firste is that if a man be baptized after that he hath synned./ Seint Augustyn seith, *"But*

---

[32]Neither Petersen, *The Sources,* pp. 6–9, nor Dempster, *"The Parson's Tale,"* pp. 731–32, makes it apparent exactly how much Chaucer has borrowed from this passage in Raymond and how much he has left out.

he be penytent for his olde synful lyf, he may nat bigynne the newe clene lif. "/ For, certes, if he be baptized withouten penitence of his olde gilt, he receyveth the mark of baptesme but nat the grace ne the remission of his synnes, til he have repentance verray./ Another defaute is this: that *men doon deedly synne after that they han receyved baptesme./ The thridde* defaute *is that men fallen in venial synnes after hir baptesme fro day to day./ Therof seith Seint Augustyn that penitence of goode and humble folk is the penitence of every day./*

The speces of Penitence been three. That oon of hem is solempne, another is commune, and the thridde is privee./ Thilke penance that is *solempne* is in two maneres; as to be put out of hooly chirche *in Lente* for slaughtre of children, and swich maner thyng./ Another is, whan a man hath *synned openly, of which synne the fame is openly spoken in the contree,* and thanne hooly chirche by juggement destreyneth hym for to do open penaunce./ *Commune* penaunce is that preestes *enjoynen men* communly in certeyn caas, as for *to goon peraventure* naked *in pilgrimages,* or barefoot./ *Pryvee penaunce is thilke that men doon alday for privee synnes, of whiche we shryve us prively and receyve privee penaunce./*

Now shaltow understande what is bihovely and necessarie to verray parfit Penitence. And this stant on three thynges:/ Contricioun of Herte, Confessioun of Mouth, and Satisfaccioun./ For which *seith Seint John Crisostom, "Penitence destreyneth a man to accepte benygnely every peyne that hym is enjoyned, with contricioun of herte, and shrift of mouth, with satisfaccioun, and in werkynge of alle manere humylitee."/ And this is fruytful penitence agayn three* thynges *in which we wratthe oure Lord Jhesu Crist;/ this is to seyn, by delit in thynkynge, by reccheleesnesse in spekynge, and by* wikked synful *werkynge.*

(Raymond, *Summa*, 3.34.5–7

[ed. Ochoa and Diez, cols. 800–02])

De Tribus Actionibus Paenitentiae

5. *Actiones autem paenitentiae*, ut ait Augustinus, *sunt tres.*

Una est quae novum hominem parturit, et fit ante baptismum. *Nisi enim baptizandus paeniteat vitae veteris, novam vitam inchoare non potest, et, si baptizetur, recipit characterem, sed non gratiam, nec peccatorum remissionem, donec recedat fictio de corde suo.* Non tamen tenetur iste ad exteriorem paenitentiam agendam, quia sufficit ei paenitentia interior. Ab hac paenitentia, cum baptizantur, soli parvuli sunt immunes, eo quod non possunt uti libero arbitrio.

Altera vero paenitentia est, sive actio paenitentiae, quam *quis facit post baptismum de mortalibus peccatis.*

Tertia est quae fit de peccatis venialibus et cotidianis. De hac Augustinus: "Paenitentia humilium et bonorum fidelium poena cotidiana." Dona sunt et vocatio Dei, quia gratia Dei in baptismo non requirit gemitum, neque planctum vel opus aliquod, sed solam fidem, et omnia gratis condonat.

Circa secundam autem actionem est quantum ad praesentem materiam principaliter insistendum.

De Tribus Speciebus Paenitentiae

6. *Species paenitentiae sunt tres, nam alia est sollemnis, alia publica, alia privata.*

Sollemnis est quae fit in capite *Quadragesimae* cum sollemnitate. Dicitur etiam sollemnis, licet non ita proprie, quando aliquis invitus ad paenitentiam agendam mittitur in monasterium. Haec debet imponi ab episcopo tantum, vel de mandato eius a sacerdote. Et debet imponi *pro crimine publico et vulgatissimo quod totam commoverit urbem.* Item non debet imponi clerico, nisi deposito. Qui semel egerit eam, non debet postea promoveri, nec ministrare in ordine suscepto. Item non debet contrahere matrimonium; si tamen contraxerit, tenebit.

Publica dicitur quandoque quae supra est dicta sollemnis, ideo quia publice fit. Proprie tamen dicitur illa quae fit in facie Ecclesiae, non cum praedicta sollemnitate, sed *cum injungitur peregrinatio* per mundum cum baculo cubitali et scapulari, vel veste alia ad hoc consueta. Hanc posset imponere quilibet sacerdos suo parochiano, quia non invenio sibi prohibitum, nisi consuetudo esset contraria in <aliqua> ecclesia. Item non debet imponi clerico, nisi deposito, nec debet imponi nisi pro crimine enormi et manifesto. Item sollemnis paenitentia non debet iterari, sed alia quaelibet potest et debet iterari quoties homo peccat.

Privata dicitur illa paenitentia quae singulariter fit cotidie, cum quis peccata sua secrete sacerdoti confitetur.

Quae Sunt Necessaria Ad Veram Paenitentiam

7. Sequitur videre quae sint necessaria in paenitentia vera et perfecta. Et quidem tria, videlicet: cordis contritio, oris confessio, operis satisfactio. Ioannes, Os aureum: "Perfecta *paenitentia cogit peccatorem omnia libenter sufferre; in corde enim contritio, in ore confessio, in opere tota humilitas, haec est fructifera paenitentia.*"

Quia enim *tribus* modis *Deum offendimus, scilicet: delectatione cogitationis, impudentia locutionis et* superbia *operis,* secundum regulam ut contraria contrariis curentur, tribus modis oppositis satisfaciamus. De his etiam Hieronymus, exponens verba Amos: "Super tribus sceleribus Damasci et super quattuor non convertam eum. Iuxta tropologiam hoc possumus dicere. Primum peccatum est cogitasse quae mala sunt. Secundum, cogitationibus acquievisse perversis. Tertium, quod mente decreveris opere complesse. Quartum, post peccatum non agere paenitentiam et suo sibi complacere delicto."[33]

---

[33]Note that Raymond's text continues on the topic of true penitence for another column in the edition by Ochoa and Diez. *Apparatus*: aliqua] ed. aliquia. *Translation*: ON THE THREE EFFECTS OF PENITENCE. 5. Now the effects of penitence, as Augustine says, are three. One is that which brings forth a new man, and this is done before baptism. For unless the person to be baptized repents of his old life, he cannot begin a new life, and if he is baptized, he receives a sign, but not grace nor the remission of sins, until the pretending removes itself from his heart. Nevertheless, he is not held to do external penance, since internal penance suffices for him. From this penitence only children are exempt, once they have been baptized, because they are not capable of using a free will. But the second penitence, or effect of penitence, is that which someone does concerning the deadly sins after baptism. The third is that which is done concerning venial and daily sins. Concerning this one, Augustine: "The penance of the humble and of those who are good among the faithful is to suffer daily." They are gifts and God's calling, since the grace of God in baptism does not require an act of moaning or wailing or something else, but faith alone, and it gives all things freely. Now as far as the present material is concerned, issues dealing with the second effect ought to be emphasized chiefly. ON THE THREE SPECIES OF PENITENCE. 6. There are three species of penitence, for one is ceremonious, one public, one private. The ceremonious one is that which is done at the height of Lent with a ceremony. It is also called ceremonious, although not in such a strict sense, when someone who is unwilling to do penance is sent to a monastery. This penitence ought to be imposed only by a bishop or, on his orders, by a priest. And it ought to be imposed for a public and widely notorious crime which has moved the entire city. Likewise, it ought not to be imposed on a cleric, unless he has been removed from office. Whoever has once done this penance ought not to be promoted afterwards, nor ought he help at the mass in the order which he has entered. Likewise, he ought not to enter into matrimony; however, if he is already married, he will remain so. Sometimes that which was called ceremonious above is called public, for the reason that it is done publicly. Nevertheless, strictly speaking public penitence is that which is done in sight of the church, not with the aforementioned ceremony, but when a pilgrimage through the world is enjoined, with

Chaucer adds dramatization to the material in the mention of child murder not found in his source, while the necessity of pilgrimage without clothing may be a further addition along this line, or it may depend on nothing more than a scribal variant (i.e., *mundum* > *nudum*?); he is also apparently confused about what should be the focus of the first section: the effects of penitence, or the defects for which one must do penitence. On the whole, however, it is clear that Chaucer's text represents a compression of the material found in Raymond by reproducing only the opening phrases or sentences of

---

pilgrim's staff and scapular or other clothing customary for this purpose. It should be possible for any priest to impose this on his parishioners since I do not find it to be prohibited to him, unless there is a contrary custom in some church. Likewise, it ought not to be imposed on a cleric, unless he has been removed from office, nor ought it be imposed at all except for an enormous and clearly evident crime. Likewise, ceremonious penitence ought not to be repeated, but any other one can be and ought to be repeated as often as a person sins. That penitence is called private which, unlike the previous two species, is done daily, when someone confesses his sins in private to a priest. WHAT THINGS ARE NECESSARY FOR TRUE PENITENCE. 7. Next, one should understand what things are necessary for true and perfect penitence. And, in fact, there are three things, namely: contrition of the heart, confession by mouth, and satisfaction in deed. John, the Golden-mouth: "Perfect penitence compels the sinner to suffer all things willingly; for contrition in heart, confession in mouth, total humility in deed, this is fruitful penitence." For since we offend God in three ways, namely: by delighting in a thought, by shamelessness in speech, and by pride in a deed, then according to the rule that diseases are cured by their opposites we should make amends in three opposing ways. Concerning these also Jerome, explaining the words of Amos: "'For three transgressions of Damascus and for four I will not alter it' <Amos 1.3>. We can say this according to the tropological manner of speaking. The first sin is to have thought things which are evil. The second, to have acquiesced to the perverse thoughts. The third, to have completed in deed that which you have decided on mentally. The fourth, not to do penance after the sin and to be very pleased with oneself for one's transgression."

the sections present in the source text, and that Chaucer has paid more attention to the rhetorical finish of what he has adopted than to the reproduction of all of his source's theological niceties.[34]

Chaucer's attention to dramatization and rhetorical elaboration can be documented elsewhere, as well, in particular in his treatment of the sins, for he often does not speak of sin in a detached way, but of "foul sin," not of a sinner committing unspecified evils, but of the sinner's acts of arson and murder. A view of Chaucer's use of *Quoniam* near the end of his treatment of the sin of envy will make this clear. In the following, italicized words indicate variants in the manuscripts of *Quoniam*:

(Chaucer, ParsT X.513–14)

Thanne comth malignitee, thurgh which a man anoyeth his neighebor prively, if he may;/ and if he noght may, algate his wikked wil ne shal nat wante, as for to brennen his hous pryvely, or empoysone or sleen his beestes, and semblable thynges.

(*Summa de vitiis*, "*Quoniam*")

[57va] Undecima est malicia, qua quis malum vel dampnum *occulte* molitur, ut dicit Glossa, Romanorum i.

Duodecima est nequicia, qua quis *temere* presumit quod nequit. Contra utrumque dicitur Corintheorum 5: "Non in fermento veteri [57vb] neque," etcetera. Fermentum est invidia, utriusque mater, et bene fermentum, quia amarum tumidum mutat, *pascam* et corrumpit.

Terciadecima est malignitas, que malam voluntatem habet, cum mala non possit, vel ut dicit Glossa, Romanorum i: "Malignitas est de *acceptis* beneficiis gracias non referre." Hec concludit mundi potentibus et divitibus

---

[34]Cf. Patterson, "The 'Parson's Tale'," pp. 343–44.

dicentibus Sapientie 5: "In malignitate nostra consumpti sumus. Talia dixerunt in inferno hii, qui *peccaverunt*."[35]

Beyond compressing the material here, Chaucer has also added a great deal of vividness to the imagination of evil, something which one might expect from a literary artist, though it has not generally been appreciated in The Parson's Tale. This vivid imagery is not limited to the depiction of evil, of course, since much of what Chaucer adds to his major sources makes the moral good more concrete as well. Perhaps the clearest example of Chaucer's attention

---

[35]From Durham, Cathedral Library MS. B.I.18, fols. 14ra–136va [Du] as the base text, collated with London, British Library MS. Harley 3823, fols. 50r–407v [Ha], and Dublin, Trinity College MS. 306, fols. 1ra–121vb [Tr]. The relevant folios for this passage are: Du, 57va–vb; Ha, 185v–186r; Tr, 38va. I have italicized passages in the text for which there are significant variants in the MSS; the entries in the apparatus below then indicate where an italicized word or passage in the text has been omitted by other witnesses (*om.*), where it is followed by another word in the other witnesses (+), or where another passage replaces the italicized one represented in the text. *Apparatus*: occulte DuHa] in occulto Tr; temere DuHa] tenere Tr; pascam HaTr] pascit Du; acceptis DuHa] *om.* Tr; peccaverunt Du] in peccato Ha, positi sunt Tr. *Translation*: The eleventh is malice, by which someone undertakes something evil or cursed in secret, as the *Gloss* on Romans 1 says. The twelfth is villany, by which someone heedlessly anticipates what he is unable to do. Against both it is said in <1> Corinthians 5<:8>: "Not with the old leaven nor" etc. The leaven is envy, the mother of both and truly leaven, since it changes what is bitter into what is swollen, and it corrupts the pascal feast. The thirteenth is malignity, which has an evil will although it cannot perform evil deeds, or as the *Gloss* on Romans 1 says: "Malignity is not giving thanks for assistance which has been received." This includes the rich and powerful of the world who say, Wisdom 5<:13–14>: "In our malignity we have been consumed. They who had sinned said such things in hell."

to such imagery is his addition of the tree of contrition (X.112–27) to material limited otherwise to what he would have found in Raymond's *Summa de paenitentia*, an image which has a close verbal parallel in a similar section of the Old French *Compileison de Seinte Penance*.[36] All of this makes it apparent that as much as Chaucer's work is well within the genre boundaries of the penitential manual, there is a degree of vigorousness in the imagery of The Parson's Tale which goes beyond the function of merely making penitential doctrine concrete for an unlearned audience. In effect, some of what we see in Chaucer's more "literary" touches in this tale amounts to the possibility of aesthetic enjoyment, even in a form such as the penitential handbook, a blending of generic functions between "mimetic" and "didactic" kinds of literature.

While Heinrich of Langenstein follows the same practice of adopting the outline of his material from Raymond as does Chaucer, his text represents a more schematic reworking of it, with a sharper view to theological technicalities than is found in The Parson's Tale. In the first section on the effects of penitence, for example, Langenstein reorganizes the discussion of the three effects to make them parallel to three kinds of sins (original, deadly, and venial), and he uses the sins then as the principle of organization for this section (*Erchantnuzz*, chap. 3 [ed. Rudolf, pp. 53–54]). His analysis presents baptism as the penitential effect required for original sin (which is discussed briefly in its historical and theological dimensions), follows Raymond closely in the presentation of deadly sin, and develops the material on venial sin by elaborating the image of the ship of penitence with which he began the treatise. In the same way, in the section on true penitence, Chrysostom's triad of perfect penitence is combined with the threefold ways in which human beings offend God and the three steps of

---

[36]Wenzel, "Notes," pp. 241–43.

penitence, the combination then elaborating in this schematic way on Raymond's mere mention of a common notion in moral theology, namely that spiritual ills are cured by their opposites:

> Vnd darvmb schol der svnder mit dreyrlaÿ püzz vnd ablegung sein svnd gen got ablegen, als ich vör geschriben hab: dez ersten mit der rew des herczen, wan dÿ rew der svnd ist wider dÿ wollust der gedênkchen; darnach mit der peicht, wann dÿ peicht ist wider den vbermůt der red; des dritten mals mit der volfůrung der aufgesaczten půzz, wann dÿ volfůrung der püzz ist wider dÿ hoffart der werich. (*Erchantnuzz*, chap. 4 [ed. Rudolf, p. 55]).[37]

Langenstein's work, like Chaucer's, is also not without important additions to the sources, but his interest in the genre of the penitential manual is demonstrated by how he directs the larger discussion of some more technical issues of theology, such as those connected with original sin, to their ecclesiastical function in a treatise designed more to prepare the sinner for penitence than to act as a text for meditation on the part of the sinner alone. The *Erchantnuzz der Sund* is the work of a trained theologian writing to educate others, perhaps even including those in the laity, in the practical matters of moral theology.[38] As such, it goes beyond simply teaching catechesis and participates in what is generally known as the "Deutsche Scholastik,"

---

[37] *Translation*: And for this reason the sinner should remove his sin against God by a threefold penitence and elimination, as I have written above: first, by the contrition of the heart, because the contrition for sin is against the lustfulness of thoughts; after that by confession, because confession is against the vaingloriousness of speech; third by the completion of the prescribed penance, because the completion of penance is against the pride of action.

[38] Cf. *Erchantnuzz*, ed. Rudolf, p. 25, who notes Langenstein's special care in writing for the laity in this treatise.

a movement with the aim of popularizing Scholastic forms of thought through the development of a vernacular prose which was intended to be on the same level of complexity as what was found in Latin.[39] Such interests can be noted in some of those passages which represent additions to Langenstein's sources—in particular a long discussion of contritionism and the efficacy of the *sacrament* of confession, as opposed to confession in merely a general sense—which are found in chapters 15 and 18 (ed. Rudolf, pp. 66–67, pp. 69–72). These sections represent a critical use of Raymond of Penna-forte, and they demonstrate Langenstein's professional interest in ensuring that his material was up to date in somewhat more technical matters of theology.

Where the sources contained material which was particularly important for the task of moral education, Langenstein's text is more expansive in what it represents in relation to those sources. It is particularly inclusive of the material adopted from Peraldus. In the treatment of envy, for example, it stays very close to Peraldus's original in describing some of the species of the sin, though it severely limits the overall number of species enumerated by Peraldus. In one case, its rendering is almost word for word in an entire section. Here again, italicized passages in the edition of Peraldus's text which follows indicate variants in the manuscripts of the *Summa*:

(*Erchantnuzz*, chap. 55 [ed. Rudolf, p. 181])

Das sechst ist: wann neid ist vnd hat gar grozze pozzhait dauon; das mag man daran pruefen, wann ein igleichs gůts dink ist liepleicher peÿ der

---

[39]Georg Steer, "Geistliche Prosa," in *Die deutsche Literatur im späten Mittelalter 1250–1370—Teil 2*, ed. Ingeborg Glier (Munich, 1987), pp. 306–70; on catechetical literature in Germany, see Egino Weidenhiller, *Untersuchungen zur deutsch-sprachigen katechetischen Literatur des späten Mittelalters* (Munich, 1965).

gemain wann allain, als Poecius spricht vnd Seneca: Chains gůts oder
chainerlaÿ hab besiczet ist liebleich an ainn gesellen. Aber der neidige wil
des güten vil lieber mangeln vnd an sein mit samt andern lewten, ee das er
well ainn gesellen haben an gůten sachen, vnd doch hat er hernach gern
gesellen in nottichait vnd in leiden. Des hat man ein ebenpild von ainem
chunig, der verlech einem geittigen menschen vnd ainem neÿdigen ein gab
paiden mit einander vnd sprach, das sÿ wellen scholten vnd ïr igleicher
besundrer pitten; wes sÿ gerten, das wolte er sÿ gewern, also weschaiden-
leich: was in der erst pêt, das im der chunik das gêb, so wolt er dem
andern, der hernach wůrd pittent, zwïr als vil geben als dem ersten. Also
wart ir igleicher auf den andern vnd verzugen, das sÿ lang nichcz paten.
Des verdros den chunikch vnd gepot dem neidigen, das er dÿ wal hiet vnd
vör pêt. Da pat der neidig mensch den chunikch mit allem fleizz, das er im
das ain aug hies auzprechen; der worten, das man seinem gesellen, dem
geittigen, seine augen paide ausprêch. Vnd der neidige wolt vmb
chainerlaÿ güt pitten, darumb das seinem gesellen nicht zwïr als vil
hernach wůrd.[40]

---

[40]*Translation*: The sixth is: since envy is a great evil and great evil comes from it;
one can prove this since any good thing is better in common than alone, as Boethius
says, and Seneca: it is not desirable to possess goods or property without a companion. But the envious person would much rather be lacking in goods and, along
with other people, be without what belongs to him, rather than have a companion
with goods, and yet he takes pleasure in having companions in need and in suffering.
About this, one has the exemplum of a king who granted an avaricious person and
an envious one a wish together, and said that they should choose and each should
make a request separately; whatever they desired, he would grant them, and do so in
this way: whatever the first one requested the king to give him, he would give to the
other one who asked after him twice as much as to the first one. Now each one
waited for the other one and they delayed, so that for a long time they did not make
a request. This began to bore the king, and he ordered the envious person to make a
request and to ask first. So the envious person with great zeal asked the king to have
one of his eyes put out, on condition that both eyes of his companion, the avaricious

(Peraldus, *Summa de vitiis*, 7.1)

[192ra] Tertiodecimo facit ad detestationem huius vitii hoc, quod *ipsa* est perversitatis magna. Cum enim omne bonum in commune deductum pulcrius elucescat, secundum Boecium, et secundum Senecam, nullius rei possessio iocunda sit sine socio, invidus *tamen* potius vult carere bono, quam *habeat socium in eo, quia potius vult* habere socium in *miseria* [192rb] quam in felicitate, sicut patet per exemplum de quodam rege, qui concessit cuidam avaro et cuidam invido munus, quod *eligerent*, ita tamen quod donum eius, qui *posterior* peteret, duplicaretur. Et cum uterque differret petere munus, precepit rex invido, *ut prius peteret;* qui petiit, ut erueretur sibi unus oculus, volens quod proximo eruerentur ambo. Noluit enim petere aliquod bonum, ne proximus illud duplicatum acciperet.[41]

---

person, would be put out. And the envious person did not want to ask for anything good, so that his companion would not have twice as much of it later.

[41]The text is cited here from MS. M (Paris, Bibliothèque Mazarine MS. 794), fol. 192ra–rb, collated with MS. N (Paris, Bibliothèque Nationale MS. 15919), fol. 295ra; cf. Guilelmus Peraldus, *Summa virtutum ac vitiorum* (Lyon, 1668), 2:347. MS. M is a *pecia* exemplar of Peraldus's *Summa de vitiis* of the thirteenth century; MS. N is a deluxe copy of the text prepared for Stephan of Abbeville, also of the thirteenth century. The folios with the table of contents of the *Summa de vitiis* at the beginning of MS. N were numbered by a modern hand; those with the text of the *Summa* follow the table of contents and were foliated by a medieval hand contemporary with that of the scribe. I have followed the medieval foliation here. For the editorial policy I have followed here, see above, n. 35. *Apparatus*: ipsa M] ipsum N; tamen M] *om.* N; habeat . . . vult M] *om.* N; miseria M] + esse N; eligerent M] elegentem N; posterior M] posterius N; ut . . . peteret M] *om.* N. *Translation*: Thirteenth, the fact that it [=invidia] possesses a great perversity creates hatred of this sin, for although every good thing held in common shines forth more beautifully, according to Boethius, and according to Seneca possessing something cannot be pleasant without a companion, nevertheless, the envious person wants to be without

The implied functions of the vernacular penitential manual implicated in such close rendering of this source text locate its primary objective very close to the sacramental nature of late-medieval penitence itself.

In spite of their important differences in emphasis, it should be clear from the presentation above that The Parson's Tale and the *Erchantnuzz der Sund* exhibit all of the dominant traits of the genre of the penitential manual. By limiting their choice of material to penitence and the vices and virtues alone, they announce their allegiance to the genre in unmistakable terms. But the question of the generic affiliation of Chaucer's text cannot rest there, for one can note, however briefly, that if there is nothing unusual about the form and content of the Parson's penitential manual, it is clear that the context and result of that "meditacioun" do make the work distinctive. Although we might expect the penitential form to lead to a purely religious confession, as was clearly its primary objective as an instrument of institutional policy, we are surprised to find, in effect, a text of literary penance following The Parson's Tale, in the form of Chaucer's Retraction (X.1081–92). Not sins, but the ethics of literary works and a literary consciousness are at the center of the Retraction, as in the same way The Parson's Tale itself partakes in the question of literature's usefulness by steadfastly denying fiction a place when it comes to the Parson's turn to narrate in *The Canterbury Tales*, and

---

some benefit rather than to have a companion with it, since he wants to have a friend in misery rather than in happiness, as is apparent in the exemplum of the king who granted to an avaricious person and to an envious person a gift which they would choose—in such a way, however, that the present of the one who chose second would be doubled. And when both delayed in choosing a gift, the king ordered the envious person to choose first; he chose that one of his eyes should be put out, wanting that both of his companion's should be put out, for he did not want to choose anything beneficial, lest his companion receive twice as much of it.

by limiting the use of exempla and other small narrative forms which could have been used to expand the penitential manual.[42] The questions implicated here involve the issue of the possible irony of Chaucer's narration in The Parson's Tale and the appropriateness of the Parson's manual as a conclusion to *The Canterbury Tales*, and as such these questions go beyond the limits of this article and will be dealt with elsewhere,[43] but it is worth noting that the Parson's use of meditative prose can be seen to lead ultimately to the "makere" of *The Canterbury Tales* speaking in his own right in the Retraction, revealing, that is to say, a remarkable subjectivity and individuality precisely where we had come to expect the subsuming of the individual in a "corporate" system of ecclesiastically regulated ethics. The privileged position of this penitential manual and meditative treatise on the vices and virtues at the end of the Canterbury pilgrimage thus may not herald Chaucer's simple adoption of religious orthodoxy at the end of the *Tales*, as some have argued,[44] but may be part of the same careful steps in developing a literary subjectivity with which the journey first began.

---

[42] See Patterson, "The 'Parson's Tale'," p. 345. Cf. Lynn Staley, "Julian of Norwich and the Late Fourteenth-Century Crisis of Authority," in David Aers and Lynn Staley, *The Powers of the Holy: Religion, Politics, and Gender in Late Medieval English Culture* (University Park, Pa., 1996), p. 144.

[43] For opposed statements of the question of irony, see Siegfried Wenzel, "Chaucer's Parson's Tale: 'Every Tale's Strengthe'," in *Europäische Lehrdichtung: Festschrift für Walter Naumann zum 70. Geburtstag*, ed. Hans Gerd Rötzer and Herbert Walz (Darmstadt, 1981), pp. 86–98; and Lee W. Patterson, *Chaucer and the Subject of History* (Madison, Wisc., 1991), pp. 316–17.

[44] Cf. for example Stephen Knight, "Chaucer's Religious Canterbury Tales," in *Medieval English Religious and Ethical Literature: Essays in Honour of G. H. Russell*, ed. Gregory Kratzmann and James Simpson (Cambridge, 1986), pp. 156–66.

Prolegomenon to a Print History of The Parson's Tale: The Novelty and Legacy of Wynkyn de Worde's Text

Daniel J. Ransom

Over the past several years, as opportunity has allowed, I have been collating texts of the Parson's Prologue and Tale for a Variorum edition of the work. At present I have completed collations for that portion of the text that appears in the Hengwrt manuscript (following the conventional numeration, lines 1–550 and the opening phrase of line 551). Until collation is complete, one cannot speak definitively about textual relationships in these parts of *The Canterbury Tales*, but substantial information has come to light and a progress report seems now in order.

The most intriguing fact is that the text of The Parson's Tale in Wynkyn de Worde's 1498 printing (WN) is clearly derived from a manuscript of considerable quality. John Manly and Edith Rickert evidently recognized this fact—their collation cards for The Parson's Tale, unlike their cards for many other tales, record the variants in WN—but in their massive edition of *The Canterbury Tales* (MR) they do not report their findings except to observe that Wynkyn de Worde probably supplemented "his principal MS" (not identified) with Ph[1], a fragmentary manuscript "of high textual value," "very close to Gg" but free from its "numerous accidental variants"

(1940:1.416). Unfortunately, Ph^1 lacks the first 586 lines of The Parson's Tale, but analysis of WN tends to corroborate and clarify MR's proposal.

It is generally known that the early editions of *The Canterbury Tales* are linked by enchainment: Caxton's second edition (CX^2, ca. 1482) is based on his first edition (CX^1, ca. 1476; on the dating see Hellinga 1982:81–83); Richard Pynson's two editions, PN^1 (1492) and PN^2 (1526), are reprints of CX^2, as is WN, for the most part. Variorum editors have demonstrated, however, that portions of WN's text—the end of The Prioress's Tale, all of Sir Thopas, the "Modern Instances" (placed at the end of The Monk's Tale), and the Monk-Nun's Priest Link (short form)—do not repeat the characteristic readings of CX^2 but show instead superior readings (and idiosyncratic punctuation) that must have come from a manuscript source (Garbáty 1978, Pearsall 1984a:109–10, Boyd 1987:93–95, Haller [in progress]; MR's collation cards also record WN in Group B^2 1653–4652). WN's text of The Parson's Tale shows the same peculiarities and adds the remarkable feature of printed marginal glosses. Moreover, whereas WN's text of B^2 1839–2156 does not have progeny, WN's text of The Parson's Tale (as well as WN's text of The Monk's Tale and The Nun's Priest's Tale) became copytext for William Thynne's edition (TH^1, 1532) and hence, in a cascade effect, for all subsequent editions until Thomas Wright's in 1851. I would like to show what this means for the tale's textual history.

First it will be useful to measure the relative accuracy of WN's text of The Parson's Tale (i.e., lines 75–551) by reporting the numbers of variants from my text in a few manuscripts and in editions contemporary with WN. My edition, while derived from the Hengwrt manuscript (Hg), emends the base text 62 times. The Ellesmere manuscript (El) has 284 variants from my edited text; the Petworth manuscript (Pw), 687 variants. CX^1 has 1,040 variants. CX^2 diverges from CX^1 only 32 times, substituting a different variant in 9 instances, agreeing with my text against CX^1 in 9 more instances, and introducing 14 variants where CX^1 agrees with my text. Thus in The Parson's Tale CX^2 has 1,045 variants. In other tales the text of CX^2 improves on that in CX^1; Caxton himself says (Preface to CX^2, ed. Crotch 1928:90–91) that he introduced better readings by way of a manuscript manifestly superior to that used for CX^1. But of the 32 divergences separating CX^2 from CX^1, 12 get no support from extant manuscripts. Caxton seems not to have made use of his better manuscript in reprinting The Parson's Tale. Pynson's first edition (PN^1) makes no pretense of deliberate editorial activity, yet PN^1 differs from its copytext, CX^2, 91 times (in 63 instances the new reading has no manuscript support), and it varies from my text in 1,102 readings. PN^2 is a more faithful reprint of CX^2, departing from it only 36 times (1,064 variants from my text).

Before comparing the numbers for WN I should point out that WN's Parson's Prologue, like most of WN's text of *The Canterbury Tales*, was set from a copy of CX^2, departing from it only 6 times, to correct obvious typographical errors (at lines 17 and 23) and to introduce its own errors (at lines 4, 5, 16, 49). In the Parson's Prologue WN and CX^2 both have 36 variants from my text. Of course, WN's text of The Parson's Tale 75–550 shares some variants with CX^2, 127 to be exact, but 63 of these represent omission of words or letters, a common kind of error that tends to create accidental convergence among unrelated texts. Furthermore, 20 of these omissions (at lines 155, 164, 168, 209, 270, 275, 323, 365, 371, 377, 379, 422, 433, 443, 481, 489, 504, 506, 514, 548) are supported by MS Cambridge Gg 4.27 (cf. Gg at line 307), a text that is very close to Ph^1 (formerly Phillipps 6570, now University of Texas Humanities Research Center MS. 46) where that text preserves The Parson's Tale (lines 587–1092 only). Gg, owing to damage, is unavailable for comparison with 17 other omissions. Nine other variants shared by WN and CX^2 are transpositions (e.g., *it is* for *is it*), at lines 98, 115, 271, 315, 325, 353,

354, 358, 387. These errors, like errors of omission, are easily shared by accident. Further accidental convergence may be seen in the tendency in WN and the CX group to replace the word *thilke* with some analogous word or phrase (*that, those, the, such*, etc.); for while they converge in 10 of these adjustments (at lines 103, 122, 230, 238, 248, 419, 465, 528, 529, 542), they diverge in 20 others (at lines 106, 134, 189, 228, 235, 322, 324, 350 [2], 352, 365, 369, 374, 396, 413, 440, 441, 442, 470, 495). Among the 20 divergences WN has manuscript precedent only at lines 106, 134, 352, 365, 413, 470, 495.

We have seen so far that 82 shared variants—the 63 omissions, the 9 transpositions, and the 10 replacements of *thilke*—do not constitute firm evidence for CX^2's influence on WN's text of The Parson's Tale. We may note further that Gg supports 16 of the remaining 44 variants shared by WN and CX^2—at lines 212, 258, 293, 319, 320, 368, 382, 409, 432, 450, 484, 486 (2), 487 (2), 504—and is unavailable for comparison with 8 others of these 44 variants. Among the 28 remaining variants that WN shares with CX^2 but not with Gg are readings that WN introduces elsewhere with no manuscript support, presumably as part of an editorial strategy to modernize or streamline the text in order to make it more accessible or readable. For example, at line 270 CX^2 and WN replace *fortherover* with *forthermore*, a change made independently in WN at lines 304, 313, and 437 (each without manuscript precedent) and at lines 271 and 305 (each with manuscript support). WN also departs from CX^2 in altering *fortherover* to *also* at lines 196, 199, 207, 321 (all without manuscript support), and to *more ouer* (with Mm only) at line 421. Again, *everich* becomes *eche* in both CX^2 and WN at lines 201 and 203 but only in WN at lines 202 (twice) and 389, all three without manuscript support, and at lines 200 (Ph^2) and 261 (Bo^1). At line 224 both CX^2 and WN replace *lorn* with *lost*, but only WN does so at line 231 (with Ra^2). At line 327 both CX^2 and WN have *sayd* for *quod*, but only WN does at line 309 (without manuscript support). And at line

378 *tale* becomes *talke* in both CX^2 and WN, but at line 257 only WN has *walkynges* for *wakynges*.

Probably the strongest evidence to show that WN's text of The Parson's Tale is unaffected by CX^2 is the sheer number of times that WN diverges from CX^2. As noted above, WN shares only 127 of CX^2's 1,045 variants from my text; thus CX^2 has 918 variants not shared by WN. In 174 instances WN has a different variant from that in CX^2; thus CX^2 has 745 variants where WN has the reading of my edition. Since conversely WN has 369 variants where CX^2 is not variant, their texts diverge 1,287 times in substantive readings. Their rate of divergence is 10 times their rate of convergence in variant readings. WN has a total of 670 variants.

I have suggested that Gg is, of all extant manuscripts, closest to the manuscript from which WN's Parson's Tale was printed. WN's relation to any manuscript is made obscure by its 242 readings for which no manuscript offers support. Moreover, 73 variants printed for the first time in WN get support from only one manuscript, and 25 manuscripts are involved. Thirteen of this group appear but once: at lines 92 Cn, 95 Ha^3, 144 La, 247 Hg, 258 Ii, 280 Ox (cf. 282), 365 He, 442 El, 445 En^3 (but corrected by a later hand), 446 Ne, 462 Ln, 470 Fi, 500 Ch. Five manuscripts appear twice: at lines 197, 200 Ph^2; 293, 470 Ll^2; 327, 354 Ra^3; 382, 448 Tc^2; 387, 390 Se. Two manuscripts appear three times: To at lines 136, 283, 352; and Bo^1 at lines 171, 261, 315. Two manuscripts appear four times: Ra^2 at lines 93, 229, 231, 455; and Dl at lines 165, 210, 389, 510. Mm appears seven times, but three involve omissions (at lines 320, 326, 331), one (at line 401) involves a substitution that WN makes independently at line 487 (twice), and one (at line 421) involves *fortherover*, which, as we have seen, WN habitually emends. The remaining two variants that WN shares solely with Mm are at lines 171 and 177. Ht appears eight times—at lines 231, 264, 306, 374, 444, 458, 461, 482—but all involve the change of *eek* to *also* (cf. Dl at lines 165, 510), a change that WN makes independently at lines 117, 386, 419, 461, 487 (at line 526 WN simply omits *eek*).

More impressive than these manuscripts is Gg, which provides unique precedent for 22 variants in WN: at lines 273, 276, 283, 290, 299, 321, 336, 350, 351, 355, 357, 420, 421, 443, 445, 447, 458, 467, 476, 481, 484, 550. Most of these convergences could be coincidental, but the relatively high number (to which we might add the *peyne/pyne* convergences at lines 277, 335, 339, 343) makes Gg stand out from the other manuscripts. Also, the convergences at lines 273, 350, and 476 seem unlikely to have come about by chance:

> To muchel] And therfore resonabely may be seyd of Jesu in
>   this manere T. m. Gg WN
> in what manere that] how Gg WN
> and that is humylitee or mekenesse] h. o. m. i. the remedye
>   ageyns pride Gg WN

In sum, Gg joins WN and CX^2 in 36 variants, offers unique manuscript support for 22, possibly 26, other variants in WN, and joins with other manuscripts in 95 more variants printed for the first time in WN. Further, given that WN, by error or by editing, introduces 242 variants without manuscript support and 51 other variants for which a manuscript origin is unlikely, it is necessary to suppose that WN's copytext was of relatively high quality (under 500 variants?) to have introduced so many correct readings where earlier editions and manuscripts were corrupt. Gg is just such a manuscript.

Gg belongs to the second of two lines of manuscript descent for the Parson's Prologue and Tale (Hg is at the top of line I); these lines are distinguished in MR (2.463, 470) on the basis of 95 variations to which 15 more may be added (at lines 296, 311, 329, 338, 368, 452, 460, 464, 471, 491 [two], 518, 531, 536, 548). Of these variations 8 appear in the Parson's Prologue and are therefore not relevant to a

discussion of WN's Parson's Tale. WN appears with line II in 75 of
the remaining 102 variants and is clearly related to the line-II variant
in 8 other instances (at lines 107, 260, 315, 338, 467, 471, 472, 483).
Of the 19 divergences from line-II variants, 10 are shared with Gg: at
lines 197, 336, 345, 350, 386, 405, 452, 460, 476, 482. The remaining
divergences are at lines 91, 186, 329, 372, 387, 397, 433, 478, 530.

The task remains to characterize the editing that helped to create
WN's text. We have already seen that the "editor" tended to replace
fortherover, *everich*, *eek*, *thilke*; and twice replaced *quod* with *sayd*,
lorn with *lost*. The direction of change seems to be from terms now
archaic to words still current today. The same tendency is apparent
in the following substitutions (no manuscript support unless otherwise indicated; + means more manuscripts are recorded in MR's
collations, vol. 8):

> *agilte* > *offendyd*: at lines 131 (2), 132, 150; > *trespassyd*:
>   at line 280
> *amenuse* > *(a)mynyshe* (diminish): at lines 359 (Gl+), 360,
>   377, 481, 496
> *anguissous* > *anguysshyd*: at line 304 (Cn+)
> *bihovely thyng* > *exspedient*: at line 387
> *bynymeth* > *taketh away*: at line 461
> *clepe* > *calle*: at lines 81, 82, 181 (Ha^4+), 182, 192 (2),
>   284, 286, 289, 293 (Ll^2), 338, 357 (Ds+), 387, 444, 468
>   (Cn+), 508
> *drencheth* > *drowneth*: at lines 363, 364 (2)
> *by thilke enchesoun* > *per chaunce*: at line 374
> *enchesoun* > *occasyon*: at line 458
> *forlete* > *leue*: at line 93 (2, once with Ra^2)
> *gabbere* > *lyar*: at line 89
> *gerdone* > *rewarde*: at line 283 (To)
> *gleedes* > *coles*: at line 548
> *halwes* > *sayntes*: at line 225
> *malisoun* > *curse*: at line 443

oneden (united) > *knyt*: at line 193

shendshipe > *shame*: at line 273

soothly > *truely*: at lines 314, 315 (*for* Gg+ *soothly*)

undernome > *rebukyd*: at line 401

werreyeth > *denyeth*: at lines 401 (Mm), 487; > *repentyth*: at line 487

woned > dwelled (Ne+ CX^1–PN^1)

woot > *knowyth*: at line 487

The tendency toward modernization, then, is too pronounced to be entirely accidental. And to such instances of apparent editing we may add two other passages: at lines 456, 459, 461, 470 WN rejects usage that makes *pride* a verb rather than a noun; and at lines 234, 236, 237 WN consistently substitutes *do/dyde* for *werke/wroghte*.

Of course, not all changes of the sort listed above result from editing. Unconscious substitution, inevitable in the making of texts, doubtless accounts for some of the variation in WN. Consider the following instances (no manuscript support unless otherwise indicated; + means more manuscripts are listed in MR's collations):

170 *stierne* > *fiers*

171 *harye* > *hale* (Bo^1)

177 *grisly* > *ferefull* (Mm)

208 *waymentynge* > *waylyng*

224 *evere* > *alway*

363 *thurrok* > *tymbre* (conscious emendation?)

414 *degisynesse* > *disguynge* (error for *disguysynge*?)

431 *skantitee* > *quantite*

433 *vicious* > *nyce*

455 *withstondynge* > *vnderstondynge*

461 *ful* > *ryght*

464 *contenaunce* > *continuaunce*

493 *detraccion* > *detractyng*

503 *murmure* > *murmurynge*

Other ambiguous adjustments to the text seem to show a conscious effort to streamline the prose:

229 *establised and > om.* (Ra²)
235 *while he was > beynge*
288 *For in . . . wel to do > om.* (Gl+)
312 *the soule > it*
314 *body and al his herte > herte and body*
314 *to the servyce of Jesu Crist > to serue C.*
315 *swete . . . Jesu Crist > om.* (Bo¹)
325 *no thyng ne hadden shame > shamyd not therof*
326 *that was most wily > wylyest*
327 *ne nat touche it > and it*
529 *venym of the devel > deuylles v.*

Sometimes, however, WN lengthens the phrasing:

273 *Jesu Crist > oure lorde J. C.* (La+)
304 *withinne me I hadde > and sorowful w. m. thenne h. I*
384–85 Expanded by 17 words
387 *dedly synnes > the vii d. s.* (Se)
397 *synne > pryde ne s.*
548 *quyke > reuye or q.*

While some alterations are clearly deliberate and others may be, some obviously or likely result from misreading or missetting:

 75 *come > torne*
276 *prosperite > prooprytee*
298 *swyche > su suche* (*su* ends a line of type)
328 *deth > de deth* (*de* ends a line of type)
355 *preye > proye*
376 *blaundise > braundyse*
387 *chieftaynes > vii Ceynes* (?)
425 *whit > whiche*
432 *to manye > company*

Let us turn now to WN's descendants. None reproduces the marginal glosses in WN, but in each the text has a clear genetic relation to WN. William Thynne's use of WN's Parson's Tale is made most clear perhaps in the fact that TH[1] has only 743 variants from my edition and shares 577 of these with WN. By contrast TH[1] converges with the other early printed editions in no more than 157 variants. TH[1]'s differences from WN, all trivial, are owing largely to 57 new variants that have no precedents, 37 variants supported by a previous edition but not by WN, and 74 variants supported by manuscripts but printed for the first time in TH[1]. The latter group shows little evidence of manuscript influence. In 35 of these 74 variants the new reading results from omission of a word or letter; transposition accounts for 6 of the other new variants with manuscript support. Of the remaining 33 cases (involving addition or substitution of words), no manuscript supports more than 9 of the variants. To illustrate the kinds of readings at issue, I list the 10 variants that are supported by single manuscripts:

308 *wherof* > *wherfore* (Cn)
339 *in* > *within* (Gg; WN reads *win*)
347 *body* > *bodies* (Py)
384 *a* > *one* (Ii)
389 *hise* > *her* (Ii)
415 *may man nat* > *may nat a man* (Ph[2])
430 *of* > *or* (Gg)
450 *and I say* > *I say that* (Ii)
458 *certes* > *truly* (Ln)
532 *pas* > *place* (Ad[1])

Since it is unlikely that Thynne combed through these manuscripts to glean so few and such paltry emendations, one must conclude that the convergences are accidental, owing in each case to the same kinds of inadvertence and editorializing. Similar changes characterize the 52 readings in which TH^1 departs from WN to agree with the text of my edition.

The same phenomena may be observed in TH^2 (1542). Thynne's second edition departs from the first in 71 readings, agreeing with my edition 8 times, substituting a different variant 14 times, and introducing variants where TH^1 agrees with my text 49 times. Thirty-three of the new variants are unique to TH^2; only 26 of the other variants printed for the first time in TH^2 have manuscript support. The changes again are trivial and their support among manuscripts random. When a third reprint was undertaken (ca. 1550), the typesetters clearly used TH^1, not TH^2, as copytext. TH^3 diverges from TH^2 82 times but from TH^1 only 18 times; and TH^3 agrees with TH^2 against TH^1 only at line 127 (TH^1 omits *he*). Nine of the divergences have no precedent whatever. Clearly no comparison of texts was attempted. In turn, John Stow (ST, 1561) merely reprinted TH^3. ST differs from TH^2 100 times, from TH^1 34 times, and from TH^3 20 times. ST agrees with TH^1 against TH^3 only once (at line 345) but with TH^3 against TH^1 15 times.

Thomas Speght's first edition (SP^1, 1598) seems to have been set from ST. Though nearly all the variation among TH^1-SP^1 is trivial, the tabulation of convergences shows SP^1 to be more like ST than like any other edition in the TH^1-ST sequence. For example, SP^1 shares 10 of the 14 readings printed for the first time in ST; in 4 other readings ST SP^1 join CX^1-PN^1 PN^2 against WN TH$^{1-3}$. Textual evidence indicates that Speght's second edition (SP^2, 1602) was also set from ST. SP^2 diverges from SP^1 35 times, and in 17 instances it rejoins ST. ST and SP^2 disagree only 19 times, and 15 of these disagreements result from variants printed for the first time in SP^2 (5 with manuscript support, 10 without). SP^2 joins SP^1 against ST only once, and that is a phantom convergence. At line 496 SP^2 reads *amenishe*, wherein the medial *e* more likely represents a misreading of original *o* (*amonishe*, i.e., admonish, in TH^3 ST) than an emendation that brings the spelling closer to the form in TH[1, 2] SP[1] (*amynish*, i.e., diminish). The typesetter of SP[3] in his turn either interpreted the *e* in SP[2] as an error for *o* or misread *e* for *o* and reversed the error. It is noteworthy that in ST-SP[3] the word is split between lines and always is hyphenated between the vowel and *n*. SP[3], a bookseller's venture undertaken in 1687 (see Pearsall 1984*b*:91), is clearly a reprint of SP[2]: its rubrics at the beginning of The Parson's Tale and between lines 74 and 75 replicate those first printed in SP[2], and it also preserves 9 readings printed for the first time in SP[2]. Nevertheless, SP[3]'s text of The Parson's Tale diverges from that of SP[2] in 23 readings. Eight of these are printed for the first time in SP[3] (3 without manuscript support); the other 15 are shared with an assortment of previous editions. SP[3]'s convergence with CX[1]-PN[1] PN[2]—and with no other edition previous to SP[3]—to read *sheres* for *sheres forch* at line 418 is achieved merely by correcting SP[2]'s unique *shetes*. It is most unlikely that the typesetters of SP[3] made any comparison of SP[2] with previous editions.

There are so few differences separating ST-SP[3] (each has somewhere between 763 and 772 variants from my text) that textual analysis cannot determine which of these editions had the most influence on John Urry's text (UR, 1721) of The Parson's Tale. According to Alderson (1970:98), Urry collated manuscripts by entering variants into the margins of a copy of ST; selecting from these gathered readings, he then emended a copy of SP[2] (Alderson suggests), which was transcribed to create a copytext for the printer. If Urry collated any manuscripts of The Parson's Tale (I have not seen the copy of ST that contains his collations), they had little or no effect on his text. However, Timothy Thomas, who helped to complete the edition after Urry's death in 1715, collated the Delamere manuscript (Dl, now Takamiya MS. 32), intending that its readings appear at the bottom of the printed page; his directions were misunderstood and the printer substituted the recorded readings for those in the copytext (see Pearsall 1984a:117). Dl supports 35 of UR's 66 departures from SP^2; in 14 instances UR agrees only with Dl. In 14 other instances UR agrees with ST against both SP^2 and Dl. There is no precedent for 11 readings in UR. Of the remaining 6 divergences of UR from SP^2, 2 are supported by SP^3 (in line 443), 1 by WN TH^{1-3} SP^1 (line 447), 1 by CX^1-PN^1 PN^2 (line 351), and 2 only by meager manuscript evidence (Ht Se at line 111; Ha^2 Ma Py Ra^2 Ry^2 at line 505). UR has 770 variants from my edition and is slightly closer to ST than to SP^2.

Thomas Tyrwhitt (TR, 1775), perhaps like Urry, used a copy of SP^2 as a copytext (see Windeatt 1984:123), but he made a much more wide-ranging and judicious use of manuscripts than did Urry, even in The Parson's Tale, which up to now had never in any real sense been edited. TR preserves 388 of the variants in SP^2 but departs from that text 586 times. Departures include 306 agreements with my edition, 202 variants where SP^2 agrees with my edition, and 78 variants where SP^2 has a different variant. Hence TR has 668 variants from my edition and shows a net improvement over SP^2 of 104 amendments. In 418 departures from SP^2, TR rejoins other editions; 399 of these instances include CX^1-PN^1 PN^2 (345 times with no other edition prior to TR). The influence of CX^2, which Tyrwhitt singles out for praise (TR 1.vi), is apparent here. One may assume that the readings adopted are frequently supported by manuscript evidence as well. TR introduces 168 readings never before printed; 133 of these have manuscript support. This is not the place to introduce an analysis of the manuscript influence on TR. It is sufficient to emphasize the reduction of WN's influence (now certainly indirect; cf. TR 1.viii) on TR.

WN's influence effectively ends with the texts that reprint TR; all new editions done after TR are based on manuscripts. WN does have, however, at least one interesting legacy that persists. At line 247 for *al mortefied* WN reads *alle amortised*, a reading for which only Hengwrt and, in part, Harley 7334 (Ha^4) and Laud 600 (Ld^1) offer manuscript support (WN and these manuscripts do not ordinarily converge in variant readings; note too that MR's collation is inaccurate in its report of Ha⁴ and Ld¹). This reading stands in TH¹ TH³-TR (TH² missets or miscorrects to *all amortified*); it does not occur elsewhere in Chaucer's work, except at Parson's Tale 233, where Ha⁴ and Ld¹ also substitute *amortised* for *al mortefied* (again MR's collation is inaccurate). The word *amortised* is evidently not Chaucerian, but because of its print history it appears in Chaucer glossaries, from that in SP² up to and including that of Davis (1979); and as a consequence its "Chaucerian" use is recorded in the five seventeenth-century editions of Edward Phillips's *The New World of English Words* (see Kerling 1979:96, 307) and even in the *OED* and the *MED*, which cite only the manuscript variant in support of the particular meanings "killed" (SP²-TR) and/or "deadened" (UR, Davis), "destroyed" (Morris 1866:1.259). In *OED* and *MED* the word otherwise has only its usual legal denotation. John Alford, who indicates that its first known English use is in *Piers Plowman* (1988:xviii, 6), mistakenly assumes that Chaucer used this word in The Parson's Tale, and that he intended its legal sense (p. xv).

BIBLIOGRAPHY

Alderson, William L., and Arnold C. Henderson. *Chaucer and Augustan Scholarship*. University of California Publications, English ser., 35. Berkeley, Los Angeles, and London: University of California Press, 1970.

Alford, John. *Piers Plowman: A Glossary of Legal Diction*. Cambridge: D. S. Brewer, 1988.

Boyd, Beverly, ed. *The Prioress's Tale: A Variorum Edition of the Works of Geoffrey Chaucer*, vol. 2, pt. 20. Norman: University of Oklahoma Press, 1987.

Caxton, William, ed. 1476 [1477]. [*The Canterbury Tales*]. *STC* 5082.

———, ed. 1482 [1483]. [*The Canterbury Tales*]. *STC* 5083.

Crotch, W. J. B., ed. *The Prologues and Epilogues of William Caxton*. EETS, o.s., vol. 176. London: Humphrey Milford/Oxford University Press, 1928.

Davis, Norman, et al. *A Chaucer Glossary*. Compiled by Norman Davis, Douglas Gray, Patricia Ingham, and Anne Wallace-Hadrill. Oxford: Clarendon Press, 1979.

Garbáty, Thomas J. "Wynkyn de Worde's 'Sir Thopas' and Other Tales." *Studies in Bibliography* 31 (1978): 57–67.

Haller, Robert S., ed. *The Monk's Tale. A Variorum Edition of the Works of Geoffrey Chaucer*, vol. 2, pt. 8. (In progress.)

Hellinga, Lotte. *Caxton in Focus: The Beginning of Printing in England*. London: British Library, 1982.

Kerling, Johan. *Chaucer in Early English Dictionaries: The Old-Word Tradition in English Lexicography down to 1721 and Speght's Chaucer Glossaries*. Germanic and Anglistic Studies of the University of Leiden, 18. Leiden: Leiden University Press, 1979.

Manly, John, and Edith Rickert, eds. *The Text of* The Canterbury Tales: *Studied on the Basis of All Known Manuscripts*. 8 vols. Chicago: University of Chicago Press, 1940.

Morris, Richard, ed. *The Poetical Works of Geoffrey Chaucer*. The Aldine Edition. 6 vols. London: Bell and Daldy, 1866.; rev. ed. 1872, reprinted London: George Bell & Sons, 1902.

Pearsall, Derek, ed. *The Nun's Priest's Tale. A Variorum Edition of the Works of Geoffrey Chaucer*, vol. 2, pt. 9. Norman: University of Oklahoma Press, 1984.

———. "Thomas Speght (ca. 1550–?)." In *Editing Chaucer: The Great Tradition*. Ed. Paul G. Ruggiers. Norman, Okla.: Pilgrim Books, 1984. Pp. 71–92.

Pynson, Richard, ed. 1492. [*The Canterbury Tales*]. *STC* 5084.

———, ed. 1526. *Here begynneth the boke of Caunterbury tales/dilygently and truely corrected/and newly printed*. Pt. 3 of an edition of the works. *STC* 5086.

Speght, Thomas, ed. 1598. *The Workes of our Antient and lerned English Poet, Geffrey Chavcer, newly Printed*. *STC* 5077.

———, ed. 1602. *The Workes of Ovr Ancient and learned English Poet, Geffrey Chavcer, newly Printed*. *STC* 5080.

————, ed. 1687. *The Works of our Ancient, Learned, & Excellent English Poet, Jeffrey Chaucer*. STC C3736.

Stow, John, ed. 1561. *The woorkes of Geffrey Chaucer, newly printed, with diuers addicions, whiche were neuer in printe before*. STC 5076.

Thynne, William, ed. 1532. *The workes of Geffray Chaucer newly printed/ with dyuers workes whiche were neuer in print before*. STC 5068.

————, ed. 1542. *The workes of Geffray Chaucer newlye printed, wyth dyuers workes whych were neuer in print before*. STC 5069.

————, ed. [1550]. *The workes of Geffray Chaucer newly printed, with dyuers workes whiche were neuer in print before*. STC 5071.

Tyrwhitt, Thomas, ed. *The Canterbury Tales of Chaucer*. 4 vols. London: T. Payne, 1775. Additional 5th vol., containing glossary, 1778. Reprint. New York: AMS Press, 1972.

Urry, John, ed. *The Works of Geoffrey Chaucer*. London: Bernard Lintot, 1721.

Windeatt, B. A. "Thomas Tyrwhitt (1730–1786)." In *Editing Chaucer: The Great Tradition*. Ed. Paul G. Ruggiers. Norman, Okla.: Pilgrim Books, 1984. Pp. 117–43.

Worde, Wynkyn de, ed. 1498. *The boke of Chaucer named Caunterbury tales*. STC 5085.

Wright, Thomas, ed. *The Canterbury Tales of Geoffrey Chaucer: A New Text with Illustrative Notes*, vol. 3. Percy Society, 26. London: Percy Society, 1851.

THE WORDS OF THE PARSON'S "VERTUOUS SENTENCE"

PEGGY KNAPP

Chaucer's Parson occupies a place of some importance in the larger fiction of *The Canterbury Tales*, both structurally—as the one who "knyttes up" its motifs and genres—and ethically—as one who has been regarded by many readers as the arbiter of the whole debate in which the Canterbury pilgrims have been engaged.[1] Formerly regarded as one of Chaucer's "idealized" pilgrims—perhaps the pilgrim most obviously idealized—the Parson has found a number of detractors in the last two decades. It is of some importance, therefore, to look into the social location of the Parson within the world created and addressed by the *Tales*. I propose to do that through an analysis of a few of the English words Chaucer uses to translate his source texts, Raymund of Pennaforte's *Summa de poenitentia* and the

---

[1]Frederick Tupper made a detailed case for this position early in this century by arguing that each of the Seven Deadly Sins comments specifically on a pilgrim in the *Tales* ("Chaucer and the Seven Deadly Sins," *PMLA* 29 [1914]: 93–128). D. W. Robertson, Jr., *A Preface to Chaucer* (Princeton, 1962), treats the Parson's *sentence* as the last word in matters of exegesis (p. 335) and doctrines concerning marriage (p. 376). Florence Ridley makes a similar, though hermeneutic, assessment of the importance of the tale: "all the individual Canterbury tales must be seen in the context of the last, *The Parson's Tale*" ("The State of Chaucer Studies: A Brief Survey," *Studies in the Age of Chaucer* 1 [1979]: 14).

Summa vitiorum of William Peraldus. It is my underlying argument that linguistic change and social change are linked, that certain words in a particular language are appropriated by one group or another to impel or impede a particular understanding of the world.[2] (An obvious example from the era of the Reformation would be the struggle to translate *ecclesia* as either "church" or "congregation"). It follows from this that the semantic choices through which Chaucer creates his voice provide clues to the Parson's self-presentation, or rather to Chaucer's presentation of the Parson, as a social being in late medieval England. The little cluster of English words I would like to consider in order to explore the Parson's social situation and ideals are *glose*, *lewed*, *estat*, and *fre*, terms which could be used to calibrate social status and articulate social and religious ideals. It is a commonplace of current hermeneutics that every utterance is issued from a situated historical vantage point, even seemingly timeless truths. I am trying to locate that vantage point for the Parson's "vertuous sentence." This "consciously sociohistorical" approach to The Parson's Tale through semantic choices helps to sharpen a reading of the Parson's relation to Lollardy (bearing on the odd mismatch many readers have seen between strong hints of Wycliffite reformism in the Parson's portrait in the General Prologue and conventionality in the tale), social hierarchy, and linguistic innovation.[3]

---

[2] I will adopt the three-fold scheme of Raymond Williams in *Marxism and Literature* (Oxford, 1977) by calling terms and discourses *dominant*, *residual*, or *emergent*.

[3] The phrase "consciously sociohistorical" is from Stephen Knight's *Geoffrey Chaucer* (Oxford, 1986), p. 3. Many scholars now take this vantage point on Chaucer, but it has a long history; see, for example, Roger Loomis's discussion of Chaucer's social location in "Was Chaucer a Laodicean?" in *Essays and Studies in Honor of Carleton Brown* (New York, 1940), pp. 129–48; repr. in *Chaucer Criticism: The Canterbury Tales*, ed. Richard J. Schoeck and Jerome Taylor (Notre Dame, Ind., 1960), pp. 291–310.

The Lollard controversy swirls around the Parson's performance, deriving from his portrait as learned, poor, outspoken toward his betters, unwilling to curse for tithes, and, although not an itinerant "poor priest," a walker with a staff in his hand. Such congruences with Wycliffite positions and practices suggest the usefulness of looking closely at the diction of The Parson's Tale to see if, after all, a "Lollere" lurks under the surface conventionality of the Parson's penitential guide. This semantic investigation will not, I think, adjudicate the issue decisively, but it may serve to moderate some recent assessments of the Parson's positions. Anne Hudson has demonstrated that late medieval English provides a distinctive "Lollard vocabulary," a small group of words given particular valences in Wycliffite arguments.[4] The words she cites are: *ground, found, Goddis lawe, mannis lawe, anticrist, prelate, newe ordris, pore priestis, pore men, caytif, accydent, sugette, glose,* and *fable. Goddis lawe, mannis lawe, prelate, newe ordris, pore priestis, pore men,* and *accydent* are not found in The Parson's Tale at all. *Ground* appears only once, "al the ground of the tale [concocted by a congenital liar] is fals" (X.610), and bears little resemblance to the frequent Lollard sense of grounding theological tenets. *Found* is also not used in that sense and only occurs as "discovered" (lines 881, 889). *Anticrist* appears once, marking simony as the greatest sin except "the synne of Lucifer and Antecrist" (line 788). *Sugette* appears only in its sense "subjected" and never, as in Wycliffite usage, for the philosophical distinction between substance and accident. Lollard writing frequently uses *caytif* in a kind of modesty topos, taking on the role of

---

[4]Anne Hudson, "Is There a Lollard Vocabulary?" in *From Ockham to Wyclif*, ed. Anne Hudson and Michael Wilks (Oxford, 1987).

the captive or outcast as that of a latter-day prophet.[5] Instances of that word in The Parson's Tale are more straightforward. Two occur in translating Romans 7.24: "Allas, I caytyf man! Who shal delivere me fro the prisoun of my caytyf body?" (line 344); another, in a quotation from Gregory on captives in hell (line 214); one, on the body as a captive rebel (line 271); and one, on the prideful being reduced to captivity (line 471). The Parson as teller never refers to himself as a *caytif*, as did Wycliffite tracts and the wills of some "Lollard knights."[6] These semantic choices display no deference to Wycliffite usages.

FABLE

Fable does strike a Wycliffite chord. Wycliffite objections to including non-biblical stories in sermons are well known. They objected particularly to friars who drew large crowds by preaching *fablis*—rhymes, gabbings, falsehood, dreams, or the wisdom of men—instead of the gospel.[7] The Parson's Prologue refuses *fablis* in much the same spirit. When Harry Bailly asks him to "Telle us a fable anon, for cokkes bones!" (line 29), he offers the Parson two affronts (perhaps deliberately) in that single line, swearing by God's body, which the Parson has objected to earlier, and tauntingly requesting a fable. The Parson answers that Paul proscribed fables in

---

[5]The Wycliffite sermon cycle in Thomas Arnold's three-volume edition (*Select English Works of John Wyclif* [Oxford, 1869–71]) frequently alludes to contemporary licensing practices which prevent "Goddis lawe" from being freely preached in the countryside "for jurisdiccioun or other cause" (I.361), probably an allusion to Lollard "poor priests" and the antipathy their preaching aroused from orthodox powers.

[6]K. B. MacFarlane, *Lancastrian Kings and Lollard Knights* (Oxford, 1972).

[7]See Arnold, *Select English Works*, I.176–77, 361; II.19, 192, 216, 361.

his letters to Timothy, and indeed the three passages (I Timothy 1.4, 4.7, and II Timothy 4.7) which bear on the point underwrite the Parson's indignation. His tale contains no instance of the word *fable* and no interpolated story that might qualify as a fable.[8] Of the remaining words in Hudson's list, only *glose* shows any resonance with Lollard senses.

GLOSE

Glose is featured in one of Chaucer's most direct references to the Wycliffite controversies. It occurs in two widely separated passages. In the first of these the Shipman (or perhaps the Wife[9]) objects to the Parson as the next teller because he has scolded the pilgrims for swearing. The residual and, in the late 1300s, still important mainstream use of *glose* is "interpretation, exegesis," a scholarly term clerics used for accreted commentaries on scripture, but it also refers to the lay practice, which Chaucer both uses and produces, of adding marginal comments to secular works. Strong Wycliffite objections to current preaching styles, especially those which did not sufficiently acquaint lay people with the simple truths of "Goddis word," joined with another strand of usage—*glose* as "flatter"—to discredit glosses from the traditional commentaries. Wycliffite preachers favored presenting the text for the day in English adorned only with explanatory

---

[8]The tale is not itself, of course, a sermon. Nonetheless, its teaching function places it in the same relation to lay knowledge of the duties of Christians as a sermon should, i.e., a parson who objects to *fablis* in this context may be expected to distrust them in sermons as well.

[9]The textual and interpretative problems connected with this passage are summarized in the notes to II.1172–83 in *The Riverside Chaucer*, p. 863.

remarks about difficult terms and appropriate moral lessons.[10] In time, these unadorned textual commentaries themselves came to be called "gospel glosses." Both the Parson's headlink and his tale are involved in the issue begun by the accusatory exchange. The Parson rebukes the Host for swearing "by Goddes dignitee" and the Host replies:

> "O Jankin, be ye there?
> I smelle a Lollere in the wynd," quod he.
> "Now! goode men," quod oure Hoste, "herkeneth me;
> Abydeth, for Goddes digne passioun,
> For we schal han a predicacioun;
> This Lollere heer wil prechen us somwhat."
> "Nay, by my fader soule, that schal he nat!"
> Seyde the Shipman, "Heer schal he nat preche;
> He schal no gospel glosen here ne teche.
> We leven alle in the grete God," quod he;
> "He wolde sowen som difficulte,
> Or springen cokkel in our clene corn." (II.1172–83)

---

[10]The five sermon cycles in Arnold's *Select English Works* explain the text for each Sunday and holiday and draw out its ethical (and sometimes social) significance. Although the traditional "four senses" are mentioned (I.30 and II.277–78), there are no attempts to explain all four and few to go beyond the simplest moral ideas. *Glossing* as orthodox preachers were using it is often directly condemned: "bastard dyvynes seien algates that thes wordis of Crist ben false, and so no wordis of Crist bynden, but to the witt that gloseris tellen" (I.367); these priests do not teach "bot flatren hom and glosen and norischen hom in synne" (III.377); "her Anticristis tirauntis [the official church] speken aȝen the newe lawe, and seien that literal witte of it shulde never be takun, but goostli witt; and thei feynen this goostli witt after shrewid wille that thei han" (II.343). The manuscripts of these "sermons" probably functioned as guides or outlines for Wycliffite preachers.

The Parson "answers" (but much later, in the prologue to his tale), " I wol nat glose — / I wol yow telle a myrie tale in prose/ To knytte up al this feeste and make an ende" (X.45–47). My reading of this exchange is that the Host and Shipman or Wife object to the Puritanical tone they hear in the Parson's objection to swearing and take his somber manner as evidence of Lollard leanings. The Parson bides his time and when his turn comes proposes to instruct, "under correccioun" (line 56), about the true way to Jerusalem. His "I wol nat glose" might be construed as a direct answer to the accuser who thinks he will disseminate the "cokkels" of Lollardy, a vowing not to do so. "I wol nat glose" might also mean something like, "I'll be direct—I won't try to fool or dazzle you," especially since syntactically it occurs as an interruption of another sentence. It could equally well announce that he will forgo the elaborate scholarly glosses, often allegorical, he disclaims when he describes himself as "nat textueel" (line 57)—perhaps continuing his reference to Paul's advice to Timothy to avoid speculations and vain discussions of theological controversies (as well as fables) in favor of emphasis on the love that issues from a pure heart and good conscience.

Which possibility explains the Parson's remarks best? Although his "tale" is not a Wycliffite "gospel glose," it is single-mindedly intent on teaching morality and contrition, and it avoids both storytelling (*fablis*) and allegorical elaboration. Taken as a disavowal of Wycliffite preaching practice, it clashes with the straitlaced tone of calling fables "swich wrecchednesse" (line 34), which is the kind of gesture that called forth the suspicion of Lollardy in the first place, nor does it seem entirely adequate to his project of teaching in English. Taken as an aside which promises not to dazzle or falsify, it affirms his intent to address the pilgrims directly and seriously about "[m]oralitee and vertuous mateere" (line 38), and follows smoothly from his disavowal of both fables and rhyme. Taken to signal an avoidance of "patristic exegesis," it eschews subtlety and over-elaboration about moral precepts. Robert Knapp describes The Parson's Tale as "ultimately achieving in relatively spare and unmetaphorical language an expository lucidity unparalleled in other penitential manuals," a spareness and lucidity which seem consonant with "not glossing" in this third sense. Knapp goes on to say that Augustine is quoted in the tale "just as slogans and tags," rather than as a probing of Augustine's densely argued positions on signs and the sacrament of penance.[11] I agree with this characterization of the Parson's use of Augustine, and I see it as a deliberate feature of his address to a lay audience which bypasses the scholarly terrain of debate over Augustinian semiotics.[12] The Parson's Augustinian learning provides him with judicious phrasings for clear moral directives like "But he be penytent for his olde synful lyf, he may nat bigynne the newe clene lif" (line 97), and "If thou hast desdayn of thy servant, if he agilte or synne, have thou thanne desdayn that thou thyself sholdest do synne" (line 150). In such instances, the Parson may be seen as quoting Augustine for his pithiness and authority and at the same time keeping his promise not to "glose."[13]

---

[11]Robert S. Knapp, "Penance, Irony, and Chaucer's Retraction," *Assays* 2 (1982): 51.

[12]Oxford debates on current doctrines of the sacraments were often waged over quotations from Augustine. Wyclif regarded himself as a strict Augustinian realist in philosophical allegiance; see Anthony Kenny, *John Wyclif* (Oxford, 1986). His sermon outlines contain only glancing allusions to Augustinian doctrine, scrupulously avoiding such controversies.

[13]The Parson's quotations from other authorities observe the same style and function as those from Augustine, a style and function similar to quotation practices in Wycliffite sermons. The Parson's choice of authorities quoted closely parallels those of the Wycliffite writing in Arnold's *Select English Works*; see my tabulations in *Chaucer and the Social Contest* (New York, 1990), p. 93. What I make of this is not a direct Lollard influence on ParsT, but an indication of widely shared assumptions about religious discourse.

Chaucer's usage elsewhere suggests that *glose* was capable of all three inflections. The "gospel glosen" of the original charge against the Parson establishes the first, the Wife of Bath's use of *glose* to describe her fifth husband's fancy sexual maneuvers (III.509) the second, and the oily Friar Thomas's "But I shal fynde it in a maner glose" (Summoner's Tale, III.1920) the third. Moreover, several of Chaucer's instances make use of more than one sense at a time, as when Fortune "list to glose" (VII.2140) with tragic protagonists in The Monk's Tale, thus suggesting both her lack of literalness or directness and her propensity to deceive. I think the Parson's Prologue presents us with such a case. The first sense is present as an echo of the earlier refusal to let the Parson speak, but it does not register an unambiguous refusal of the Lollard preaching style. The second and third senses, often implied together in Chaucerian instances, operate here directly: the Parson will not deceive, and he will not enter into arcane doctrinal disputes.

If this reading is right, it neither demonstrates nor refutes the Parson's Lollardy. A poem from the Vernon manuscript, called "Who says the Sooth, He shall be Shent" (No. 103 in Carleton Brown's *Religious Lyrics of the Fourteenth Century*), uses *glose* in much the same way:

> Thus is the sothe I-kept in close,
> And vche mon maketh touh and queynte;
> To leue the tixt and take the glose,
> Eueri word thei coloure and peynte. (lines 13–16)

Brown regards the author as a friar (p. xx) because he refers to the silencing of a friar who teaches the "trewe tixt,"[14] but whether or not he himself was a friar, his poem describes a friar who took the same

---

[14] Carleton Brown, *Religious Lyrics of the XIVth Century* (Oxford, 1924; repr. 1970).

attitude toward text and gloss that the Parson seems to be taking. (Early in Wyclif's career, he regarded the friars as potential allies, but he later became their implacable opponent, and the English sermons and tracts tirelessly inveigh against them.) What I want to make of this attitude toward friars is that criticism of over-elaborate glossing was widely shared, although we have come to know it primarily through Lollard writing. Much in The Parson's Tale positions itself in a rather broad band of late medieval moral indignation and discontent with ecclesiastical practice which only later (and of course especially after Parliament's edict *De heretico comburendo* of 1401) became incriminatingly Lollard. In The Parson's Tale itself, neither the practice nor the word *glose* appears; like fables and *fablis*, its omission is a signifying absence.

LEWED

In Middle English, *lewed* usually meant "unlearned, untaught in Latin," lumping together most of those who rule and those who work and distinguishing them from the clerical estate, often in the phrase "the lerned and the lewed." There are, however, some Middle English instances of the word in its surviving sense "licentious," as in Trevisa's translation of *De proprietatibus rerum*, in a condemnation of joking about the sexual members.[15] Chaucer's narrator in The Franklin's Tale warns his audience against a premature judgment of Arveragus which would hold him "a lewed man" (V.1494) for allowing Dorigen to meet Aurelius in the garden, an instance which may be read as an indictment of the husband's learning and/or sexual

---

[15]"Translation of Bartholomew de Glanville's *De proprietatibus rerum* (1398)," British Library MS. Add. 27944. Photostat in the *Middle English Dictionary* library, Ann Arbor, Mich.

propriety. Wycliffites argued that "Goddes word" belonged to the *lewed* as well as the *lerned*, that the saving truths of scripture are not linked to their Latin representations and should be taught directly to lay people. Without abandoning the idea of society's three estates, they gesture toward a kind of spiritual egalitarianism.[16] In some obvious ways Chaucer's deployment of *lewed* resembles Wyclif's closely. The description of the Parson in the General Prologue stresses his respect for lay people in his parish, though he was himself "a lerned man, a clerk" (I.480), and his contempt for unworthy priests:

> For if a preest be foul, on whom we truste,
> No wonder is a lewed man to ruste;
> And shame it is, if a prest take keep,
> A shiten shepherde and a clene sheep. (lines 501–04)

The Parson's plainness of speech and lack of automatic reverence for institutional authority match that of Lollard documents, and so does his image of shepherd and sheep, though nothing in this passage is exclusively Lollard. Although hardly subversive in its outlines, the tale does attack simony by saying that "lewed men" respect the sacraments less when they are administered by the unworthy (X.791), hinting at a more precarious version of priestly efficacy than strict

---

[16]For example, "Therfore this prayere, declared en Englyssche, may edify the lewede peple, as it doth clerkes in Latyn," (*Pater Noster*, in *Works Hitherto Unprinted*, ed. F. D. Matthew, EETS, o.s., vol. 74 [London, 1880], p. 2). In *De veritate sacrae Scripturae*, Wyclif alleges that, "ʒif a lord or a laborer loue betere god than thes veyn religious & proude & lecherous possessioneris, the lewid manys preiere is betere" (ed. Rudolf Buddensieg [Leipzig, 1904], p. 117).

orthodoxy called for[17] and sharply contrasting with the Pardoner's cynical disrespect for the deductive powers of the "lewed peple" sitting before him as he preaches (VI.392). The other instance of *lewed* in The Parson's Tale explains the term "develes *Pater Noster*," used by simple people to mean murmurings against their "betters": "lewed folk yeven it swich a name" (X.508). The "lewed folk" here are uneducated, since the devil, says the Parson in his rather literal-minded way, never had a Pater Noster.[18] The emergent tilt of the word toward "licentious" occurs nowhere in The Parson's Tale.[19] Like *glose*, then, *lewed* in the Parson's discourse marks a social space shared by devout orthodox reformers and Wycliffites, who may not be all that distinct from one another among Chaucer's first hearers and readers.

ESTAT

The Middle English term *estat* can indicate a general condition, as in "the *estat* of virginity or widowhood," but is used more commonly to refer to the three estates—the first who pray and study, the second who rule and fight, and the third who labor. An emergent use highlights the material holdings that accompany and sustain what traditional social thought had regarded as essential states of being. Thus *estat* as "what one is" gradually gives way, in general after Chaucer's time, to *estat* as "what one has or controls."

---

[17]The *Postquam* contains no parallel passage. See *Summa virtutum de remediis anime*, ed. Siegfried Wenzel (Athens, Ga., 1984), p. 20.

[18]Again, there is no parallel in the source; see Wenzel, *Summa virtutum*, p. 14.

[19]Elsewhere in *CT* the word *lewed* does signify wickedness, notably in referring to the wolf in MancT (IX.184).

The Parson's Tale acknowledges the traditional social sense of the word and interprets it. The tale concurs in the general consensus that temporal high and low are ordained by God and "everich sholde be served in his estaat and in his degree," but stresses that this formulation entails mutual obligations, the man to the lord and the lord to the man (lines 771–72). (The Parson even mentions that some converts to the faith set their chattel slaves free.) To the person who is placed in "heigh estaat," that gift is like God's other gifts, given to test human ability to resist sin (line 153). The very definition of the sin of "[v]eyneglorie" is "to have pompe and delit in his temporeel hynesse, and glorifie hym in this worldly estaat" (line 405). The Parson offers another status hierarchy, also threefold: innocence, sinfulness, and grace. Like the three social estates, these spiritual conditions are defined by the work they require: in innocence, praise; in sinfulness, prayer for amendment; in grace, penitence (lines 681–84).

The Parson's Tale also comments on clothing as a sign of *estat* and as an occasion for sin. The wastefulness of current styles for the high-born is sinful in its use of scarce materials and its design (trailing gowns which easily become threadbare and dung-stained). Such clothing is also impossible to give to the poor: it is "nat convenient to were for hire estaat" since it is so "pownsoned and dagged" (pierced and slit) that it will scarcely keep an outdoor worker warm, not to mention its immodesty (lines 416–21). Denunciations of clothing styles are the subject of some of the most colorful prose in The Parson's Tale, including his charge that they make men look as if they had developed "the maladie of hirnia," their buttocks resembling "the hyndre part of a she-ape in the fulle of the moone" (lines 423–24). David Aers sees such descriptions as evidence of the Parson's disgust for the body and the temptations it offers for sin, finding him more rigorous than other orthodox writers on penitence, in consequence of his "platonic-manichean" metaphor of the soul imprisoning the body.[20] I read the Parson's stance very differently. These passages occur in his discussion of pride; they inveigh against stylish distortions of the body, not the body itself. Furthermore, they follow directly and logically from his attack on the extravagance of fashionable garments, which lists all the reasons why they cost so much and waste resources needed elsewhere. The fact that fashionable clothing does not enhance the dignity of the wearer is just the capstone of a larger, more socially (one might even say ecologically) responsible line of reasoning. In that this reasoning unsparingly "snybbes" the rich, it recalls the Parson introduced in the General Prologue, who admonishes the obstinate "of heigh or lough estat" (I.522). Note, too, that the Parson most sharply targets men's clothing rather than women's, hardly justifying Aers's allegation that he here reveals "his own obsessions and his own participation in what he sees as the sins of fallen man" by his "prurient fascination" with sex.[21]

These emphases emerge from the Parson's references to the estates: (1) he acknowledges their rightness for temporal governance; (2) he considers membership in the ruling estate to provide temptations to pride and indulgence; (3) the particulars of his rebukes to those who misuse social power show a detailed sense of the lives of the poor; and (4) he provides an analogous threefold layout for spiritual estates, which are the ones that count at the end of the

---

[20]David Aers, *Chaucer, Langland and the Creative Imagination* (London, 1980), pp. 109–12. I particularly object to Aers's assertion that the Parson is to be held responsible (either as a deliberate move on Chaucer's part or not) for mistranslating Romans 7.24. St. Paul does figure the captivity of the soul within the body, a captivity which leads ultimately to death.

[21]Aers, *Chaucer*, p. 110. The phrase "prurient fascination" is quoted by Aers from John Finlayson's "The Satiric Mode and the Parson's Tale," *Chaucer Review* 6 (1971): 114–15.

earthly pilgrimage. These inflections acknowledge the social reality of earthly *estat* while they reduce its ultimate value, making, for example, Walter's gift to Griselde or January's to May worth less than their stories seem to imply. This deference toward dominant discourses of governance demonstrates that support for social hierarchies does not necessarily endorse irresponsible behavior of the high toward the low, nor does it inhibit envisioning the lives of the poor. Wycliffite tracts also strongly supported estates theory, sometimes going so far as to argue that the duty of the knightly class to protect the faith authorized its seizure of unlawful clerical landholdings.

FRE

Fre as an adjective in Germanic and Celtic senses, the *Oxford English Dictionary* tells us, denotes "dear," with the implication of blood ties to the family and non-servitude. The word entered the Middle English period in two main developments from that "dear" or "kindred": "noble" (in its various senses) and "unconstrained." The connection between noble birth and liberty reflects and buttresses feudal modes of production and social hierarchy. Nobility as high birth itself remained an important use of *fre* as an adjective or a noun (the free person) throughout the medieval period. In William of Palerne, for example, we find "When the fre was in the forest founde / In comely clothes was he clad" (lines 505–06), and the issue is exclusively one of his birth.[22] Very often this usage appears in salutation, in phrases like "my lady fair and fre." During the period, though, the social fact of high birth was broadened by its association

---

[22]*The Romance of William of Palerne*, ed. W. W. Skeat, EETS, e.s., vol. 1 (1887, repr. 1898), pp. 8–175.

with the spiritual *fredom* of all souls in a state of grace[23] and became a key term in debates about divine foreknowledge and human will. Secularization extended usage still further to "unconstrained, un-coerced" in more quotidian venues. What progressively dropped out after the Middle Ages is the sense "noble" or "gracious," and what began to be hinted at is an implication of looseness which became so strong by the early seventeenth century that Thomas Middleton's *A Trick to Catch the Old One* (1607) could feature a character named "Freedom" as the son of Mistress Lucre.[24]

The various potential relationships between *fre* as a term marking social class and a term carrying religious weight are amply explored in The Parson's Tale. There are ten instances of *fre* in the tale (the other tales have four or fewer), and they represent the major medieval uses: as markers of social estate and spiritual estate, as the counter term in the predestination debate, and in constructions like "free from." When the Parson teaches that the degree of sin is determined in part by the situation of the sinner—"male or femele, yong or oold, gentil or thral, free or servant" (X.961)—he uses the word in its social sense, but in "thurgh synne ther he was free now is he maked bonde" (line 149), the powerful social *fredom* (nobility, membership in the family) is shifted to a spiritual arena. References to high and low status surround this passage, further linking the prestige of *fre* to noble standing even while democratizing it by placing it within the grasp of everyone who resists sin. The Parson even says that "in

---

[23]The mingling of senses is developed from both ends. The value of the souls of poor, but saved, Christians comes to be indicated by the word *fre*, and images of noble life are conferred upon the holy family, especially the Virgin, who is very frequently "that fre" or "our lady free," as is the case in PrT (VII.467, 532, 664).

[24]Thomas Middleton, *A Trick to Catch the Old One*, ed. Charles Barbar (Berkeley, 1968).

somme contrees, ther they byen thralles, whan they han turned hem
to the feith, they maken hire thralles free out of thraldom" (line 772),
which mildly suggests that Christian communities must be egalitarian
in this "time of grace."

The Parson's best example of an emergent use for *fre* may be his
excoriation of wicked priests as

> the sones of Belial — that is, the devel./ Belial is to seyn, "withouten
> juge." And so faren they; hem thynketh they been free and han no juge,
> namoore than hath a free bole that taketh which cow that hym liketh in the
> town./ So faren they by wommen. For right as a free bole is ynough for al
> a toun, right so is a wikked preest corrupcioun ynough for al a parisshe, or
> for al a contree. (lines 897–99)

What I see here is a negotiation between the old association with
nobility—the priest thinks that his membership in the first estate
makes him *fre*—and the new meaning of "unfettered" with a tilt
toward "licentious"—in what the Parson alleges about him—through
the analogy with the bull's sexual proclivities.

Stressing the importance of voluntary confession, the Parson
urges that "he that trespaseth by his free wyl, that by his free wyl he
confesse his trespas" (line 1012). This passage, like so much else in
the tale, focuses on the individual Christian's responsibility in accounting for his or her spiritual life. The word *fre* here does not differ
greatly from its uses in other debates about the will, but the position
the Parson takes leans toward the anti-sacramental stance of contemporary Lollards without being openly unorthodox.

Critics like Aers are of course right to see the Parson's prose as
far less self-reflexive and playful than Chaucer's intertext concerning
him. The playful uses of *glose* in the intertext and the Parson's Prologue are not continued in the tale. *Lewed* and *estat* are used

exclusively in their old-fashioned senses in the tale, and *fre* only once in an emergent and punning formulation.[25] The Parson does not emerge from this sort of scrutiny looking very trendy as a sign user. The very moral certainty that earlier critics valued in the Parson's teaching and behavior makes him suspect in today's climate of semiotic self-consciousness: "idealization" is not only more difficult to convey, it is more difficult to imagine. "Unlike his maker, he fails to attend to the mediations through which all knowledge and moral judgment are constructed," writes Aers. I agree; he does not make the grounds of his discourse on penitence a subject for his instruction in it, but soberly assumes its force and urgency. (He is also unlike the Wycliffites in this method, in that they relentlessly attend to the founding and grounding of their own assertions and those of their opponents.) But does this constitute, as Aers goes on to claim, "a grave and debilitating failure of imagination and critical intelligence"?[26] I think rather that it presents the Parson as a stern and untroubled moral teacher who attempts to empower his lay audience by laying out the particulars of the sins and their remedies. Rather than hoarding his knowledge as a clerical and masculine privilege—with the threat of "cursing" always there to enforce it—he publishes what he knows to lay pilgrims to help them avoid sin when they can and repent when they have sinned. Moreover, he speaks to them "under correccioun." These features do not clash with the uncompromising diligence conveyed by his portrait in the General Prologue.

Nonetheless, the tale does not fully deliver what the General Prologue and the intertext have led us to expect. Loomis explains this

---

[25] The Parson also uses *kynde* to mean "semen," as he warns against polluting the church by spilling "kynde inwith that place" (X.965), a residual usage for the end of the century.

[26] Aers, *Chaucer*, p. 109.

fact through a chronology of authorship in which the frame is written early, when a broad consensus between Lollard and other devout reformers was in evidence, but the tale and Retraction written later, when it might have proved dangerous for Chaucer to "round off his *magnum opus* with a heretical sermon."[27] Such a biographical account may or may not be true, but I do not wish to invoke it. More interesting, I think, is a consideration of the textual effects produced by the feisty portrait of the Parson and his traditional tale. Early readers or hearers could understand the Parson as an uncompromising reformer and yet a preacher of familiar doctrine. The Wife of Bath's Prologue and Tale provide a useful analogy: the woman is strikingly unconventional, indeed threatening to "normal people" and to social order, but her tale is nostalgic and doctrinally sound. Outrageous as her ideas look, they can, under the right textual management, be represented as acceptable, and even inspiring. The Parson also worries some of the pilgrims and doubtless some members of the early audiences of *The Canterbury Tales*, but he can reprove sin with the best of his less suspicious-looking colleagues. Perhaps The Parson's Tale delineates moral terrains shared by devout Christians of "orthodox" and "heterodox" views and in some measure functions to neutralize the demonization of Lollardy which would soon render ecclesiastical reform in England so difficult.

---

[27]Loomis, "Was Chaucer a Laodicean?" p. 304.

Chaucer's Parson and the "Idiosyncracies of Fiction"

Judith Ferster

To those modern critics who see Chaucer as a relativist, the Parson is an embarrassment. They want to read the structure of *The Canterbury Tales* as a refusal to search for a single absolute truth in favor of an accumulation of partial truths. To anyone who interprets Chaucer's epistemology in this way, however, the absolutist Parson is a serious problem. Especially because he is the final storyteller and the discussion in his prologue hints at the end of the storytelling game,[1] and because his tale is followed by the narrator's (or perhaps Chaucer's) own doubts about stories and a meditation on the state of his soul, the Parson can seem to be presenting the ultimate truth, the single answer to the many questions posed by the earlier tales.[2] His absolutism raises the question of whether he represents Chaucer's views on knowledge and on the meaning of the work as a whole. The perception that his "tale" has very little to do with him personally

---

[1] Judson Boyce Allen, "The Old Way and the Parson's Way: An Ironic Reading of the Parson's Tale," *Journal of Medieval and Renaissance Studies* 3 (1973): 255–71, argues that the position of ParsT at the end of *CT* does not give it special weight or authority. Allen uses as evidence medieval readings of Aristotle's *Poetics*.

[2] Many critics have noted the way the Parson picks up some of the material introduced by the other pilgrims. One of the first was Frederick Tupper, "Chaucer and the Seven Deadly Sins," *PMLA* 29 (1914): 93–128.

adds to this impression. While other pilgrims tell tales that reveal their personalities, the Parson seems to some to present material that is entirely impersonal, even unsuited to him.[3] His tale then seems all the more objective and universal. According to Robert M. Jordan, The Parson's Tale "shows the true way . . . for it moves beyond the symbolic game of illusion to the reality of revealed truth. . . . Because the Parson's Tale is Truth it lacks the idiosyncrasies of fiction."[4]

Some recent critics, however, have argued that the Parson is not an exponent of uncontroversial truth, but rather is an arguer taking sides on contemporary issues, and thus must be seen as partial—like all the other pilgrims—in both senses of the word. That is, he presents only part of the truth and is prejudicially committed to his own view. David Aers and Carol Kaske show that the Parson's interpretation of Christian doctrine is much narrower than it has to be. One could disagree with the Parson on a number of issues and still be an orthodox Christian. His way may be one way, but it is not the only way.[5] If the Parson is choosing from among a range of options on the issues he

---

[3] See Jill Mann, *Chaucer and Medieval Estates Satire: The Literature of Social Classes and the* General Prologue *to the* Canterbury Tales (Cambridge, 1973), pp. 61, 63; Donald R. Howard, *The Idea of the Canterbury Tales* (Berkeley, 1976), p. 175; Charles A. Owen, Jr., *Pilgrimage and Storytelling in the Canterbury Tales: The Dialectic of "Ernest" and "Game"* (Norman, Okla., 1977), p. 210.

[4] Robert M. Jordan, *Chaucer and the Shape of Creation: The Aesthetic Possibilities of Inorganic Structure* (Cambridge, Mass., 1967), p. 240. See also Derek Pearsall, *The Life of Geoffrey Chaucer: A Critical Biography* (Oxford, 1992), p. 269: in ParsT, there is no "dramatic voicing."

[5] David Aers, *Chaucer, Langland and the Creative Imagination* (London, 1980), pp. 109–14; Carol V. Kaske, "Getting Around the Parson's Tale: An Alternative to Allegory and Irony," in *Chaucer at Albany*, ed. Rossell Hope Robbins (New York, 1975), pp. 147–77. See also Allen, "The Old Way."

addresses, then he sounds less like the voice of Truth. He also sounds less like the voice of Chaucer giving his final and "real" opinion about the work and more like himself, one equal voice among many.

My goal here is to show that The Parson's Tale fits the Parson. He does not present "pure" doctrine (as if that were possible) and is not exempt from the human condition: he does not speak Truth, but truth-according-to-the Parson. In order to show that the Parson's truth is relative to the Parson, I shall examine some of his themes—especially the relationship of the individual to larger social and religious contexts. I am interested in the Parson's treatment of these themes not merely for themselves, but also for the way they reflect the tensions in the Parson's biases and interests. I shall explicate parts of The Parson's Tale that seem impersonal and doctrinal in order to show how personal they really are. I do not intend to psychoanalyze the Parson. Some of the relevant facts about him are not even particuarly intimate. Chaucer seems to me to be interested in the way bias and prejudgment influence our knowledge. The sources of prejudgment include one's position in the world, to which the Parson is very sensitive. Insofar as his tale is in harmony with his sense of who he is and what he ought to be as a parson, he demonstrates the relationship between identity and knowl-edge. And since his material seems so impersonal, the evidence that even he has shaped his tale in accordance with his own occupation and preoccupations is all the more striking.

My general approach here will be "dramatic," in Robert M. Lumiansky's sense of the word: I am interpreting the way the speech is appropriate to the speaker.[6] A number of critics have spoken about

---

[6]Robert M. Lumiansky, *Of Sondry Folk: The Dramatic Principle in the Canterbury Tales* (Austin, Tex., 1955). Lumiansky's explication of the way the tale is "suited" to the Parson is on pp. 239–45. For the original formulation of this idea, see George Lyman Kittredge, *Chaucer and His Poetry* (Cambridge, Mass., 1915), chap. 5.

the Parson's relationship to his tale. John Finlayson is not as concerned with subject matter as with tone, but his argument that the tale is "to a discernible extent the product of a distinctive personality" is important for my purposes here.[7] So is James Dean's idea that the "Parson's style reflects the man's plainness."[8] In contrast, Lee Patterson contends that The Parson's Tale provides not a fulfillment of the game in which tellers produce tales that are in some way related to them, but an alternative to it, "a complete and exclusive understanding of character, action, and even language." The Parson rejects "all personal speaking that does not confront, in the sacramental language of penance, the sinfulness of the human condition."[9] Nevertheless, as Patterson also reminds us, the tale is paradoxically part of the game in which tellers are bound to tales: it "takes its origin in the very dramatic and realistic context which it will dismiss, and it is a denial of the tale-telling game that in the first instance quits the Manciple."[10]

In this essay I want to expand on the part of the paradox that locates the Parson in the tale-telling fiction and relates penitential writing on penance to the Parson himself. In this, I am attempting to take seriously Marshall Leicester's judgment that we often give up too soon on the pilgrim narrators as the speakers of their tales. He advises us to see the tales as "individually voiced, and radically so" and argues "that each of the tales is primarily (in the sense of 'first,'

---

[7]John Finlayson, "The Satiric Mode and the *Parson's Tale*," *Chaucer Review* 6 (1971): 115.

[8]James Dean, "Dismantling the Canterbury Book," *PMLA* 100 (1985): 755.

[9]Lee W. Patterson, "The 'Parson's Tale' and the Quitting of the 'Canterbury Tales'," *Traditio* 34 (1978): 379.

[10]Patterson, "The 'Parson's Tale'," p. 380. Patterson relates the pentitential act of writing a treatise on penance to Chaucer speaking in his own voice.

that is, the place where one starts) an expression of its teller's personality and outlook. . . ."[11]

My concerns are also hermeneutical. Knowledge is affected by the nature of the knower and his viewpoint—his place in the world. Perception is conditioned by prejudgment—what the knower already, perhaps unconsciously, knows.[12] This idea, a cornerstone of modern hermeneutics, would have been familiar to Chaucer through Boethius, who, in the *Consolation of Philosophy*, says (in Chaucer's translation):

> al that evere is iknowe, it is . . . comprehendid and knowen, nat aftir his strengthe and his nature, but aftir the faculte (*that is to seyn, the power and the nature*) of hem that knowen. (Book V, pr. 4, lines 137–41; my emphasis)[13]

---

[11]H. Marshall Leicester, Jr., *The Disenchanted Self: Representing the Subject in the Canterbury Tales* (Berkeley, 1990), p. 6.

[12]See especially Hans-Georg Gadamer, *Truth and Method* (London, 1975); Paul Ricoeur, *Interpretation and the Surplus of Meaning* (Fort Worth, Tex., 1976); *Paul Ricoeur: Hermeneutics and the Human Sciences: Essays on Language, Action, and Interpretation*, ed. and trans. John B. Thompson (Cambridge, 1981).

[13]Boethius needs this form of relativism in order to distinguish between the different human faculties (seeing is different from touching, reason is different from imagination) and between man's perception and God's. The latter distinction is important to his argument that God's foreknowledge is separate from and does not interfere with man's free will. God's mode of perceiving is different from man's in that it is eternal, not temporal, and therefore not causative. Thus, for Boethius, the fact that knowledge is relative to the knower is the key to the compatibility of God's omniscience and man's freedom.

Boethius and modern hermeneutics have in common the belief that this relativism is not the result of a mistake correctible by care or method, but rather one of the constant conditions of perception.[14]

The fact that Boethius articulates this idea so clearly makes more plausible the modern interpretation of *The Canterbury Tales* as an experiment in perspective.[15] But the Parson remains a crucial test case for that interpretation. This is the context for my view that The Parson's Tale fits the Parson as well as any of the tales fit their tellers. I want to show the close correspondence between the Parson's interests and situation in life on the one hand and, on the other, the ideas in his tale. I will explore some of the themes or preoccupations that appear in the tale—including the relationship between the self and the group, the relationships among parts of the self and among parts of the group—and then show how he shapes them and how they fit with what we can know about him.

THE PARSON'S TALE

The Parson's Tale contains at least five different models of the self, society, and their interrelations:

1. the self as separate from the outside world;
2. the self as an integral part of a larger system;
3. the self as a collection of warring parts, hierarchically arranged, the lower members most corrupt;

---

[14]Gadamer, *Truth*, p. xvi, says, for instance, "My real concern was and is philosophic: not what we do or what we ought to do, but what happens to us over and above our wanting and doing."

[15]For hermeneutical interpretations of several dream visions and several of the *CT*, see Judith Ferster, *Chaucer on Interpretation* (Cambridge, 1985).

4. the society as a collection of warring parts, hierarchically arranged, the higher members most corrupt;
5. society as a group of individuals who are, by some criteria, all equal.

The first of these models for the individual is the commonplace medieval notion that each person is a house that ought to be shut off from harmful outside influences. The integral self is closed, walled off from temptation:

> An ydel man is lyk to a place that hath no walles; the develes may entre on every syde, or sheten at hym at discovert, by temptacion on every syde. (X.714)

This idea of the self-as-fortress[16] suggests that the individual needs protecting.

Not only devils, but some people as well, are dangerous:

> Certes, the commendacioun of the peple is somtyme ful fals and ful brotel for to triste; this day they preyse, tomorwe they blame./ God woot, desir to have commendacioun eek of the peple hath caused deeth to many a bisy man. (lines 473–74)

The passage is Boethian in its exploration of the inconveniences and dangers of the goods of Fortune. Lady Philosophy warns Boethius that those who want honor become vulnerable to others. They must beseech and supplicate the powerful and will "defoule thiself thurw humblesse of axynge" (Book III., pr. 8, lines 13–14). For both the

---

[16]This image resembles Prudence's elaborate allegorical interpretation of the attack on Melibee's house in Mel (VII.1424–26).

Parson and Lady Philosophy, there is danger in desire that opens one to other people.

This suspicion of commerce between the self and the outside world is reflected in the Parson's attitude toward bodily functions that effect such an exchange. It is bad to take in too much food or drink (X.372, 913, 947) or let out too many words (lines 373, 947) or too much semen (lines 912–14). The body's commerce with the outside world easily goes wrong and leads to sin. The Parson acknowledges that human beings must eat to live (line 372), but the body's commerce with the world endangers spiritual health and must be carefully regulated.

The Parson also presents a different model of the relationship between self and not-self, however. At times he describes a self which is not and need not aspire to be a closed fortress. Sometimes the individual is linked to others as part of a larger system. We cannot be separated from God because "alle oure thoghtes been discovered as to hym" (line 167). The Parson picks up the Christian emphasis on man's relationship with God when he lists as one of the reasons for penitence "remembrance of the passioun that oure Lord Jhesu Crist suffred for oure synnes" (line 255). Men and Christ have made an exchange that unites them; when Christ "suffred for my synnes, and no thyng for his gilt" (line 259), He made a bond between Himself and man which man can honor through penitence. God is ideally almost one of the mental faculties by which man controls his unruly body:

> For it is sooth that God, and resoun, and sensualitee, and the body of man been so ordeyned that everich of thise foure thynges sholde have lordshipe over that oother,/ as thus: God sholde have lordshipe over resoun, and resoun over sensualitee, and sensualitee over the body of man. (lines 261–62)

God and humans are part of a seamless but hierarchical system of feudal relationships in which each faculty has sovereignty over the one below it.

A similar system is formed when a couple marries. Man and wife are "two in o flessh" (line 842). In fact, adultery is theft, for an adulterous wife steals her body from her husband when she gives it to her lover (line 878), or even homicide, "for it kerveth atwo and breketh atwo" the single creature formed by marriage (line 888). The metaphor is extended when the Parson says that the punishment for adultery is appropriate: the stink of fire and brimstone matches "the stynk of hire ordure" (line 841). Those who go outside the unit of marriage are characterized by a bad smell like the smell of excrement, which was once inside but is now outside the body.

Marriage partners do not control their own bodies. The unit of the couple takes priority. One partner cannot withdraw from the sexual relationship without the other's consent because each owes the other "the dette of hire bodies, for neither of hem hath power of his owene body" (line 940). Paying one's marriage debt is perhaps not as worthy a justification for sex as the desire for children, but it is an important obligation, binding even on those who would prefer abstinence. The two concepts—the sinfulness of lust in marriage and the marriage debt—together form a sort of shell game of desire. Desire is acknowledged to exist, but whichever partner is being scrutinized, it is the other one whose desire is responsible for the continuation of their sexual activity, which is justified only when they are considered as a unit.

The couple also appears to be a unit in the allegorical interpretation of the Fall, in which Eve plays the part of the body and Adam the part of the head and thus reason. The Fall occurs through "the delit of the flessh," that is, Eve, who seduces Adam, that is, "resoun" (lines 331–32). This story emphasizes the hierarchical nature of marriage, but also the way man and wife together constitute a single person.

Marriage also bonds the couple with Christ because He endorsed marriage. A female adulterer not only steals her body from her husband but also "steleth hir soule fro Crist and yeveth it to the devel" (line 878). Both the body and the soul belong to Christ, and adultery is like stealing "the vessel of grace" from the church (line 879).

These two models of the self—as closed to the outside world or as open to and integrated with the outside world—are both reflected in the Parson's poetic description of the perfections of virgins. If a virgin is "hooly in herte and clene of body,"

> Thanne is she spouse to Jhesu Crist, and she is the lyf of angeles./ She is the preisynge of this world, and she is as thise martirs in egalitee; she hath in hire that tonge may nat telle ne herte thynke./ Virginitee baar oure Lord Jhesu Crist, and virgine was hymselve. (lines 948–50)

The virgin's holiness has something to do with wholeness. But her wholeness comes at the expense of physical satisfaction: she is like a martyr. She is simultaneously open to Christ, as his spouse, and closed to other humans ("she hath in hire that tonge may nat telle"). She is also like Christ, who was both virgin and martyr, and like the Virgin Mary, who is both virgin and mother. The virgin unites both models that the Parson uses to describe the relationship between self and world.

The Parson's third model of the self complicates what I have already said about the relationship between the individual and the larger context because it emphasizes the way the self may not be a whole. That is, at times the self seems to be not a unit capable of shutting out or including some piece of the world, but rather a bunch of disparate parts in conflict with each other.[17] At times the Parson

---

[17]St. Paul reports "another law in my members warring against the law of my mind" (Rom. 7.18).

speaks as if the self is not unified because the body is inherently and obstinately bad. Reason must struggle to dominate the body, and its failure to do so turns the proper order "up-so-doun" (line 260). Sin makes the "free" (line 149) self who is "born to gretter thynges" (line 145) inappropriately "thral to [his] body" (line 145). The Parson quotes St. Paul's exclamation (Romans 7.24), "Allas, I caytyf man! Who shal delivere me fro the prisoun of my caytyf body?" (line 344).

Man's higher and lower natures are irrevocably hostile because the body is the source of original sin, as the Parson makes clear when he allegorizes the story of the fall, which I quoted above. Since the body is a source of temptation to sin, one should not cultivate its health: a healthy body can cause the sickness of the soul and thus threaten spiritual well-being (lines 458–60).

Perhaps as a corollary to his hostility to the physical, the Parson emphasizes mental experience over deeds. Just going through the motions of penitence is not enough. Penitence must be sincerely meant (line 983) and motivated by the right reasons (line 1023; also lines 1045–46 on the sincerity of prayer). Gluttony is always bad, but fasting for the wrong reason is also bad (especially if it is done for the health of the body). Fasting is good only when done "for Godes sake, and in hope to have the blisse of hevene" (line 832; also see the role of the will in obedience [line 675]). Anger is often bad, but it is worse if intended rather than impulsive (lines 541–43). And lechery, even if *only* desired, is sinful (line 846).

In the Parson's scheme, the individual is ideally an integrated whole in that virtue requires cooperation between body and soul because while each can sin alone, they can be righteous only together. Nevertheless, the Parson's view of the body makes this cooperation less likely than conflict because the body, in its strength and contrariness, is likely to rebel (line 271). The self should ideally be closed to temptation (sin means letting in the devil), and the mind should be impervious to the influence of the body (line 145). The

Parson's view of man is individualistic in that each person is responsible for his own salvation, but for each individual, internal peace is not likely.

The war among the parts of the self has an analogue in the Parson's description of the war among the parts of society. This parallel is not surprising considering the popularity of the metaphor of the body politic in the Middle Ages.[18] However, in the body, according to the Parson, it is the lower members who are apt to behave badly while in society it is the higher.

In the ideal society, acceptance of hierarchy is the remedy for conflict between inferiors and superiors. "[C]ommune profit" and "pees and rest in erthe" depend on a hierarchy in which everyone obeys those above him (line 773). If all members know their places, the hierarchy prevails peacefully. Thus, individuals who combat their own pride contribute to social harmony.[19] But the Parson is well aware of the forces that threaten to disturb peace and rest. In particular, since he is concerned that the aristocracy takes advantage of the people, he chastises

> thilke lordes that been lyk wolves, that devouren the possessiouns or the catel of povre folk wrongfully, withouten mercy or mesure. . . . (line 775)

---

[18]For an anthropological discussion of this use of the body as a metaphor for society, see Mary Douglas, *Purity and Danger: An Analysis of Concepts of Pollution and Taboo* (London, 1966), p. 115. On the metaphor of the body politic see E. Kantorowicz, *The King's Two Bodies* (Princeton, 1957).

[19]There may be a catch-22 in advising everyone to "chese the loweste place over al" (line 482). The Parson does not address the idea of a competition in humility, nor the paradox of seeking the "loweste" place "over al."

In addition to this rapacity, there are sinners who deprive the poor of alms or workers of wages (line 568) and who oppress workers in other ways. They "maken hir servantz to travaillen to grevously or out of tyme, as on haly dayes . . ." (line 667). Since these last two sins against the peaceful social hierarchy are sins of anger, it is fitting that the remedy for them includes "mansuetude," "debonairetee," "pacience," and "suffrance" (line 654). It is less fitting that the remedy is offered not to the perpetrators, but to the victims. Out of love for Christ, who was patient with his tormentors, those who are tormented should "lerne to be pacient" (line 669). They "do greet synne" who demand "outrageous labour" from their workers (line 667), but nothing is offered to cure their wickedness. Not only is this a departure from the usual application of remedies to sinners; it makes workers analogous to Christ and their employers analogous to His crucifiers.

Thus, the hierarchy of society, like the hierarchy of the body, is not free of the tension that comes from conflicting interests. The Parson, however, has another way of seeing social relations, this one more egalitarian. For instance, since all men are descended from the same parentage, they are all, "bothe riche and povre," equals in sin (line 461). All men die (line 762) and high rank is no protection from the torments of hell because "namoore reverence shal be doon there to a kyng than to a knave" (line 188).

Having accumulated these five different models for the self, society, and their interrelations, we can look for ways in which the Parson himself is implicated in them—how he shapes them and how his own traits and interests are embedded in them.

THE PARSON IN THE PARSON'S TALE

The Parson's Rhetoric of Narration

The Parson's rhetoric of narration offers evidence about how his language structures his relationship to his material and to his audience. Much of The Parson's Tale reproduces the rhetoric of the sources, treatises on penance and the sins that present their material as if it existed objectively—as if the definitions of terms and the order of presentation existed outside of discourse, and as if the discourse were a mere copy. "Post vitium avaritie sequitur de vitio gule," says one.[20] The Parson translates straightforwardly—"After Avarice comth Glotonye" (line 818)—with no hint that the order of sins is a product of mind. This kind of formulation is what gives the impression that treatises are impersonal, "unvoiced." Although in the past the tale has been treated as a sermon, only a few critics today dwell on its orality. Siegfried Wenzel's work on the sources that provide its content and Lee Patterson's exploration of the fourteenth-century penitential manuals that provide its literary context have taken us back to Chaucer's own word for it, "tretys" (Retraction, X.1081).[21]

But to label the tale a treatise is not to obviate the need to study its rhetoric. The rhetoric of objectivity, as our own technological age has found, is extremely powerful. It often implies that the information offered, the speaker, and the audience are independent of one another. Sentences like "The speces of Penitence been three" (X.102) discourage questions like "According to whom?" Such uses of the

---

[20]Siegfried Wenzel, "The Source of Chaucer's Seven Deadly Sins," *Traditio* 30 (1974): 370 (108r).

[21]Wenzel, "The Source for the 'Remedia' of the Parson's Tale," *Traditio* 27 (1971): 433–53; "The Source of Chaucer's Seven Deadly Sins," pp. 351–78; and the "Explanatory Notes" in *The Riverside Chaucer*; Patterson, "The 'Parson's Tale'."

verb *to be*, very common in The Parson's Tale, block inquiry about origins that would attack the "naturalness" of the divisions. The claim is not only that God created everything "in right ordre" (and numbered it [line 218]), but also that the Parson merely follows that godly order.

I would claim that even if the Parson merely copied the rhetoric of his sources, we could interpret it as his own because he has adopted it. The impersonal becomes personal when it is chosen. But the Parson also uses different rhetorical strategies that make much more explicit his shaping of the material. For instance, at the beginning of the discussion of the first sin, he says,

> And thogh so be that no man kan outrely telle the nombre of the twigges and of the harmes that cometh of Pride, yet wol I shewe a partie of hem, as ye shul understonde. (line 390)

Here is acknowledgment not only of the limitations of the human mind in counting, but also of his own activity in showing, and the audience's in receiving what he shows.

Sometimes the Parson uses such formulations where he is adding something to the source, so that there is no direct parallel. At other times, however, he is translating, but very freely. Here are some examples, with literal translations of the source (my own), to show what the Parson has done to "voice" the tale:[22]

---

[22]I have taken the passages from the treatise on sin from Wenzel, "The Source of Chaucer's Seven Deadly Sins," and use his line numbers. I have taken the passages from the treatise on remedies for sin from Wenzel's edition, *Summa virtutum de remediis anime* (Athens, Ga., 1984), and use his chapter and line numbers.

THE PARSON'S TALE	SOURCE	TRANSLATION
now shul ye undestonde which is the remedie agayns the synne of Pride; and that is humylitee (line 476)	et primo de humili- tate quia ipsa est remedium superbie (II.3)	and first is humility, for it is the remedy for pride
Now wol I speke (line 515)	Dicendum est (III.3)	Now shall it be spoken of
in the name of thy neighe- bor thou shalt understonde the name of thy brother (line 516)	Et nomine 'fratis' intelligitur omnis homo (III.839–40)	And by the name 'brother' is every man understood
I seye, thyn enemy shaltow love for Goddes sake (line 523)	Amicos debemus dili- gere in Deo . . . et inimicos propter Deum (III. 862–63)	We must love our friends in God and our enemies because of God
Now shul ye understonde (line 804)	sequitur (VII.2)	[it] follows
Now lat us speke (line 840)	[not in source]	
Of Leccherie, as I seyde, sourden diverse speces, as fornicacioun (line 865)	Sequitur de specibus luxurie . . . quarum prima est fornicatio (118v)	The species of lust, of which the first is fornication
I ne kan seye it noon ootherweyes in Englissh, but in Latyn it highte (line 869)	[not in source]	

I have spoken (line 873)	Et dicitur (120v)	And it is said
Now shaltow understonde that matrimoyne is leefful assemblynge of man and of womman (line 917)	Est autem matrimonium "legittima uiri et mulieris coniunccio" (IX.20–21)	Marriage is the lawful union of man and woman
I woot wel that they sholde setten hire entente to plesen hir housbondes (line 932)	Item studere debet uxor qualiter "uiro [suo] placeat" (IX.109)	Also, a wife should study how she can please her husband
Ful ofte tyme I rede (line 955)	[not in source]	

In these passages the Parson introduces the first and second person pronouns, which hardly ever appear in his sources. He is much readier than the sources to acknowledge his audience and himself as manager of the discourse. In the eighth passage, he even mentions a translation problem and, in the twelfth, mentions the fact that he has sources.

Several times the Parson even speaks as though he is shaping the material, for instance when he justifies classifying flattery as anger: "I rekene flaterie in the vices of Ire . . ." (line 618). The reason is, in fact, a little strained, but in the use of the verb "rekene," he acknowledges himself as one of the sources of his treatise.

He also begins and ends with modesty tropes, in the Prologue putting his "meditacioun/ . . . under correccioun/ Of clerkes" (lines 55–57) and at the end of the tale distinguishing between what he can and cannot do:

Now after that I have declared yow, as I kan, the sevene deedly synnes, and somme of hire braunches and hire remedies, soothly, if I koude, I wolde telle yow the ten comandementz./ But so heigh a doctrine I lete to divines. (lines 956–57)

According to Patterson, a number of analogues to The Parson's Tale do include the Ten Commandments.[23] The Parson's refusal to take them on and his admission that all the previous teaching has been "as I kan" acknowledge his limits and their influence on the material he presents. He selects and grooms his material as all authors do. A number of the pilgrims mention the sources of their tales. The Clerk, for instance, even admits cutting a part of Petrarch's introduction that he feels is irrelevant (IV.39–55). Of course Chaucer stands behind his characters. But, just as inside the fiction of the frame we must call the Clerk a pilgrim-author who adjusts his tale to suit himself, we must also give the Parson that status.

The Parson as Editor

Two examples of the way the Parson modifies his material might be useful here. We have already seen how the treatise denigrates the body, treating it as a source of sin. We can see an aspect of the Parson's attitude toward the body in his discussion of the motives for marital sex, a touchstone for many medieval theologians and teachers of confession. According to Pierre J. Payer, the conventional organization of the kinds of marital intercourse in one mid-thirteenth century source of The Parson's Tale, the *Summa vitiorum* of William Peraldus, was itself a synthesis of several other sources. The scheme the Parson adopts is the result of much sifting and synthesis.[24] But the Parson does not adopt the results of this process passively. Although his categorization of the four motives for sex follows the convention (procreation, paying the marital debt, avoiding lechery, and "amorous

---

[23]Patterson, "The 'Parson's Tale'," p. 340.

[24]See Pierre J. Payer, *The Bridling of Desire: Views of Sex in the Later Middle Ages* (Toronto, 1993), pp. 84–86, for the emergence of the four motives in the work of Raymond of Pennafort (another of Chaucer's important sources) from two different schemes.

love," X.939–43), when he announces the moral weight of each of the four, he adds his own coloring to the scheme.[25] In the Parson's source, the first and second are not sinful, the third is a venial sin, and the fourth is a venial sin unless the act is so pleasurable that the man "does not discern whether it is his wife or another woman." Such blind pleasure is mortal sin.[26] In the Parson's scheme, the first and second are "meritorie," and the third is venial sin. But, as Kaske notes, the Parson goes beyond the rigor of his source when he adds, speaking of the first three motives together, "scarsly may ther any of thise be withoute venial synne, for the corrupcion and for the delit" (line 942).[27] Thus the Parson destroys the distinctions among the three because pleasure makes all sexual acts sinful. Kaske also notes the Parson's increase in the moral penalty for the fourth motive: it is *always* mortal sin.[28]

According to Thomas N. Tentler, the question of the moral culpability of marital sex for pleasure rather than the three other reasons was one of the key ways to distinguish between "rigorist" and "laxist" writers. Sexual pleasure, then, gives us the key to the Parson's rigorism. There were ways to restrict the grip of mortal sinfulness on sexual pleasure. An important one was to divide pleasurable sex that

---

[25]For the relevant lines in ParsT aligned with those in the source, see Wenzel, "The Source for the 'Remedia'," pp. 449–50.

[26]For the very useful juxtaposition of the Parson on the four motives and his source, the *Remedium contra peccatum luxurie*, see Wenzel, "The Source for the 'Remedia'," pp. 449–51. Kaske, "Getting Around," pp. 167–68, translates the Latin.

[27]Kaske, "Getting Around," p. 169.

[28]See Kaske, "Getting Around," p. 169. Wenzel, "The Source for the 'Remedia'," p. 452, agrees that the source is more "sophisticated, lenient, and as it were, 'modern' than Chaucer" (cited in Kaske, p. 168). I agree with this assessment but attribute the "rigorism" of ParsT first to the Parson.

occurs naturally and pleasurable sex that was artificially incited. Only the use of artificial aphrodisiacs leads to damnation.[29] That this distinction is easier to make (one has to examine one's conscience to know whether one has forgotten the identity of the woman with whom one is having sex, but there's a somewhat less blurry line between using and not using artificial stimulants) highlights the choices the Parson makes. At a time when he could have left a little room for sexual pleasure, he refuses to sanction it at all.

Another sign of the Parson's aggressive translating is in the ordering of the motives. The source announces that there are four, then defines three and goes back to say what kinds of sin they are. It then defines the fourth, saying that one has to distinguish between sex when one is too carried away to be aware of the identity of the woman and sex when one remains aware. As we have seen, the reason for the distinction is that they are different kinds of sin.[30] In contrast, the Parson announces that there are *three* motives for marital sex, defines them, and then, without defining it, announces what kind of sin the fourth is: "The ferthe is for sothe deedly synne" (line 940). The Parson thus miscounts, inserts the fourth and his "for sothe" where the fourth is not mentioned in the source, and reverses the order of defining the sins and giving them their moral labels. As Wenzel says, the arithmetic mistake may be the result of a mis-translation of a faulty text copied hastily by candlelight,[31] but the listing of four motives was so common in the Middle Ages that perhaps we may also take it and the other anomalies in this passage as marks of the Parson's own thought on the questions about marital

---

[29] Thomas N. Tentler, *Sin and Confession on the Eve of the Reformation* (Princeton, 1977), p. 178.

[30] See Wenzel, "The Source for the 'Remedia'," p. 450.

[31] Wenzel, "The Source for the 'Remedia'," p. 452.

sex. Wenzel speculates that Chaucer might have been synthesizing several different sources.[32] So the anomalies might be the result of Chaucer's own discomfort with the cumbersome family of texts and/or system of judgment on sexuality. Or it could be Chaucer's joke at the expense of his sources. Or, whether it is a sign of discomfort or humor or both, if we follow Leicester's logic, it could be the Parson's.

Another subject on which the Parson leaves his mark is the relationship between the higher and lower estates of society. We have already seen how he treats the imbalance between the estates mostly as the fault of the members of the higher orders. But his criticism of them puts him squarely in the middle of some of the most prominent causes of social unrest in late fourteenth-century England—complaints against attempts to suppress wages, which rose after the plague reduced the number of agricultural workers, and complaints about the injustices of the differences in power and status between landowners and the peasantry. Both of these played a part in the Rising of 1381. The 1351 Statute of Labourers, Parliament's attempt at wage control, was much resented and, because it was not entirely successful, it had resulted in the conviction and imprisonment of many workers.[33] One of the demands in the Rising was amnesty for all those in prison because of the statute.

Besides the depredations of landowners, there is another target of the Parson's criticism: excessive taxes and those who impose them. This grievance, too, was expressed in the Rising of 1381. The

---

[32]See Wenzel, "The Source for the 'Remedia'," "The Source of Chaucer's Seven Deadly Sins," and the "Explanatory Notes" in *The Riverside Chaucer*, p. 956.

[33]R. B. Dobson, ed., *The Peasants' Revolt of 1381*, 2nd ed. (Houndmills and London, 1983), pp. 63–68. For Dobson's comments on the enforcement of the statute as a cause for the rising of 1381, see p. 69.

Rising's *tax célèbre* was the poll tax of 1380, the last in a series levied to support the war with France. The Parson's are "custumes and taillages" (line 567; see also line 752). Although these were not linked explicitly to the Rising, they were often the focus of resentment. Tallage had long associations with social unrest. One sympathetic early account tells of William FitzRobert's leadership in 1194 of an uprising in London against the mayor and aldermen, who both imposed a tallage and refused to pay it themselves.[34] According to Barbara Hanawalt, even when they did not stir open rebellion, tallages were the subject of court cases as people tried various legal maneuvers to avoid paying them.[35]

Even though they were supposedly abolished in 1340,[36] tallages continued to be imposed. Richard II did it in 1398 and 1399, for which *Richard the Redeless* chastises him. Included in the retrospective of the sins that caused his deposition was the "tallage of youre townes without any werre."[37] Thus, at the beginning of his reign, Richard's administration got into trouble with the lower classes for war taxes and, despite his later attempts to pursue a policy of peace, which stirred much trouble among the nobility,[38] he did not

---

[34] From Matthew Paris's addition to the *Flowers of History*, excerpted in *The Portable Medieval Reader*, ed. James Bruce Ross and Mary Martin McLaughlin (New York, 1949), pp. 177–79.

[35] Barbara Hanawalt, "Peasant Resistance to Royal and Seigneurial Impositions," in *Social Unrest in the Late Middle Ages*, ed. Francis X. Newman (Binghamton, N.Y., 1986), pp. 32–33.

[36] May McKisack, *The Fourteenth Century, 1307–1399* (Oxford, 1959), pp. 163–64.

[37] *Richard the Redeless*, in *The Piers Plowman Tradition*, ed. Helen Barr (London, 1993), Passus 1., line 102. This poem is, of course, at least a little later than ParsT.

[38] Anthony Tuck, *Crown and Nobility, 1272-1461* (Totowa, N.J., 1985), pp. 186–99, esp. p. 196.

take the opportunity peace offered to reduce his expenses and reduce taxation, and thus continued to arouse discontent. If we accept an early date for the tale, it would have been closer to the Rising. If we accept a later date for the tale, it could have been contemporary with the re-imposition of the tallage, and thus stirred corollary resentments.[39] No matter what the date, the memory of the Rising was vivid and connected to fears all through the rest of the century that it would be repeated.[40]

One peculiar aspect of the Parson's treatment of "wrongful" taxes is that in one passage taxes appear under the rubric of "ire" and are tucked into a section on the varieties of manslaughter. Giving advice to levy taxes serves as an analogy for giving deceitful advice, which constitutes homicide:

> Homycide is eek in yevynge of wikked conseil by fraude, as for to yeven conseil to areysen wrongful custumes and taillages. (line 567)

Odd as this analogy is, it may have had a contemporary ring to it: during the Rising of 1381, no blame for the unjust poll tax was attached to Richard, who was a minor at the time. As in many cases of opposition to royal policy, the king was not held accountable. The

---

[39]Patterson, "'The Parson's Tale'," p. 380, accepts a late date. Pearsall, *Life*, p. 228, does not think think that the tale was "likely to have been written last or even late."

[40]Steven Swindell, "'Cokkel in the Clene Corne': Preaching, Penitence and Politics in the *Canterbury Tales*," unpublished Master's Thesis, North Carolina State Univ., 1994, p. 1, argues that ParsT registers many of the tensions that produced the Rising and its uneasy aftermath. He notes a number of topical allusions but also sees the whole mechanism of confession and penance as contributing to social unrest because emphasis on the sins of the nobility justified the complaints and aspirations of the lower estate.

fault was seen to lie in the bad advice he was getting. The scene the Parson invokes replicates one of the conditions of life in Richard's reign: unjust taxes imposed by the king's advisers. As Steven Swindell points out, the lines mentioning tallage do not come from the Parson's sources.[41] The Parson seems to be going out of his way to make his critiques explicit enough to invoke the actual causes of social unrest in his own time.

Thus we have seen how the Parson shapes the material of his tale; in the case of the material on the estates of society, the shaping has the result of making the tale seem to refer very specifically to actual social conditions in his own time. We have also seen how his rhetoric of narration acknowledges his active manipulation of his material. Wenzel affirms that the tale demonstrates "a great freedom to select source material and to mold it according to the author's own structural principle."[42] I differ from Wenzel only in following Leicester's experiment of seeing what happens when we attribute the authorial activity to the Parson.

The Parson and the Pilgrimage

Along with the tale's relationship to its historical context, we can also see the signs of its relationship to the Parson himself, his role as priest, and his relationship to the "society" of the pilgrimage. The Parson begins by quoting Jeremiah 6.16, a passage that provides the metaphor of the path that makes the comparison of penance and pilgrimage so natural. Jeremiah advises Christians to ask "which is *the* goode wey" to salvation (line 77; my emphasis). When the Parson restates this idea for his own purposes, he does not claim that there is only one option:

---

[41]Swindell, "'Cokkel in the Clene Corne'," pp. 43–44.
[42]Wenzel, "The Source for the 'Remedia'," p. 453.

Manye been the weyes espirituels that leden folk to oure Lord Jhesu Crist and to the regne of glorie./ Of whiche weyes ther is *a* ful noble wey and *a* ful covenable . . . / and this wey is cleped Penitence. . . . (lines 79–81; my emphasis)

The and *a* are small words, but important ones, especially because of the change from one to the other in such close proximity. For the Parson, the one "righte wey" (line 80) to heaven is to avoid sin in the first place. Penitence provides those who have strayed a way back to it. Actually, on the Parson's map, penitence provides three paths: repentance every time one sins (line 91), repentance at the end of life (line 94), and repentance followed by a sinless life (line 93). Of these, he recommends the last as the "siker wey" (line 94), and the form of his treatise—an explication of penitence plus a manual on the Seven Deadly Sins and how to avoid them—will help. But as he himself says, it is but a single way to salvation. The Parson is not a transparent medium of truth but an advocate.

The Parson's advocacy allows us to explore his ambivalent relationship to the pilgrimage because penitence and pilgrimages, both ways to salvation, are competitors. Whereas the Parson seems to be a willing member of the pilgrimage who agrees to the election of Harry Bailly as governor of the group and his plan for the storytelling contest, casts no dissenting vote, and makes no move to withdraw along the route, his storytelling performance undercuts his relationship to the group.[43] His allegorical interpretation of pilgrimage may be seen as undercutting the actual pilgrimage to Canterbury: he hopes to show the Canterbury pilgrims the way "Of thilke parfit

---

[43]It is nonetheless important to note that his storytelling performance also participates in the game. This is the kind of paradox Patterson, "The 'Parson's Tale'," p. 380, refers to. See also Dean, "Dismantling," on ParsT as a response to MancT, fitting into the final group of tales by taking up the "closing" theme of transformation.

glorious pilgrymage/ That highte Jerusalem celestial" (lines 50–51). He is reminding them that Canterbury is only an interim goal on the way to heaven. As Donald R. Howard points out, the Parson changes the itinerary from a two-way to a one-way journey.[44] The pilgrims are not going back to London, but forward to death and judgment. So just as the Parson criticizes the storytelling contest by refusing to tell a fable (lines 31–41), he criticizes the pilgrimage by putting it into a spiritual context.

The Parson's criticism of the pilgrimage may extend as well to his choice of subject. Whereas pilgrimage is a physical activity, penitence is a mental one. It is not a physical journey on a physical road but one of the "weyes espirituels" (line 79). Unlike a pilgrimage, penitence cannot be done mechanically; it demands proper intention. While pilgrimage can be a sightseeing trip that celebrates spring, offers thanks for a return to physical health, and creates a fellowship that promises to confer praise for excellent storytelling, confession must include sorrow for past sin and a resolve not to sin in the future (line 84) and, as we have seen, is based on a denigration of the body that assumes that physical health is dangerous and on a suspicion of "commendacioun of the peple" (line 472).[45] The material the Parson presents emphasizes the spiritual over the physical, with repeated underscoring of intention. His attempt to transform the pilgrimage road into a spiritual path conforms perfectly to the content of his treatise.

Another way the tale criticizes the pilgrimage is that this pilgrimage is a group activity with an *ad hoc* structure while confession is solitary and institutionally mandated. The collectivism, spontaneity,

---

[44]Howard, *The Idea*, p. 69.

[45]The narrator has mentioned in GenPro that many people make pilgrimages to repay the saint for restoring their physical health (I.18). The Parson suggests that physical health is spiritually dangerous (X.457).

and voluntarism of the pilgrimage emphasize the contrasting aspects of confession: it is an individual activity and a matter of obligation.[46]

The Parson is behaving somewhat like the unscrupulous Pardoner in offering a spiritual service that only he can provide.[47] The Pardoner works by fear—advising people to buy his pardons because death can strike at any moment (VI.923–40). Although we have no indication that the Parson is eager for personal gain (see I.486–89),[48] he is like the Pardoner in promoting his way, his service, and his institution.

All these criticisms of the pilgrimage are present in the Parson's Prologue. The Parson agrees to "tell," as the rules say he must, but not a tale. He implicitly criticizes the foregoing "fables" as "draf" (X.35), cites the authorized (that is, biblical) source for his rejection of fiction, and yet engages with the pilgrims in an elaborate ritual of

---

[46] As Colin Morris, *The Discovery of the Individual: 1050–1200* (London, 1972), pp. 70–79, says, the church's emphasis on confession by a single person to a single priest (as opposed to group or public confession to a congregation) promotes individual piety. See also Michel Foucault, *The History of Sexuality*, vol.1, *An Introduction*, trans. Robert Hurley (New York, 1978), p. 58. According to Patterson, "The 'Parson's Tale'," p. 348, there is another debate the Parson is taking sides in: that with nominalism about whether the forms of piety should be left up to individuals or legislated by the church.

[47] During much of the Middle Ages there was a range of opinion on what accomplished justification: God, the contrite sinner, or the priest. But the Fourth Lateran Council of 1215 decreed that private confession to a priest was obligatory. Between the ninth and thirteenth centuries, says Tentler, "the meaning of the priest's role was more carefully defined and its implications in the process of forgiveness radically enhanced" (*Sin*, p. 16).

[48] According to Tentler, *Sin*, p. 87, the clergy could not require payment for hearing confession, but those who confessed were sometimes encouraged to give their confessors gifts.

permission-asking and permission-granting that implicitly reaffirms their *ad hoc* contract:

"For which I seye, if that yow list to heere
Moralitee and vertuous mateere,
And thanne that ye wol yeve me audience,
I wol ful fayn, at Cristes reverence,
Do yow plesaunce leefful, as I kan.
.   .   .   .
And if ye vouche sauf, anon I shal
Bigynne upon my tale, for which I preye
Telle your avys; I kan no bettre seye."
.   .   .   .
 Upon this word we han assented soone,
For, as it seemed, it was for to doone —
To enden in som vertuous sentence,
And for to yeve hym space and audience,
And bade oure Hoost he sholde to hym seye
That alle we to telle his tale hym preye.
 Oure Hoost hadde the wordes for us alle. . . . (lines 37–41, 52–54, 61–67)

The Parson secedes from the pilgrimage by making it clear that his authority lies elsewhere and by changing the rules to include a "meditacioun," yet does so with the permission of the group while Harry Bailly acts as intermediary. Some of the vocabulary of the original agreement in the General Prologue returns ("vouche sauf" [I.812]; "assent" [I.777, 817]), and the Parson promises "plesaunce" but under the correction of his own institution's authority (the "clerkes" of X.57). Thus the Parson is both of and not of the pilgrimage, an ambivalent position that is consistent with his complex stand on the relationship between individual selves and groups and his own position in his social context.

Thus, the very fact of being a parson both separates the Parson from and unites him with others. This is clear not only from his behavior on the pilgrimage but from what the narrator learns about him and reports in the General Prologue. For instance, he believes that he must be better than his parishioners, but he must be better to provide an example to them (I.496–506). As a number of critics have said, the voice in this passage sounds like that of the Parson himself.[49] The narrator's voice seems to give way to the pilgrim's. In this case, the pilgrim's emphatic repetition creates a paradox because what he repeats is his principle that parsons should teach by example before teaching by precept (line 497). The principle emphasizes his claim about his own practice—instruction by behavior before instruction through words. All his talk about not talking is just slightly contradictory (like the repeated "shut up" in The Manciple's Tale, IX.309–62) and makes "ensample" (I.496) slightly ambiguous: does it refer to his being a model or to the aphoristic metaphors he is about to quote? There is something a little difficult here. Perhaps it is merely that the Parson is being overly self-righteous and that if there is any way in which he is not ideal, it is in this slightly pretentious self-congratulation. Or perhaps this too-much-protesting is the sign of some anxiety. Although we cannot determine exactly what is behind this slightly discordant self-righteousness, it is important to notice that its subject matter is the relationship between the Parson as leader and his congregation. Jill Mann has argued not only that his virtues are set off against the complaints against parsons in the estates satires but also that he is *aware* of those conventional criticisms.[50] He is addressing the subject of whether he is an ideal or a corrupt parson.

In the context of the passage from the General Prologue, it is interesting to look at the Parson's comments in his treatise on the

---

[49]See Mann, *Chaucer*, p. 66; Owen, *Pilgrimage*, p. 74.

[50]Mann, *Chaucer*, p. 66.

illicit sex of priests because they emphasize his concern with a religious leader's responsibility to and for his flock:

> Preestes been aungels, as by the dignitee of hir mysterye; but for sothe, Seint Paul seith that Sathanas transformeth hym in an aungel of light./ Soothly, the preest that haunteth deedly synne, he may be likned to the aungel of derknesse transformed in the aungel of light. He semeth aungel of light, but for sothe he is aungel of derknesse./ Swiche preestes been the sones of Helie, as sheweth in the Book of Kynges, that they weren the sones of Belial — that is, the devel./ Belial is to seyn, "withouten juge." And so faren they; hem thynketh they been free, and han no juge, namoore than hath a free bole that taketh which cow that hym liketh in the town./ So faren they by wommen. For right as a free bole is ynough for al a toun, *right so is a wikked preest corrupcioun ynough for al a parisshe, or for al a contree.* (X.895–99; my emphasis)

Despite the extra responsibility of his religious office, he is a man, and he indirectly but clearly indicates that *no one* is exempt from temptation. No one, no matter how holy, is immune, not even saints who have mortified the flesh. Although St. Jerome lived for years alone as an ascetic in the desert, "yet seyde he that 'the brennynge of lecherie boyled in al his body'" (lines 345–46). The Parson's use of the first person acknowledges that he is implicated:

> that is to seyn, that everich of us hath matere and occasioun to be tempted of the norissynge of synne that is in his body./ And therfore seith Seint John the Evaungelist, "If that we seyn that we be withoute synne, we deceyve us selve, and trouthe is nat in us." (lines 348–49)

Perhaps the incriminating witness of the saints explains the inclusion of the Parson's own activities in the list of those that count as satisfaction, which consists of doing good works (alleviating the physical and mental suffering of others) and bodily pain (suffering physically and mentally). Bodily pain

> stant in preyeres, in wakynges, in fastynges, in vertuouse techynges of orisouns./
>
> . . . .
>
> [and] in disciplyne or techynge, by word, or by writynge, or in ensample. . . . (lines 1038, 1052)

The Parson classifies his life-work and his activity on the pilgrimage as suffering to make restitution for sin.[51] The acknowledgment has special meaning in the context of his emphatic denunciation of priestly sin. Priestly sin is a social problem. The Parson is like all others but has the special responsibility not to be like all others, for the sake of all others. Mimicking his ambivalent relationship to the pilgrimage, his relationship to all mankind is "of" and "not of."

Some of the tensions among the various models of self and other reflected in the Parson's treatise and in his actual position among parishioners and pilgrims are reconciled in the utopian vision at the end of the sermon. There are three related passages that lead up to the final resolution of the various images of the self and its relationship to the world. When the Parson describes hell early in his tale, he says that the damned have no meat or drink, only endless appetite and thirst; no clothing; no peace, only rebellion and hate among friends, parents and children, and siblings; and all this lack lasts forever (lines 194–206).

---

[51]One of the sins of which he may be guilty is chiding. He calls it a sin in X.622–23 and speaks of himself as a chider of sinners in I.521–23. This is another indication of the difficulties of being a parson.

A similar series of human requirements appears when the Parson lists ministering to others' needs as good works that count as satisfaction:

> a man hath nede of thise thinges generally: he hath nede of foode, he hath nede of clothyng and herberwe, he hath nede of charitable conseil and visitynge in prisone and in maladie, and sepulture of his dede body. (line 1031)

This list, an allusion to the corporal acts of mercy, describes the openness to environment which, as we have seen, can lead man to sin and which *constitutes* his eternal punishment. The problem of vulnerability is solved in heaven, where the resurrected body is transformed:

> ther as the body of man, that whilom was foul and derk, is moore clcer than the sonne; ther as the body, that whilom was syk, freele, and fieble, and mortal, is inmortal, and so strong and so hool that ther may no thyng apeyren it;/ ther as ne is neither hunger, thurst, ne coold, but every soule replenyssed with the sighte of the parfit knowynge of God. (lines 1078–79)

All the needs the Parson previously listed are abolished: food, drink, clothing, shelter, advice, and visiting are now all unnecessary. Body and soul are no longer vulnerable to evil influences but are open to God and to the equal joy of others: "ther as is the blisful compaignye that rejoysen hem everemo, everich of otheres joye . . ." (line 1077). Now mutuality, not hierarchy, resolves class conflict. *All* selves are transformed from subjects to lords and participate in "This blisful regne" (line 1080). Denial of needs on earth earns their abolition in heaven through God, and all shall be equally elevated to high status. The conflicts between the parts of the body, generated by the body's sinfulness and human needs, and the conflicts between the strata of society, generated by the sinfulness of rulers, are resolved. The body's greed and the rulers' greed are abolished: each person, by his own spiritual efforts, has earned eternal sovereignty and mutually enriching, joyful companionship.

The "fit" between the utopian vision and the particular complexities of his position among his lay fellows is striking. The vision answers the concerns that we have seen reflected in his discussion of the relationship between the self and the outside world and of his own position as parson. This is orthodoxy, but a version of orthodoxy filtered through the special lens of a man in a specific position in a group.

The Parson's truth, although consistent with revealed Christian truth, is no less a truth revealed from a particular standpoint in time and place. It echoes the ideas that make up the framework for the complaints in the Rising of 1381 against the Statute of Laborers and regressive taxes—dissatisfaction with the whole system of villeinage that subjected workers to particular landowners. In the accounts of Froissart and Walsingham, the rebels articulated the idea of human beings' equality before God and called for the abolition of the estates system.[52] As the famous couplet of the Rising puts it, "When Adam delved and Eve span / Who was then the gentleman?" The Parson's vision of heaven also recalls some of his own language about serfdom from earlier in the tale, including its incompatibility with Christian belief (line 772) and a passage we have examined before about human beings' equality in origin and equality in sin (line 461).[53]

---

[52]See Dobson, *The Peasants' Revolt*, pp. 371, 374–75. For Rodney Hilton's comments on these accounts, see *Bond Men Made Free: Medieval Peasant Movements and the English Rising of 1381* (London, 1983).

[53]According to Pearsall, *Life*, p. 149, Chaucer (and by implication the Parson) is "quite unalive" to the possible allusions to the rhetoric of equality of the Rising of 1381. But see Swindell on these passages, e.g., "'Cokkel in the Clene Corne',," pp. 24–26, 47–53.

As when the Parson admitted that the nobles sometimes oppressed their workers but advised peasants to be patient, here the Parson is not being revolutionary: we must wait until we get to heaven for equality. But the Parson's language of equality resonates with the accounts of the Rising and with his own impulses toward equality when he chides all sinners equally, "[w]hat so he were, of heigh or lough estat" (I.522), even as it goes them one better, abolishing rank by elevating everyone to lordship. Again, the Parson's vision is particular to himself and his time.

We can better understand the ways in which the Parson's vision of heaven, though orthodox, is particular to him if we compare the end of his tale with that of the narrator's Retraction. The Parson emphasizes the efficacy of human beings' actions and attitudes in winning heaven, and his economic metaphor of purchasing (X.1080, implicitly repeated four more times) reaffirms the idea that man can accomplish his salvation. In contrast, the narrator of the Retraction emphasizes his own inability to win heaven and his dependence on Jesus, Mary, and the saints for his moral writings (lines 1088–89) and asks for grace,

> bisekynge hem that they from hennes forth unto my lyves ende sende me grace to biwayle my giltes and to studie to the salvacioun of my soule, and graunte me grace of verray penitence, confessioun and satisfaccioun to doon in this present lyf,/ thurgh the benigne grace of hym that is kyng of kynges and preest over alle preestes, that boghte us with the precious blood of his herte,/ so that I may been oon of hem at the day of doom that shulle be saved. *Qui cum Patre et Spiritu Sancto vivit et regnat Deus per omnia secula. Amen.* (lines 1090–92)

He mentions his moral works not to claim credit, but rather to offer thanks for them. He mentions grace three times and turns the economic metaphor around so that man is not buying heaven, but God is buying man.[54] He then effaces himself further by offering a well-known Latin invocation.

The differences between the Parson and the narrator of the Retraction (whether the persona "Geffrey" or Chaucer himself, or some indefinable amalgamation of the two) reflect the differences in medieval theories of confession that I have outlined. In discussing the efficacy of confession, different writers emphasized different aspects of the sacrament. The contrast between The Parson's Tale and the Retraction highlights the fact that even if he never strays from orthodoxy, the Parson is making choices within it. His choices represent neither Truth nor Chaucer. The Parson's voice is a voice among the others, one marked by the preoccupations and social context of its speaker. He represents, no less than the other pilgrims, Chaucer's interest in Boethius's idea of the ways in which what is known is known not according to the thing known, but according to the knower.

I do not mean to imply that there is no final, absolute voice in *The Canterbury Tales*; there is, but it is God's and therefore can only be alluded to. At the end of the Retraction, Chaucer defers to God and submits himself to God's judgment on Judgment Day.[55] And

---

[54]The connotation of "purchace" is not necessarily economic. According to Norman Davis et al., *A Chaucer Glossary* (Oxford, 1979), *OED*, and *MED*, it can mean "acquire," but in the late fourteenth century it also has the sense of "pay money for." The Parson uses this meaning in several places, and it is not excluded in line 1080, especially in the context of "boghte" in Retr.

[55]See Ferster, *Chaucer*, p. 156.

significantly enough for the two leaders of the pilgrimage, the one who becomes "oure governour" (I.813) at its start and the one who takes over to "knytte up al this feeste" (X.47) at the end, Chaucer refers to Christ as "kyng of kynges and preest over alle preestes" (line 1091). The final word is not spoken in poems, or in treatises, or on earth.[56]

---

[56]I am grateful to James Dean, David Ferster, Robert C. Lane, and the late John Hazel Smith for their helpful comments on earlier drafts of this essay. While I was advising him on his master's thesis, Steven Swindell and I had many bracing discussions that influenced my view of the relationship between the Parson and the Rising of 1381. I also appreciate the comments and suggestions offered in my 1999 graduate Chaucer seminar.

Dropping the Personae
and Reforming the Self:
The Parson's Tale and the End
of *The Canterbury Tales*

Gregory Roper

Thanks to the work of many scholars, each working on a different part of the puzzle, we now know a great deal about the social, historical, and theological background to The Parson's Tale and the sacrament of penance in the later Middle Ages.[1] Texts have been established, though only a few have been edited in modern critical editions.[2] The development of the theology and practice of the

---

[1]This article was originally presented, in much briefer form, at the New Chaucer Society Ninth International Congress, Trinity College, Dublin, July 24, 1994. I would like to thank the Society for its travel subvention, which made it possible for me to attend the Congress and thus begin to develop this article.

[2]Several of these are published in the venerable Early English Text Society series from the turn of the century, but only *John Mirk's Instructions for Parish Priests*, ed. Gillis Kristensson (Amsterdam, 1974); F. Broomfield, *Thomae de Chobham Summa confessorum* (Louvain, 1968); Robert Mannyng of Brunne, *Handlyng Synne*, ed. Idelle Sullens (Binghamton, N.Y., 1983); and Robert of Flamborough, *Liber poenitentialis*, ed. J. J. Francis Firth, C.S.B. (Toronto, 1971) have seen a recent edition. The older edition of Mirk is edited by Edward Peacock, EETS, o.s., vol. 31 (London, 1868). Other penitential manuals consulted for this essay include the

sacrament in the Middle Ages has been elucidated by historians, who show the development from the *paenitentia una* of the early church, through the reforms of the Irish monks in the ninth century and the canon lawyers of succeeding centuries, past the contritionist controversy begun by Abelard into the full and in some ways terminal articulation by the scholastics, especially Thomas Aquinas.[3] We know about the massive and continuous campaign to teach this sacrament, first to the clergy who would have to administer it, and then to the lay parishioners who would be required to practice it, after the Fourth Lateran Council required annual penance in 1215. And we know that in England the movement was particularly strong due to the influence of activist friar bishops (Grosseteste, Pecham, and others) who were interested in general reform and education, and who

Aȝenbite of Inwit, ed. Pamela Gradon, EETS, n.s., vol. 23 (London, 1965); the *Ancrene Wisse*, ed. J. R. R. Tolkein, EETS, o.s., vol. 243 (London, 1962); the *Lay Folks' Catechism*, ed. Thomas F. Simmons and H. E. Nolloth, EETS, o.s., vol. 118 (London, 1901); *The Boke of Penance*, in *Cursor Mundi*, ed. Richard Morris, EETS, o.s., vol. 68 (London, 1878); the *Boke of Vices and Virtues*, ed. W. N. Francis, EETS, o.s., vol. 217 (London, 1942). Additional manuals still exist only in manuscript form, especially those written in French.

[3]For the general history of the sacrament, see Henry Charles Lea, *A History of Auricular Confession and Indulgences in the Latin Church* (1896; repr. New York, 1968). For the general history of the penitential handbooks, see John T. McNeil and Helena M. Gamer, *Medieval Handbooks of Penance* (New York, 1938). Other general studies include Homer G. Pfander, "Some Medieval Manuals of Religious Instruction in England and Observations on Chaucer's Parson's Tale," *Journal of English and Germanic Philology* 35 (1936): 243–56; Bernhard Poschmann, *Penance and the Anointing of the Sick*, trans. and rev. Francis Courtenay, S.J. (New York, 1964); and D. W. Robertson, Jr., "The Cultural Tradition of *Handlyng Synne*," *Speculum* 22 (1947): 162–85.

saw penitential reform as a crucial part of this project.[4] Thus we know that the penitential manual in its various forms—Latin *summa*-type treatise; one section of a general curriculum for instructing priests; user-friendly, sometimes exemplum-filled text for more general consumption; and handy guide for priests to use in executing the sacrament—was "one of the popular best sellers of the age."[5] We know, too, that sermon after sermon during this period was wholly devoted to preaching, teaching, and explaining the material in these handbooks. Lee Patterson sums up these activities when he writes, "Of all the ways in which the church affected the lives of medieval Christians, certainly the most ubiquitous and probably the most profound was through its administration of the sacrament of penance. . . . in succeeding centuries more and more of the religious life of medieval people came to be concentrated upon and articulated in terms of penance and the confessional."[6]

We know a great deal about this reform movement, then, and the crucial role penance played in it. But little work has been done describing the complex theological and psychological *event* of late medieval confession. Little study has been done on the crucial role the handbooks played in defining and shaping the event of confession, and few, if any, have considered how penance constructs the

---

[4]See Marion Gibbs and Jane Lang, *Bishops and Reform, 1215–1272* (Oxford, 1934); Christopher R. Cheney, *English Synodalia of the Thirteenth Century* (Oxford, 1941); and F. M. Powicke and C. R. Cheney, *Councils and Synods with Other Documents Relating to the English Church*, 2 vols. (Oxford, 1964).

[5]Broomfield, *Thomae de Chobham*, p. xx. Lee Patterson notes the various ways that the material came to the average Christian in "The 'Parson's Tale' and the Quitting of the 'Canterbury Tales'," *Traditio* 34 (1978): 337–39.

[6]Lee Patterson, *Chaucer and the Subject of History* (Madison, Wisc., 1991), p. 374.

penitent as a particular kind of self.[7] In the next few pages I would like to explore this subject briefly, giving an introduction to the penitential self. I will look at the way the sacrament, through the use of the penitential manual, constructs the penitential self through a complex dialectic of objective and subjective, listening and speaking, asserting one's "I" and submitting it to the text and God.

By 1215 penance had long since progressed from a public rite to a private affair, from the judicial and punitive sanction it had been in the early church to a more psychological and restorative process. Private confession, originated by the Irish monks, had spread across the continent (albeit erratically), finally and for all time defeating the notion of the *paenitentia una* and suggesting that penance be used to help and not merely punish and separate the sinner.[8] Abelard's emphasis on intention as the basis of sin, a position hotly debated yet vastly influential, increased theological speculation on the psychological workings of sin and confession, and increased emphasis on the sacrament as a restorative, reforming process. Finally, the

---

[7]Only Lee Patterson, and only in a small way, has begun some of this work. In his first essay on the topic of confession, "Chaucerian Confession: Penitential Literature and the Pardoner," *Medievalia et Humanistica*, n.s., 7 (1976): 153–72, he begins looking at the psychology of penance, and in his recent book, *Chaucer and the Subject of History*, he discusses it again. But Patterson is more concerned with the topic of despair and how its psychology works than he is with the specific psychological and self-constructing processes of penance. In what follows, I trust my differences from and expansion on his beginnings will be clear.

[8]We can see this, at least theoretically, in Robert of Flamborough's *Liber poenitentialis*, which was surely written before Fourth Lateran. In Robert's treatise, amidst the workings of a canon lawyer's mind engaged in cataloging sins and offenses against church law, we can see the sacrament being positioned as a way to help and reform sinners rather than merely punish them.

thirteenth-century scholastics, particularly Aquinas, achieved a synthesis of the Abelardian contritionist position with the anti-contritionist position, one in which the verbal confession is an instrumental cause of shame and contrition as well as a guarantor of the presence of true contrition.[9] This articulation of the complex theological structure of confession was a grand achievement. But in some ways the more immense accomplishment was the extension of this complex process of reform to the widest possible franchise, to every parishioner in Western Europe. Here indeed is a stunning and epochal event in the history of the Western self that often has been ignored or misunderstood. For penance, as it came to be practiced in the later Middle Ages, is a complex theological and psychological event, and to have every parishioner, from lord to villein, practicing it requires a thorough and complete process of education.[10] On the theological level, penance takes a sinful soul removed from God and, by the complex process of Examination of Conscience, Confession, and Satisfaction, restores the *Imago Dei*, the true reflection of God in the human soul.[11] On the psychological level, penance takes a broken,

[9]A splendid presentation of the contritionist controversy and its Thomistic resolution may be found in Poschmann, *Penance*, pp. 157–65. Linda Georgianna also gives a fine account of the theological problems and disputes in *The Solitary Self: Individuality in the Ancrene Wisse* (Cambridge, Mass., 1981).

[10]While it is true that penitentials existed from a much earlier date, and while these earlier manuals did accomplish some of this educational process, the breadth and depth of educational movement only began after 1215, when the hierarchy legitimized the penitentials and began supporting their production. It is hard to deny the huge expansion of penitential material after 1215 and its influence on virtually every form of medieval religious life.

[11]Credit must go to Lee Patterson here for his excellent explication of this theology in "Chaucerian Confession."

divided self and, by inducing shame and contrition and getting the sinner to speak about past events, restores to the self a wholeness, a completion, by giving the penitent in effect a new self. The handbooks taught people how to prepare for and execute a proper confession and taught priests how to administer the sacrament, but more important for my purposes (and for Chaucer's, as we shall see later), the penitential manuals taught sinners how to discover and speak forth their selves, how to construct their own sense of an "I," how to slough off one self and regain another, according to the types of Christian life. Today, when one finds advice telling one how to find oneself, fix oneself, heal oneself, and re-make oneself in dozens of magazines available at the end of every grocery store check-out aisle, it is difficult to imagine a world in which this kind of instruction was, for most people, entirely new. What the handbooks were teaching, to an audience largely ignorant, illiterate, and unused to such things, was a complete and integrated process of self-exploration, self-discovery, and self-presentation.

To accomplish this instruction, the handbooks often begin as Chaucer does in The Parson's Tale, defining sin and penitence and outlining the prerequisites for contrition and a good confession. But the handbooks' primary and most lengthy material is a long list of sins, a list which, in effect, teaches what sin is by listing which actions are sinful. This list, usually structured around the *forma confitendi* (the three-part grouping of the Ten Commandments, Seven Deadly Sins, and Five Wits), defines the sins in careful, complete, exhaustive detail. In this, Chaucer's Parson is atypical only in that he omits the Ten Commandments and Five Wits; the Parson neglects the latter and leaves the former to the theologians, who have subtler wits than he, and because he has worked them into the text:

> Now after that I have declared yow, as I kan, the sevene deedly synnes, and
> somme of hire braunches and hire remedies, soothly, if I koude, I wolde

telle yow the ten comandementz./ But so heigh a doctrine I lete to divines.
Natheless, I hope to God, they been touched in this tretice, everich of hem
alle. (X.956–57)

What is the purpose of these lists, other than to record encyclo-
pedically and taxonomically all of the possible wrongs one can do?
How does this list of sins structure the psychological act of penance?

It seems to me that the purpose of these lists is twofold. First, such
a list serves as a sort of checklist during the penitent's Examination of
Conscience. Whether penitents have the actual book in front of them
(which is not likely), or remember the material from a sermon, or, as
we shall see in a moment with John Mirk's guide, the priest goes over
this list in the process of confession, the penitents can use the list to jog
the memory, as an aid to help them recall those sins they have committed since the last confession. Penitents may sincerely want to review their lives, but as we all know, the human memory is a fallible
faculty, perhaps especially when it comes to remembering one's past
misdeeds. So the text serves first to jog the penitents' memory by
listing all of the possible sins one could have committed.

But the lists of sins are more than just aids to memory. The *forma
confitendi* is a sort of map of the interior landscape of the sinful self
and a guide to discovering that more or less unknown territory by
offering signposts for the exploration of the penitent's past. The penitential handbook's lists of sins are *sample portraits* that penitents are
asked to match up against their own experiences. As the sinners'
memories are jogged by particular sins, they in a sense "try on" those
sins. And in trying them on, the penitents specify the general definitions or descriptions in the handbook with their own experiences, and
can then describe their lives in sin. The text is thus a potential picture
of sinners, but it also helps penitents particularize, individualize, past
acts, and in this dialectic they not only recall their past acts, but also
see their actions as simultaneously their own and also as instances of

objective, common, universal sin. By probing the subjective, personal memory of the actions through the screen of the objective list of sins, the penitent comes, that is, to a moment of self-discovery that is simultaneously a discovery of how typical and unindividual that self is.

An example will help explain this process. Suppose I am examining my conscience in preparation for confession. I work through the text of a handbook as I examine my life since the last confession; for convenience's sake, let us say the text is The Parson's Tale, though a fourteenth-century person may have consulted the *Aȝenbite of Inwit*, the *Boke of Vices and Virtues*, *The Clensyng of Mannes Soule*, the *Boke of Penance* from *Cursor Mundi*, or any of the other popular versions that ultimately have their sources in Raymond or the bishops' constitutions of the thirteenth century.[12] I come to the second deadly sin listed there, and read this about Envy:

> The speces of Envye been thise. Ther is first, sorwe of oother mannes goodnesse and of his prosperitee; and prosperitee is kyndely matere of joye; thanne is Envye a synne agayns kynde./ The seconde spece of Envye is joye of oother mannes harm, and that is proprely lyk to the devel, that evere rejoyseth hym of mannes harm./ Of thise two speces comth bakbityng; and this synne of bakbityng or detraccion hath certeine speces. . . .
> (lines 491–93)

Have I committed this sin? I ask. I look at the definition and measure it against my experience to see if it "fits," to see if it accurately describes me and my past actions. Then I particularize the definition

---

[12]It is true that there are some differences in these handbooks with regard to structure, language, and so forth; often these differences, it seems, result from the adaptation of the penitential material for different types of audiences. The psychological process, however, is pretty much the same regardless of the shape of the list and the social class of penitent.

with my own instance of envious behavior. At the time, or in the intervening weeks, I might have in an unfocused way realized that these things were wrong but had no particular sense of their significance. But now, using the handbook's definitions and structures as a guide, I specify that unfocused sense of wrong and understand my actions as envy—and even more particularly, as two of the species of envy, "sorwe of oother mannes goodnesse and of his prosperitee" and "joye of oother mannes harm," that is, "bakbityng" or "detraccion." I in turn see *myself* as an example, a type, of envy, backbiting, detraction.

The sinner reviewing a life with the use of a penitential handbook, then, sees these disparate experiences of life as instances of the objective structures of sin and comes to know these acts as sinful, comes to know their meaning and significance. The penitent discovers the reality of his subjective acts and by "coming face to face with the defilement he has become . . . understands his life as an instance of moral law."[13] In other words, penitents realize that their subjective acts are instances of objective structures; their selves are defined, given significance, through matching their subjectivity with this objective structure. Seeing oneself as a "sinner" gives one's fluid, unfocused life a meaning and a form. The whole point of the handbooks' intricate lists and exhaustive categories, therefore, is to provide more, and more specific, occasions for discovering particular sins and thus to enable penitents to define themselves as sinners with more precision and accuracy. By becoming more of an individual— by particularizing sins, identifying the particular ways in which he has acted—the penitent becomes less an individual self and more a self defined as a role, a texture of relations, because sin itself is so ordinary, typical, and universal. The dialectic thus moves from

---

[13]Patterson, "Chaucerian Confession," p. 154.

objective (the "portraits" of sin that the handbook provides) through subjective (the memory of the act of sin) back to objective (seeing the self as an instance of moral law). And, finally, seeing himself as *this* sort of self (a sinner) enables the penitent to see that self for what it is, leave it behind, and convert his life to a new self, a new role: a self related to God (actually an old role and self, since it is the self which in Catholic theology the penitent gained through baptism).[14]

Part of my project here is to break down these categories of "self" and "subject" to create a richer understanding of late medieval identity than either seems to allow, to find a way between or around these terms. A fully achieved self, in medieval Roman Catholic theology, cannot be a liberal humanist self that is self-possessing, transcendent in itself, the monad of bourgeois liberal American individualism: cutting off the self's relation to its origin in the divine suggests the sin of Pride, and is, in fact, what I am trying to suggest late medieval thinkers would have considered the state, the selfhood, of the sinner before contrition. Nor could medieval Catholic theology agree that the self is merely a constructed subject, a locus of intersection of social forces in this world: that, too, cuts off identity of the person from the divine origin, the deepest relation and ultimate home of the self. Thus neither of the terms—*self* or *subject*, as current scholarship uses them—seems adequate to describe late medieval penitential selfhood. I am trying to show, by using (in a sense) a postmodern method, that is, by showing the process by which this self became "subject to" the penitential process, that the late medieval self was seen as something not individual and not "subject to," but in a sense both and neither, traveling through a private, individual list of sins

---

[14]On the self as "disenchanted," that is, aware of its own constructedness, see H. Marshall Leicester, Jr., *The Disenchanted Self: Representing the Subject in the Canterbury Tales* (Berkeley, 1990).

(when one sins, one does so always individually, not corporately) by way of an objective process that suggests sin is always typical and universal. The sinful self is seen as at once individual and typical; the penitent self is seen as crucified; the absolved self, at its deepest core, as the penitential process reveals, is a relation, not just to things of this world but to the divine. If we conceive of the self as a dialectic, which finds its individuality precisely by and through submitting to, being subject to the discourse of penance and does so precisely in order to surrender that individuality and return to a self related to God, a self which is not authoritative but spoken into being by God, then we can see how *individual* and *subject* are both partial terms which conceive of only one side of the complex dynamic that is the medieval self. The difficulty here, I recognize, is agency.

The priest's task, then, is to enable the penitent to speak forth his confession effectively; the priest must encourage the penitent—must force him, if necessary—to construct "a sort of autobiography of sin."[15] In his *Instructions for Parish Priests*, a penitential guide directed at the priest but whose contents are largely taken from the same conservative tradition (the *Pupilla oculi*, the *Pars oculi*) from which The Parson's Tale derives, John Mirk describes the way the priest is to "grope" the penitent's "sore" by asking questions. In fact, Mirk gives us our best concrete view of what a late medieval confession was like, before the invention of confessional boxes and rooms (see lines 769–804). He explains how the penitent is to kneel before the priest, who pulls his hood over his eyes so as not to see the penitent. The priest, Mirk instructs, should sit "stylle as ston" (line 777) while the penitent first confesses; he should be sure not to spit, cough, or wriggle his legs, lest he give the impression he is impatient or loathes being there. When the penitent says "I con no more" (line

---

[15]Patterson, "Chaucerian Confession," p. 155.

709), the priest is to respond immediately by aggressively questioning the penitent:

> Freyne hym þus & grope his sore,
> "Sone or doghter, now herken me,
> For sum-what I wole helpe þe,
> And when þou herest what þou hast do
> Knowlache wel a-non þer-to." (lines 799–804)

Mirk tells the priest to walk the penitent through the *forma confitendi*: he is to ask the penitent pointedly the questions that are merely passive pictures in the handbooks:

> Hast þou any tyme wytyngly,
> I-wrathþad þy god greuowsly?
> Hast þow ben inobedyent
> A-gayn goddes cummawndement? (lines 977–80)

And so on, through the entire *forma confitendi*, in effect going over the entire structure again, this time more slowly and carefully, probing each one to make sure the penitent has not left out anything. Mirk's (or his priests') questions force penitents to construct statements about themselves, that is, to reject certain pictures or to displace themselves into the roles which the questions depict. They must, in fact, state aloud their sins, claim their sinful "I"s in statements which predicate the "I" into sin—"Yes, I was envious" or "I was prideful." This act of accepting that role the priest offers, speaking it forth, predicating it of one's own "I," gives the penitent an identity. It is an act by which penitents define their selves, suggest the meaning of their lives, and yet they do so—again—by screening the individual experience through the objective standards and strictures the priest provides.

Yet even while discovering this self, the penitent is already on the way to discarding it. Penance does not merely leave sinners with knowledge of their sins, of their divided, disordered selves. Penance regenerates the self, reforming the penitent's identity on a new model, a new role. By seeing themselves—more important for our purposes, by *speaking* themselves—into the role of a sinner, penitents gain a distance from that "I." As Lacan and Benveniste note time and again, an odd slippage occurs when one predicates one's own "I" in language; one becomes the subject of the sentence, but does so only by losing oneself in language as an object. More helpful to understanding the situation of penitential speaking, though, are the terms of discourse theory, in which the "I" of the *enounced* is in the act of speaking separated from the "I" of the enunciation, which supersedes it.[16] Antony Easthope describes the paradoxical situation of someone who under interrogation admits, "I am lying," and the situation parallels sacramental confession almost exactly:

> He means that the liar is, as it were, someone else represented in his discourse, though the single shifter of the first person covers both I's. The situation would have been clearer if he had said "I have been lying," discarding one self and accepting another, that is, speaking about his previous untruthful self as a character in his own discourse as much as to say "he was lying, not me." The "I" speaking and the "I" spoken about can never be the same.[17]

---

[16]Émile Benveniste, *Problems in General Linguistics*, trans. Mary Elizabeth Meek (Miami, Fla., 1971), pp. 199–200; Jacques Lacan, *Écrits*, trans. Alan Sheridan (London, 1977), pp. 83–92; Seymour Chatman, *Story and Discourse: Narrative Structure in Fiction and Film* (Ithaca, N.Y., 1978).

[17]Antony Easthope, *Poetry As Discourse* (London, 1983), p. 44.

"A character in his own discourse": this is a pretty good summation of the medieval penitential self. Because the "I" speaking and the "I" spoken about can never be the same, as the penitent speaks about the past "I," the sacramental process is already creating—has already created?—a present "I" which is different, new, separate from that other, older "I" which sinned.

So the "I" of the penitent is one which he or she discovers by trying on another's language, traits, and description. But in that very moment of discovering the self, the penitent sets that self aside. The penitent displaces the old "I" of past sins into the role of a sinner, comes to understand the significance of that old life, and thus gains a new self: the penitent "I" who is speaking now, enacting a new role—the new Christian, the reformed penitent. Speech itself—this penitential kind of speech—becomes regenerative, re-creating, re-forming a self.

The Canterbury Tales is an investigation of the philosophical and moral basis of storytelling, of rhetorical self-fashioning, of language itself and, until The Parson's Tale, appears to give some very post-modern answers to these problems. Chaucer's main goal throughout the *Tales* has been, up to this point, to test how far language can go in describing the world, the extent to which self-interest clouds this truth-telling, how social power and rhetorical power are intertwined, how one uses the various forms of language to create—or conceal— one's self. The Pardoner's Tale asks us to consider whether authorial intent has any bearing on a text's meaning and moral effects, for the Pardoner tells an exemplum which is, as C. David Benson notes, a triumph of Christian affective narrative put in the service of despicable motives;[18] the Clerk tells a tale which he then tells us is not really applicable to life; the controversy over The Knight's Tale has always been whether his class affiliations cause the Knight to tell a tale which elides crucial problems in the narrative; the Wife, to the delight of post-Lacanian readers everywhere, shows us how the self is created in and by language, discourse patterns, the social texts we inhabit;[19] the Nun's Priest, despite his exuberant use of language, in many ways raises the question of whether language is anything but a hermetically sealed, self-reflexive land of play; the Manciple, bitterest and most negative of all, counsels silence, but of course does so at such great length as to show unconsciously both the limitations and the inevitability (as well as the inevitable limitations) of language: one must use language itself to defeat language. All the while, Chaucer *himself* is playing a game with the readers, hiding behind

---

[18]"The exemplum of the three revelers is Chaucer's defense of poetry because it proves the power of skillful art to communicate Christian themes. . . . The *Pardoner's Tale* is one of Chaucer's most audacious creations. It contains all the best and all the worst the poet had to say for imaginative literature. While illustrating the dangers when clever language and the powers of fiction are misused, the Pardoner's prologue and two tales also succeed in justifying the ways of Christian poetry to medieval (and modern) man" (C. David Benson, *Chaucer's Drama of Style: Poetic Variety and Contrast in the Canterbury Tales* [Chapel Hill, N.C., 1986], p. 63). Benson is also clear in his judgment that PardT is superior to ParsT; the former, he says, "has a power and appeal that the *Parson's Tale* does not begin to match" (p. 63). I'm not quite so sure.

[19]Lee Patterson, "The 'Parson's Tale'," pp. 360–61, writes: "In the tales the characters use the language of homiletic exhortation as the material from which they fashion nothing less than themselves. . . . [They] create themselves for us not merely in language but *as* language, giving to a generalized mode of speaking a unique voice that implies a coextensive character."

the masks of his pilgrims (including the pilgrim "Chaucer"). As Ralph Hanna notes,

> Partial and limited human perspective inheres in the gross form and manner of the poem, for Chaucer as poet can only say what he wants to say in the Tales by an act of imaginative fragmentation. To write the work he wishes, he must divide himself into a series of twenty-odd voices, each of which speaks separately and uniquely. Moreover, each voice in its primary mode offers only an interpretation, a tale . . . and since in fragmenting his voice Chaucer has denied himself the possibility of invoking any transcendent standard through authorial commentary (the voice identified as "I" is one of the poem's most clearly limited), the collision of various interpretations, of possible ways of viewing the world, is never resolved within the Tales.[20]

Chaucer never appears "himself," never claims a transcendent authorial voice, so that he can explore the limitations of point of view and point out the way rhetorical desires delimit our effectiveness as speakers. But in The Parson's Tale Chaucer uses the theological and psychological structures of penitential reform to show how to criticize, and finally to supersede, the limitations and depredations of the rhetorical self, to move beyond the limitations of rhetorical language, rhetorical self-fashioning, to find some firmer ground for the self. The purpose of The Parson's Tale is to transcend not just fiction (*pace* Patterson) but the self itself; in the process which is The Parson's Tale, the self is transcended, "quitted," answered, defeated, and re-formed. More important, the tale shows us, the readers, how to do it ourselves.

---

[20]Ralph Hanna III, "Unlocking What's Locked: Gawain's Green Girdle," *Viator* 14 (1983): 300.

Many critics have commented on the way the Parson's Prologue suggests not just a completion, but also a rejection, a cancellation, or a transformation of the literary pilgrimage. Night is approaching: "Foure of the clokke it was tho, as I gesse" (X.5), so the time is short; Libra's scales of justice, and therefore of penance and judgment, ascend (lines 10–11); the travelers seem to be approaching the shrine city, though they are not yet there. The pilgrims for once seem to be in agreement; the Host, perfectly happy to announce that the contest has gone according to plan (lines 17–18), that only one tale remains, and that the appropriate teller is at hand to complete the contest (lines 22–29). In The Miller's Prologue the Host, exuberant at The Knight's Tale, had exclaimed "unbokeled is the male" (I.3115), declaring the game begun; now, as he asks the Parson to "Unbokele and shewe us what is in thy male" (X.26), it is so that whatever is in that purse may "knytte up wel a greet mateere" (line 28). The end, thus, is coming; Barbara Herrnstein Smith herself could not have arranged a better example of poetic closure.[21] But, as Charlotte Gross notes, there are also plenty of gestures of anti-closure, of opening up, of leading the way forward: out of fiction, into reality (and the valences of *that* term will become important), towards Jerusalem, into the self.[22]

Furthermore, the Parson himself recapitulates the questions of language and selfhood that the pilgrims and Chaucer have been asking all along, suggesting both closure and opening up into a new realm. He promises to "knytte up al this feeste and make an ende" by telling "a myrie tale in prose" (lines 46–47), which seems to promise a coherent closure to the literary work, consistent with its working

---

[21]Barbara Herrnstein Smith, *Poetic Closure: A Study of How Poems End* (Chicago, 1968).

[22]See Charlotte Gross, "'The goode wey': Ending and Not-Ending in The Parson's Tale," pp. 177–97 in this volume.

principles. Much of his speech, however, is a rejection of the fictions and poetics of the work up to this point. He will do away with any fables, any rhyme, alliteration, any "chaff"; he will not "glose" (line 45); he will not "weyven soothfastnesse" (line 33)—that is, tell fictions in any way. All he is interested in is the "fruit," the fruitfulness of language—not merely how it can *describe* the truth, but something at once more transcendent and more practical. The Parson promises

> To shewe yow the wey, in this viage,
> Of thilke parfit glorious pilgrymage
> That highte Jerusalem celestial. (lines 49–51)

Thus the whole question of the rhetorical use of language is transformed, canceled, superseded. No longer is the question how to affect others with language—whether to instruct them (Monk), to please them (Nun's Priest), to "quite" them (Miller), to create a personality which can manipulate them (Wife), or to coerce them into buying fake relics (Pardoner). No longer is the purpose of this game to judge one another's tales, their rhetorical performances and self-creations. Foucaultian "power," in all of its linguistic, ideational, rhetorical, social, and political constructions, is suddenly and irrevocably beside the point. The point now, the Parson announces, is to judge not others but ourselves. What the Parson will talk about is how (notice it is the *way*, the process) to get to heaven. In its spare simplicity, the Parson's announced intention comes as a shock, both simpler and more profound than the "entente" of any of the pilgrim tellers encountered so far. And its seeming arrogance is immediately countered by humility:

> But nathelees, this meditacioun
> I putte it ay under correccioun
> Of clerkes, for I am nat textueel;
> I take but the sentence, trusteth weel.

Therfore I make protestacioun
That I wol stonde to correccioun. (lines 55–60)

No other pilgrim is willing to admit so much: that he or she does not completely control meaning, or *sentence* and *solaas*, or the construction of the self in the text. The Parson opens up his text as well to a realm where it, too, is in process, is on the way to its goal, where it may need assistance, reform, re-shaping; but he trusts that the *sentence* is essentially right—not because he controls it linguistically but because he trusts that it is guaranteed by the Word which it addresses. Human language, however, must always "stonde to correccioun" under this trusting faith; the Parson's epistemology is a realist one that suggests that language, though it might not be able to create paradise in fiction, can, for all its vagaries, do the job, show us how to get to heaven.

And the way to get there—which should be no surprise, at this point—turns out to be a penitential handbook. It is not another tale; rather, it is a handbook, a how-to guide, that teaches its readers how to "stonde to correccioun" themselves, how to speak properly, how to use language in the most significant way. Rather than telling stories *of* someone else (a carpenter and his wife, Dorigen and Arveragus, three rioters) *to* others in order to affect them and aggrandize a falsely constructed self in language, The Parson's Tale teaches its readers how to use language to change themselves, to confess their *own* stories, and thus to discover the humility of self that cancels itself in order to re-form it. What the sacrament of penance asks Christians to do is to look back over their own lives and construct a story, a narrative, an autobiography—not to impress or persuade or convince or even instruct or entertain others but to expose themselves to themselves, to confess to God, and to reform their own selves. Language, in the sacrament, is turned from an exterior power play into an inner, reforming and redemptive force—

from rhetoric to meditation and psychological restructuring. As I said above, in the theology and psychology of penance it is crucial that penance requires one not merely to think about one's sins but to confess them aloud, to put into language a "tale" of one's own life in sin, constructing one's "I" in and through the language of the sacrament. And this, of course, is where the Parson leads the pilgrimage: out of the world of language-as-power, fictional language as self-creation, social texts as constructions of personae, and into a language that, because it is guaranteed sacramentally, truly has the power to reshape the speaker's "I," to cancel the sinful self and re-create the *Imago Dei* in the soul. Therefore, after all the other pilgrims have told their tales, showing the limitations of language, the inadequacy of rhetoric, the abuses of glossing, the problems and deceptions of self-construction, the inadequacy of a socially constituted selfhood, each teller telling only his or her individual, limited truth, the Parson shows the true and effective way to use language, the proper kind of "tale" to tell. His tale is not a tale and in fact rejects the very functions of language that a "tale" suggests; it is instead a guidebook to all future speech. He suggests that the pilgrims stop listening to others' voices and begin opening their own mouths, predicating their own "I"s, in the method he lays out.[23]

---

[23]Patterson, "The 'Parson's Tale'," p. 361, argues that ParsT is "intellective rather than hortatory" and that the tale is more interested in the reader understanding sin than enacting anything. Here, clearly, Patterson misses the whole import of the penitential handbooks; he feels that ParsT simply explains sin, categorizes it, so that one can understand it intellectually. I hope that by now this view has been superseded; the point of the handbook is not simply to explain, but to get the penitent to do something—namely, begin trying on these "sample portraits" and thereby begin discovering the self in order to reform it.

Thus the Parson works through all of the categories of the typical handbook, explaining sin, telling what is necessary for a good confession, and so forth. He is a serious psychologist and theologian of sin, carefully balancing the contritionist and the sacramental theologies of the later Middle Ages, maintaining the balance between inner contrition and the speech which often produces and augments it (lines 113–16, 1015–28). Then, for the largest part of the work, the Parson plots out the Seven Deadly Sins, just as all of the penitential handbooks do. The purpose of this central part of the text is not to persuade readers with *sentence* and *solaas*, to delight them with brilliant narrative structure, but to give them sample portraits, possible pictures of themselves that they match up to their own experience. The reader of The Parson's Tale thus becomes an active participant in it, using the handbook, not merely listening to a story told.

A careful reading of the entire tale is not to my purpose here. As plenty of scholars have shown, Chaucer's adaptations and redactions of his sources are carefully done;[24] however, we should not overplay these, especially in a genre where each newly produced handbook adapted and revised its sources in minor ways. To my mind, it is how *little* adaptation Chaucer has done, in comparison with what he does in the other tales, that is important here. The Parson's Tale moves away from artfulness, artifice, and rhetoric and into a submission to the general, typical, objective penitential process. It is not so much the details of the handbook, therefore, but the very fact that it *is* a handbook, and that it is *here*, at this given place in *The Canterbury Tales*, that is important. The tale's significance thus lies not in what it reveals but in how it teaches us to reveal ourselves to ourselves and to God, who, the perfect auditor, can understand our "entente"

---

[24]Siegfried Wenzel has shown this more carefully than anyone else. See, for instance, "Notes on the *Parson's Tale*," *Chaucer Review* 16 (1982): 248–51.

perfectly.[25] It is interested not in the result but the method, the way rather than the final arrival.

Thus the function of language is transformed in The Parson's Tale. In the previous tales, as Patterson points out, the pilgrims use different forms of language—satirical, bawdy, courtly, even homiletic—to "fashion," to "create," themselves. But in The Parson's Tale Chaucer transcends not only fiction and language but the self itself. He moves out of the worldly scheme (of *sentence* and *solaas*) to suggest that language is best used for penance—for personal exploration and reform, not to re-set the self as an individual, as an independent agent "using" language, but to provide the central way in which the self can destroy and reaffirm its relational being, its relationship to God. The self, says penitential structure—and the Parson—is no more an isolated individual monad than it is merely a "subject" constructed out of social, linguistic, or political forces. But we already knew that, or should have, from seeing the failures of the strongest individuals of *The Canterbury Tales*—the Wife, the Pardoner, the Canon, among others. These pilgrims are at once the most individualistic pilgrims (which is why liberal humanist criticism was so fascinated by them) and yet are pilgrims who attempt to forge a self out of the social discourses around them (which is why late-twentieth century postmodernists are so fascinated by them). Medieval penitential theology declares that one cannot "create" or "construct" a self, nor can social forces do it for one. The best one can do with a self, the medieval handbooks suggest, is reform it—that is, re-form, re-construct, the self's relation to God and others; the worst one can do is bend the self out of shape, empty it through the privation that is sin, cut off one's relations to others and God. Penance affirms

---

[25] See Linda Georgianna, "Love So Dearly Bought: The Terms of Redemption in *The Canterbury Tales*," *Studies in the Age of Chaucer* 12 (1990): 85–116.

that the self is not isolated, individual, complete, neither a Gnostic separation from this world nor completely socially constructed; it only exists in and as a relation to God, and it does so by constructing the self through language—but a particular, sacramental use and structure of language.

The Retraction provides the opportunity for Chaucer himself to learn the lesson he taught others in The Parson's Tale. He drops the game of language, the play of rhetoric, the toying with false selves and masks and personae and pilgrims, to end his own pilgrimage of language, to come to the shrine beyond human words and the shrine of the Word. The way he does this is tricky indeed; at the beginning of the Retraction, as many have noticed, it appears that the Parson is still speaking:

> Now preye I to hem alle that herkne this litel tretys or rede, that if ther be any thyng in it that liketh hem, that therof they thanken oure Lord Jhesu Crist, of whom procedeth al wit and al goodnesse. (line 1081)

But then Chaucer gradually—so gradually that critics have debated when it happens—elides the Parson's voice and speaks in his own voice. For the first and only time, he drops all of the personae of the tales and takes up his own voice, his own self-expression. The reason for this elision is, I hope, now clear: he must take up another's voice first, as the penitent takes up the sample portraits or the priest's voice, in order to come to his own true penitential voice, finding in the other pilgrims' and now the Parson's sample portraits an accurate, objective portrayal of his own experience which he then speaks in his own auto-biographical statement. What he seems to confess, to apologize for, is first simply a lack of literary skill (he "wolde ful fayn have seyd bettre if [he] hadde had konnynge" [line 1082]), claiming his "entente" (line 1083) was good. But then, as he continues to speak, he seems to come to a deeper understanding of his self-limitations, of the moral risks he faces as a writer. Here Chaucer's anti-contritionist, pro-sacramental bias shows through: the speech itself has driven him to a deeper understanding of his failings, creating greater shame, contrition, and a more significant self-examination. Reviewing his life, he constructs an autobiography and comes to see himself, his *self*, in a new light. And what he confesses are his own individual efforts, his own "original" writings, his attempts to create his own self, his own voice, a rhetorical "I" all on his own:

> as is the book of Troilus; the book also of Fame; the book of the XXV. Ladies; the book of the Duchesse; the book of Seint Valentynes day of the Parlement of Briddes; the tales of Caunterbury, thilke that sownen into synne;/ the book of the Leoun; and many another book, if they were in my remembrance, and many a song and many a leccherous lay, that Crist for his grete mercy foryeve me the synne. (lines 1086–87)

What he thanks Christ and Mary for are the translations—those moments when he displaces his language into another's language, his self into another self:

> But of the translacion of Boece de Consolacione, and othere bookes of legendes of seintes, and omelies, and moralitee, and devocioun,/ that thanke I oure Lord Jhesu Crist and his blisful Mooder, and alle the seintes of hevene,/ bisekynge hem that they from hennes forth unto my lyves ende sende me grace to biwayle my giltes and to studie to the salvacioun of my soule, and graunte me grace of verray penitence, confessioun and satis-faccioun to doon in this present lyf. . . . (lines 1088–90)

What I am saying about the Retraction, then, is the oldest thing of all—that here Chaucer utters a confession—but I am trying to show that Chaucer understood the rhetoric, theology, and psychology of that act. And, far from simply running from his fiction in a hasty and belated attempt to save his soul, he uses The Parson's Tale and Retraction to question the very act of fiction-making and finally finds it wanting. To Chaucer fiction-making is not, finally, the highest good, the deepest and most significant use of language, or the doorway to fully achieved self-hood—as much as that might wound our humanist sensibilities today. Therefore at the end of his work he turns his own language to prayer, changing his language not in degree but fundamentally in kind. Chaucer moves out of the human, confused, limited, self-interested world of language he has explored so well in the tales toward a transcendent use of language, a use that he does not root in the autonomous and willful user of words, in the this-worldly self, but that, as Chaucer seems clearly to believe, reaches beyond that self to find the self's true home, true grounding.

The Parson's Tale, to borrow the terms of modern Speech-Act theory, is about "illocutionary language."[26] It is about action; it is about *doing* something with and through words, as J. L. Austin would say, and its import is not a matter of true or false, but whether the use of the language is felicitous or infelicitous. Here, of course, felicity—ultimate happiness—is the very core of this illocutionary language. It is about the complex way in which constructing a tale of ourselves enables us to begin changing ourselves, re-orienting ourselves, finding, and speaking into being, what a medieval Christian would have considered the true self. And that, in fact, is what makes the tale "myrie."

---

[26] J. L. Austin, "Performative-Constantive," in *The Philosophy of Language*, ed. J. R. Searle (Oxford, 1971), pp. 1–12.

"THE GOODE WEY":
ENDING AND NOT-ENDING
IN THE PARSON'S TALE

CHARLOTTE GROSS

Explaining the "subtyl art" (*Tr* 2.257) of composition to his niece, Pandarus asserts that "[the] tale is al for som conclusioun" (*Tr* 2.259)—that is, directed towards an end that gives meaning to the whole.[1] In contrast, some readers of Chaucer's Parson's Tale have found in this last Canterbury tale not the sense of fulfillment or resolution generally associated with conclusions, but rather a transcendence, denial, or even cancellation of the preceding tales, a negation of their diversity, festivity, and art.[2] Yet if the relation of the

---

[1] Playing on the double meaning of "ende" and "entencioun" (purpose, goal), Pandarus argues that the "conclusion" is of first importance. Insofar as literary conclusions aid retrospective perception of structure and meaning, his word-play well conveys the modern sense of "conclusion." On the primacy of endings according to medieval rhetoricians, see Rosemarie P. McGerr, "Medieval Concepts of Literary Closure: Theory and Practice," *Exemplaria* 1 (1989): 154–61.

[2] In addition, some Chaucerians would exclude the penitential treatise as "ill-tempered, bad-mannered, pedantic, and joyless" (E. Talbot Donaldson, *Speaking of Chaucer* [New York, 1970], p. 173) and "endless, narrow, small-minded" (Charles Muscatine, "Chaucer's Religion and the Chaucer Religion," in *Chaucer Traditions: Studies in Honour of Derek Brewer*, ed. Ruth Morse and Barry Windeatt [Cambridge, 1990], p. 258).

final tale to the entire collection remains problematic, most readers nevertheless unite in regarding The Parson's Tale as a strong ending: as Lee Patterson writes, "[I]ts very nature is terminal."[3] As a termination or ending, The Parson's Tale interrupts a linear sequence of tale-telling. It arrests our expectation of continuation simply by virtue of being "different": different in its movement from storytelling to authoritative truth (Howard 1976); from illusion to "final reality" (David 1976); from the many to the One (Lawler 1980); from fiction to biography (Patterson 1978); from "artistic . . . [to] historical consciousness" (Pearsall 1985); from sin to remedy (Lawton 1987); and from narrative fiction to unchanging doctrine (Wetherbee 1989).[4]

Implicit, perhaps, in these various critical readings is the distinction, not always fully or consistently articulated, between a simple announcement of ending—"This collection of tales stops here"—and a more complex notion of closure. According to Barbara Herrnstein Smith's classic study, closure concerns the sense of completion and stability—the reader's experience of unity, coherence, and design—that arises from the fulfillment of expectations and the resolution of

---

[3]Lee Patterson, "The 'Parson's Tale' and the Quitting of the 'Canterbury Tales'," *Traditio* 34 (1978): 380.

[4]Donald R. Howard, *The Idea of the Canterbury Tales* (Berkeley, 1976), p. 381; Alfred David, *The Strumpet Muse: Art and Morals in Chaucer's Poetry* (Bloomington, Ind., 1976), p. 239; Traugott Lawler, *The One and the Many in the Canterbury Tales* (Hamden, Conn., 1980), p. 153; Patterson, "The 'Parson's Tale'," p. 380; Derek Pearsall, *The Canterbury Tales* (London, 1985), p. 292; David Lawton, "Chaucer's Two Ways: The Pilgrimage Frame of *The Canterbury Tales*," *Studies in the Age of Chaucer* 9 (1987): 40; Winthrop Wetherbee, *Chaucer and the Canterbury Tales* (Cambridge, 1989), p. 126.

previously-deferred tensions.[5] More recently, David Hult has drawn attention to closure as an act, a closing or bringing to conclusion, and "thus the intervention of a subject effecting the work's completion." As he argues, closure is "a discourse on the frame" that also responds to the work's "inner movement in the direction of unity or completeness."[6] But despite such theoretical elaboration, the issue of closure in *The Canterbury Tales* elicits little consensus among readers of Chaucer, who not only discern differing "inner movements" in *The Canterbury Tales* but also interpret the text from differing ideological perspectives.[7] If for Traugott Lawler The Parson's Tale confers retrospective unity upon a multiplicity of tales to provide "full closure," for Robert Jordan the concluding treatise is a "digression" that abandons the fictional frame and "finally de-centers the *Canterbury Tales*."[8] And in the reading of Donald Howard, The Parson's Tale, while certainly closural, represents only one of many possible knittings, "esthetically satisfying only from one viewpoint."[9]

More recently, David Lawton has argued that the coexistence in Chaucer's frame of two conflicting "ways"—attitudes or impulses

---

[5]Barbara Herrnstein Smith, *Poetic Closure: A Study of How Poems End* (Chicago, 1968), pp. 2–3, 34–36.

[6]David Hult, ed., *Concepts of Closure*, in *Yale French Studies* 67 (New Haven, 1984), pp. iv–v.

[7]To a large degree, critical assessments of closure in ParsT have turned on the persistent issue of "transcendent truth" (that is, the implied ontological status of the Parson's words); for some readers, the transcendent precludes closure as surely as for others it confers it. In this essay I will argue that other factors, which may be considered separately, also contribute to the issue of closure in ParsT.

[8]Lawler, *The One*, pp. 169–72; Robert Jordan, *Chaucer's Poetics and the Modern Reader* (Berkeley, 1987), pp. 167–68.

[9]Howard, *The Idea*, p. 385.

which reflect historical values—invites us to read The Parson's Tale as part of a closure sequence.[10] In contrast, Paul Strohm finds The Parson's Tale to be characterized by a monovocal finality that "closes down" the varied worlds and discourses of the tales, even while Chaucer's Canterbury book itself strongly resists closure.[11] And Patterson's 1991 study of Chaucer and history sees in The Parson's Tale not fulfillment or resolution but "the definitive cancellation of the *Canterbury Tales*," an ultimate undoing of the "linear purposiveness of pilgrimage"—as I take it, a strong but non-closural ending. [12]

The assumption that "closure was an unquestioned ideal in medieval literature" recently has been challenged explicitly by Rosemarie McGerr, who argues that medieval writers, able to maintain contradictory perspectives and receptive to disjunction and tension, "appreciated the significance of suspension of closure."[13] Chaucer's final tale suggests that such suspension was self-conscious and purposeful. On the one hand, the Parson's Prologue is supersaturated with signals of ending and closure, from the long afternoon shadows to the speaker's explicit project "[t]o knytte up al this feeste and make an ende" (X.47). On the other hand, the Parson clearly defines his concept of making an end as pointing to another road forward: he will show the audience "the wey, in this viage" (line 49)—a "wey" defined as a journey of penitence to be accomplished in linear time.

---

[10]Lawton, "Chaucer's Two Ways," pp. 3–40.

[11]Paul Strohm, *Social Chaucer* (Cambridge, Mass., 1989), pp. 179–80.

[12]Lee W. Patterson, *Chaucer and the Subject of History* (Madison, Wisc., 1991), p. 246 and p. 20.

[13]McGerr, "Medieval Concepts," pp. 169–70. McGerr also finds that "medieval theorists do have a strong sense of literary closure, but that, for many of them as for many modern theorists, closure involves a complex set of ideas about the entire structure of a text . . ." (p. 161).

As I will argue, along with its strong movement towards ending and its many intimations of closure—its powerful evocation of last things—The Parson's Tale introduces an equally strong anti-closural movement of "not-ending." This is the forward-looking "goode wey" (line 77), which leads the Chaucerian audience away from the fictional world of pilgrims and tales—not towards transcendent reality, but instead towards the English here and now, towards a practical scrutiny of self guided by the Parson's careful treatment of penitence. If, as Derek Pearsall has suggested, The Parson's Tale stands at an infinitesimal distance from Chaucer himself—a distance shortly to be removed in the Retraction[14]—so too the implied audience of this penitential treatise shifts imperceptibly from the fictional pilgrims to Chaucer's contemporary and future readers. It "makes us turn from the world of [*The Canterbury Tales*] and look to our selves in the world about us."[15]

This paper focuses on two limited aspects of closure in The Parson's Tale—time and timelessness, ending and not-ending—in an effort to isolate and clarify a small part of the larger problem of "knitting up." Having distinguished literary *ending*, a manipulation of formal and thematic elements announcing a stopping point, from *closure*, a resolution of tension offering a sense of completion, unity, and fulfillment, I would suggest that in The Parson's Tale the idea of "not-ending" works in an anti-closural manner. As I will argue, time does not cease in this last "tale" of Canterbury, although narrative does; nor is temporality necessarily transcended by universal or "timeless" truth, as some readers have urged. While the ultimate goal

---

[14]Pearsall, *The Canterbury Tales*, p. 293, argues that "[t]he Parson's Tale passes from the fictional world of *The Canterbury Tales* into the real world of Chaucer's life as a Christian."

[15]Howard, *The Idea*, p. 380.

of the "goode wey" is clearly "Jerusalem celestial" (line 51)—an overwhelming signal of ending and transcendence—the "wey" itself is a forward-looking extension into the immediate future, the quotidian time of the Chaucerian audience.

This double movement of The Parson's Tale, a simultaneous ending and not-ending, finds a theoretical basis in a fundamental paradigm of Christian ontology. In his meditations on time and eternity in the *Confessions*, Augustine distinguishes between *expectatio futurorum*, the expectation of future things which carries the soul forward in time, and *intentio ad superiora*, the orientation of the soul towards the eternal.[16] The distinction follows from Augustine's conception of time as a *distentio animi*, a distension or extension of soul produced by the simultaneous activities of the faculties of memory, attention, and expectation. The soul is necessarily superior to temporal things; yet the very operations that permit the soul to measure time inevitably fragment it between past and future. As Augustine writes in a moving passage of the *Confessions*, "My thoughts are torn apart in changing time" ("[A]t ego in tempora dissilui," 11.29).[17] The distracted and fragmented soul may nevertheless be unified by a second interior motion. This is *intentio ad superiora*, which concentrates the soul, directing it "not to those things which are future and transitory"—that is, the objects of

---

[16]Jean Guitton, *Le Temps et l'éternité chez Plotin et Saint Augustin*, 2nd ed. (Paris, 1959), pp. 223–43. This distinction, a persistent theme in Augustine's work, is most clearly set forth in *Confessions* 11.

[17]Augustine, *Confessions*, 2 vols. (Cambridge, Mass., 1912), 1: 278–80. All citations will be from this text, henceforth referred to as *Conf.*, and will be noted parenthetically; all translations are mine.

expectation—"but rather towards [its] eternal goal" (11.30).[18] An imperfect and provisional medium, time allows the soul to be present to itself (through memory) and to anticipate things to come (through expectation). But when such "distending" spiritual movements are transcended by pure *intentio*—as in moments of contemplation like those experienced by Augustine and Monica at Ostia—the soul for an instant enjoys the complete self-presence and unification proper to eternity (9.10).[19]

As this account suggests, Augustine's attitude towards time is profoundly ambivalent. On the one hand, time distracts and scatters the soul in the sensible world so that it loses sight of true Being, turns away from God, and falls to the formless disorder of sin. As Henri Marrou has observed, "Dans une philosophie de l'essence, le temps apparaît toujours un peu comme un scandale."[20] For Augustine, working in the Neoplatonic tradition, time is associated with the "dissimilitude" of deficient being, the changeability of matter, and (by

---

[18]Augustine, *Conf.* 11.29: ". . . sequens unum, praeterita oblitus, non in ea quae futura et transitura sunt, sed in ea quae ante sunt non *distentus*, sed *extentus*, non secundum *distentionem*, sed secundum *intentionem* sequor ad palmam supernae vocationis. . ." (my emphasis). But Augustine concludes the chapter by expressing his sense of fragmentation in time: "[A]t ego in tempora dissilui, quorum ordinem nescio, et tumultuosis varietatibus dilaniantur cogitationes meae, intima viscera animae meae, donec in te confluam. . ." (ibid.).

[19]Guitton, *Le Temps et l'éternité*, p. 235. For Augustine's conception of memory (of self and God), see *Conf.* X and *De Trinitate* 14. See also Guitton, pp. 243–53; and Étienne Gilson, *The Christian Philosophy of Saint Augustine* (New York, 1960), p. 221.

[20]Henri-Irénée Marrou, *L'Ambivalence du temps de l'histoire chez Saint Augustin* (Paris, 1950), p. 43.

implication) with sin.[21] On the other hand, time is also the essential medium of both redemptive history—preeminently the Incarnation—and personal salvation. In enabling the soul to know or be present to itself, Augustine holds, the faculty of memory initiates a first step in the consciousness of *interiora* that leads to God.[22] With its tests and deferrals, time moreover supports the movement of will by which the soul turns and redirects itself to its Creator. For Augustine, such voluntary conversions both acknowledge the eternal and affirm the reality and importance of time itself; as Jean Guitton has observed, "[L]e temps est avant tout le lieu de salut."[23] Thus two distinct but complementary motions of the soul coexist in the journey to God. "We turn ourselves to Him temporally, that is, from some particular time," writes Augustine in his *De Trinitate*, "in order to remain with him eternally. . . . He has been made a road for us in time in order that . . . He might be a mansion for us in eternity" (7.3.5).[24]

---

[21] Augustine's negative views of materiality and temporality are largely derived from his Neoplatonism. Marrou argues that for Augustine time is "ambivalent," evil by nature but an "instrument of progress" through grace (*L'Ambivalence du temps*, p. 71). Étienne Gilson similarly sees Augustine's concept of salvation as a redemption "from the anguish of time and of becoming" (*A History of Christian Philosophy in the Middle Ages* [New York, 1955], pp. 592–93 n. 23). In contrast, Guitton, *Le Temps et l'éternité*, stresses the positive role of time in Augustine, for whom time is the testing-ground of the soul and the road to eternity. An unresolved ambivalence about temporality is central to Augustinian thought.

[22] See, e.g., Augustine, *Conf.* 10.17: "[E]go ascendens per animum meum ad te, qui desuper mihi manes, transibo et istam vim meam, quae memoria vocatur volens te attingere. . . ."

[23] Guitton, *Le Temps et l'éternité*, p. 235; see also ibid., pp. 121–45.

[24] Augustine, *On the Trinity*, trans. Stephen McKenna (Washington, D.C., 1962), pp. 226–27.

Similarly, I would argue, in the last tale of the Canterbury book the Parson's "goode wey" of penitence is a careful combination of *intentio* and *expectatio*: the journey of confession, contrition, and satisfaction is both guided by an orientation to the eternal and accomplished in linear time. As Siegfried Wenzel's studies of sources have shown, in the task of translating, combining, and composing Chaucer "not only worked selectively but also made changes and additions which reveal intelligence, purposiveness, and . . . familiarity with the pastoral-theological thought and language of his time."[25] I therefore view the temporal structure and texture of the treatise—the complex use of time and temporality—as directly indicative of Chaucer's design for ending and not-ending in The Parson's Tale.

Chaucer's recasting of Pennaforte's *Summa de poenitentia*—the ultimate source of the opening and closing sections of The Parson's Tale—foregrounds his concern for both time and eternity, *expectatio* and *intentio*. First, Chaucer's additions to Pennaforte emphasize that genuine penitence demands uninterrupted continuity in time, a movement towards the future (the dimension of *expectatio*): "[He shal] continue in goode werkes, or elles his repentance may nat availle"

---

[25]Siegfried Wenzel, "Notes on the *Parson's Tale*," *Chaucer Review* 16 (1982): 237–56. In the Notes to *The Riverside Chaucer*, Wenzel similarly proposes that "Chaucer himself made a purposeful compilation and translation from divers sources" (p. 956). For sources of this compilation, see Kate Oelzner Petersen, *The Sources of the Parson's Tale* (Boston, 1901; repr. New York, 1973) for Raymund of Pennaforte's *Summa de poenitentia*; for William Peraldus's *summae* and related texts, see Wenzel, "The Source of Chaucer's Seven Deadly Sins," *Traditio* 30 (1974): 351–78; and Wenzel, ed., *Summa virtutum de remediis anime* (Athens, Ga., 1984). See also note 30, below.

(line 88).[26] At the outset of his treatise, Chaucer replaces Pennaforte's triadic biblical allusions—e.g., the three-day journey of Moses into the desert (Exodus 5.3)—with a more temporally complex image, the allegorical tree of Penitence. Whereas the metaphor of a journey implies simple linear sequence—"passing through phases as a train passes through stations," as C. S. Lewis once wrote—Chaucer's tree-image conveys both temporal progress and the interrelatedness of parts essential to penitence, an inseparable triad of thoughts, words, and deeds (lines 478, 959).[27] Thus the root of contrition, leaves of confession, and fruit of satisfaction develop and flourish both successively and simultaneously: that is, the allegorical tree affords an atemporal overview of the stages of what must be an ongoing temporal process.[28] According to the Parson himself, penitential time

---

[26]The phrase "[T]o continue in good werkes," is an addition to Pennaforte; see Petersen, *The Sources*, p. 5. Chaucer may have worked from a short version of Pennaforte (see Wenzel, "The Parson's Tale in Current Literary Studies," in this volume). This hypothesis does not affect an argument from additions, since what is not in a long version is not likely to be in the short one. Of course, many of Chaucer's "additions" have sources and analogues in contemporary penitential literature.

[27]C. S. Lewis, *The Allegory of Love* (Oxford, 1936), p. 1. For Penneforte's text and biblical triads, see Germaine Dempster, "The *Parson's Tale*," in *Sources and Analogues of the Canterbury Tales*, ed. W. F. Bryan and Germaine Dempster (New York, 1941), pp. 732–33. Pennaforte's other biblical triads do not refer to journeys (e.g., the three dead whom Christ raised to life [Matt. 9.18–25]).

[28]Hence, it would seem, Chaucer's deliberate conflation of the fruit of satisfaction and the "fruyt" by which men are known (lines 115–16; Matt. 7.16–20), criticized by Patterson as confused ("The 'Parson's Tale'," p. 352). Chaucer associates "fruyt" with both *expectatio* or future things—"[f]or in the flour is hope of fruyt in tyme comynge, and . . . hope of grace wel for to do" (line 288)—and with *intentio* or eternal things (lines 1076–80).

is forward-looking and continuous: "contricioun moste be continueel," since it sustains hope of forgiveness (line 305); confession must be prompt and frequent, since untended sin grows worse in time (lines 998, 1027); and satisfaction must be continued in future good works (lines 88, 115).

Second, in reshaping his sources Chaucer confines nearly all references to Last Things—death, judgment, heaven, and hell—to the opening and closing sections of The Parson's Tale (lines 75–386 and 958–1080). He thus creates for the central treatise on the Seven Deadly Sins a frame which combines both *expectatio*, the forward-looking and temporal "wey" of penitence, and *intentio*, the orientation to eternal things. Chaucer's substantive additions to Pennaforte's *Summa*—for example, his amplification of the causes of contrition—work to intensify this double movement of the frame. Thus, on the one hand, he expands Pennaforte's third cause of contrition—a brief evocation of final judgment and hell—to a lengthy and vivid account of Doomsday and the pains of eternal damnation (lines 158–230), moving from "the stierne and wrothe juge" (line 170) to "the horrible develes that hym tormenten" (line 183) to the eternal absence of all good, "deeth withoute deeth and ende withouten ende" (line 214). On the other hand, Chaucer's discussion of good works as a cause of contrition (lacking in Pennaforte) foregrounds the "wey" of linear temporality, urging the reader to consider the relation of past, present, and future actions. According to the Parson, contrition arises when we meditate on good works left undone or lost, the latter "mortefied" and "dulled" by present or future deadly sin (lines 231–35). Chaucer's best-known addition to Pennaforte's six causes of contrition, a vivid "remembrance" of the Passion, similarly strengthens the double movement of the frame. As in all Passion meditations, the historical moment of the Crucifixion becomes immediately present to evoke a strongly affective response: "muchel oghte synful man wepen and biwayle" (line 282). Yet the suffering Christ, who is conflated with the Christ of Revelations, also directs the readers' thoughts to Last Things and eternity: "'I was atte dore of thyn herte . . . and cleped for to entre. . . . I wol entre into hym by my grace and soupe with hym'" (lines 289–90; Revelations 3.20).

Finally, the verb forms of Chaucer's "penitential frame" (i.e., his recasting of Pennaforte) make clear that the "goode wey" is a road in time. If the exhortations of the opening discussion of penitence and contrition call for affective response—sorrow, lamentation, fear, hope—the imperatives of the end-frame, which treats confession and satisfaction, demand action in the immediate future: "thy shrift sholde be ful of teeris" (line 993); "thou shalt shryve thee of alle thy synnes to o man" (line 1006); "lat no synne been untoold" (line 1010). Intensified by a movement from the impersonal "man" to "ye" and especially to the intimate "thou," the Parson's forceful concluding tone is clearly heard in comparison with Pennaforte's *Summa*. For instance, the participial "non tacens verum" becomes the imperative, "Thou ne shalt nat eek make no lesynges" (line 1019); the hortatory "[D]ebet confessio esse frequens" becomes the sharp command, "shryve thee ofte" (line 1025); and the simple "[Debet confessio esse] nuda" becomes the highly circumstantial "Thou most eek shewe thy synne by thyn owene propre mouth, but thow be woxe dowmb, and nat by no lettre" (line 1021).[29] Directing the audience to specific and immediate action, establishing the metaphysics of sin, the pragmatics of good works, and the ever-presence of redemption in Christian history, the frame invites the audience to meditate on both eternity and time. Insofar as we look to Chaucer's final vision of heaven, to endless bliss and perfect knowing, the frame offers a strong sense of ending. But insofar as the "goode wey" of penitence is shown to be continuous and temporal, moving from "remembrance" of past sin to

---

[29]Petersen, *The Sources*, pp. 21–22; Dempster, "The Parson's Tale," pp. 38–39.

present contrition to immediate action in future word and deed, we experience an equal sense of not-ending, or even beginning again. For in the sacrament of confession, Chaucer tells us, "alle thynges renovellen" (line 1027).

The same sense of forward-looking temporality—of *expectatio futurorum*—characterizes the Parson's central exposition of the Seven Deadly Sins and their remedies.[30] Unlike the prescriptive and often hortatory frame, however, the central treatise on sin tends to be definitional and descriptive; and thus for some readers The Parson's Tale represents a movement towards the general, universal, and timeless.[31] Strohm, for example, argues that "the *Parson's Tale* would subsume the world of varied temporality into its timeless categories," while Patterson stresses that the larger theological context of the tale "defines a pattern of sin and redemption applicable . . . to all men and all women, in any place and at any time."[32] In this latter sense, the Parson's general definitions of sin, its causes and sub-species, are

---

[30]Wenzel has shown that this central treatise draws on two redactions of Peraldus, the texts he calls *Primo/Quoniam* (for the sins); and (for the remedies) on the treatise *Summa virtutum de remediis anime* (*Postquam*); see note 25, above.

[31]Of course, there are exceptions to this non-hortatory tone; see, e.g., the Parson's well-known discussion of pride in dress (lines 416–31).

[32]Strohm, *Social Chaucer*, p. 177, and Patterson, "The 'Parson's Tale'," p. 370, approach the notion of "universality" from different perspectives. For Patterson, reading ParsT as "general" supports his argument that the penitential treatise is concerned not merely in retrospect with the Canterbury pilgrims, but with all Christians: "Sin is to be understood . . . as the central fact of the human situation" (p. 342). According to Strohm's argument, the Parson misrepresents the new social relations and impulses of Chaucer's age, "refeudalizing" society by returning to (and seeking to enforce) a hierarchical social model originally represented by its proponents as "timeless" or "universal" (pp. 176–80; see, e.g., lines 771–74).

intended to be comparable to what we would call scientific truths. That is, they are repeatable and generalizable propositions lacking specific location in time or space: "Water freezes at zero degrees Centigrade"; "Accidie maketh [a man] hevy, thoghtful, and wraw" (line 677).[33] And indeed, our sense of "scientific truth" is enhanced by Chaucer's occasional use of purely physiological definitions: "Ire, after the Philosophre, is the fervent blood of man yquyked in his herte . . ." (line 536). But in discussing the manifestations of vice or virtue, the Parson's amplifications move strongly to the particular, specific, practical, and immediate. The nature and causes of human failings are keenly observed: thus envy adds "but" to a sentence of praise, tying "a wikked knotte atte laste ende" (line 494); a lie can arise "of delit," elaborated for the sheer joy of its telling (line 610). Equally shrewd and specific is the Parson's counsel on satisfaction: for instance, the man unable to make charitable visits in person is advised to send to the sick by messenger (line 1032). As Howard observes, The Parson's Tale offers its audience "*practical* information, applied specifically to details of everyday life."[34] Nor does the relentlessly conservative outlook of this penitential treatise diminish the evidence of its frequent and significant topicality: thus we read that lords who maintain large, unruly, or dangerous retinues make public display of sinful pride (lines 437–39); that servants forced to labor "grevously" or on holidays should endure this affliction with the remedial virtue of patience (lines 667–68); and that men are oppressed by taxes, duties,

[33]On "scientific truths," see George T. Wright, "The Lyric Present: Simple Present Verbs in English Poems," *PMLA* 89 (1974): 563–79.

[34]Howard, *The Idea*, p. 377.

and services as a result of avarice—although God wisely ordained estates and degree (lines 752, 771).[35]

The issue is not, finally, whether the Parson's remarks are "timeless" in the sense of being universally applicable in some absolute way—after all, many passages clearly show strong historical inflection—but whether they are meant to be construed by the audience as theoretical or practical, whether beyond time or within the bounds of temporality. If the Parson's iterated "now shul ye understonde" (e.g., line 804) suggests a theoretical or intellectual enterprise, Chaucer's interpolation of remedial virtues among the vices, like his addition of sharp imperatives to the penitential frame, emphasizes the need for immediate and active reform of self, in time. This practical orientation of The Parson's Tale may be elucidated with reference to the historical development of medieval penitential literature. According to Leonard Boyle, Pennaforte's *Summa* exemplifies the "first wave" of confessional manuals following the Fourth Lateran Council (1215), *summa poenitentiae* largely directed towards educating priests. In contrast, the various vernacular manuals of virtues and vices that proliferated around 1260 and after—descendants of Latin treatises such as Peraldus's *Summa de vitiis*, from which the Parson's discussion of deadly sin ultimately derives—are written for the laity, designed to teach the individual Christian penitent to confess, to combat sin, to scrutinize and reform the self.[36] Part of Chaucer's

---

[35] On contemporary religious issues treated in ParsT, see Patterson, "The 'Parson's Tale'," p. 348; and Howard, *The Idea*, p. 377.

[36] Leonard Boyle, "The Fourth Lateran Council and Manuals of Popular Theology," in *The Popular Literature of Medieval England*, ed. Thomas J. Heffernan, Tennessee Studies in Literature 28 (Knoxville, Tenn., 1985), pp. 30–43. As Boyle notes, early Latin manuals of vices and virtues (like the *Summa de vitiis* of Peraldus [just before 1250]) were directed towards clerical audiences; later vernacular treatises were

work, then, was to minimize the differences between these two implied audiences, to direct The Parson's Tale clearly towards the serious-minded, educated lay reader.[37] In its thorough discussion of penitence and careful anatomy of sin—its subspecies, manifestations, and remedial virtues—The Parson's Tale, I would argue, inevitably leads the reader towards practical self-evaluation of the sort legitimized and given lasting impetus by the Fourth Lateran Council.

That Chaucer's original audience is likely to have read the Parson's "litel tretys" in good earnest is congruent with the significant growth of lay piety in the latter half of the fourteenth century. This well-documented movement is illustrated, for example, by the popularity of vernacular devotional manuals such as the *Pricke of Conscience*, of which more manuscripts survive than of *The Canterbury Tales*.[38] Within Chaucer's own circle of friends, the listeners and readers whose tastes and responses encouraged his work, we find Sir John Clanvowe, author in 1391 of *The Two Ways*, a devotional treatise which attests to the compelling power of the "nargh" or

---

written for the laity (p. 35). The Peraldian-derived treatises which provide sources for Chaucer's discussion of the deadly sins seem to represent an intermediate stage: Wenzel, for example, points to a "mixed" audience in *Quoniam* ("The Continuing Life of William Peraldus's *Summa Vitiorum*," in *Ad Litteram: Authoritative Texts and Their Medieval Readers*, ed. M. D. Jordan and Kent Emery, Jr. [Notre Dame, Ind., 1992], pp. 150–51).

[37]For an argument that the Parson's treatise is not stylistically homogeneous, but appears to address two audiences, see Beryl Rowland, "Sermon and Penitential in *The Parson's Tale* and Their Effect on Style," *Florilegium* 9 (1987): 125–45. In contrast, I have suggested that Chaucer's recasting of his sources—for example, the addition of imperatives to Pennaforte—works to direct the treatise to the penitent rather than the priest.

[38]Pearsall, *The Canterbury Tales*, p. 297.

"goode wey" for the Chaucerian audience.[39] Nor should The Parson's Tale be viewed as monolithic: in its scope, purpose, complexity, and detail this concluding treatise on penitence invites, and indeed demands, individual response. The "goode wey" offered by the Parson is thus the quotidian time through which the Chaucerian audience, responding to the tale with many voices and diverse actions, will move—a temporal and linear extension into the immediate future. In framing the central treatise on sin and its remedies with visions of hell and heaven, Chaucer invokes endings and places his study of human vice and virtue under the aspect of eternity. But insofar as the "goode wey" looks to future things, by implication leading to speech rather than silence, to diversity rather than unity, and to temporality rather than eternity, The Parson's Tale may be read as a peculiarly Chaucerian not-ending.

As a postscript to this discussion of ending and not-ending in The Parson's Tale, one may ask whether Augustinian attitudes towards time and eternity persisted in the fourteenth century. In a free rendering of Augustine, the Parson defines deadly sin as a turning from God to give one's heart "to thyng that may chaunge and flitte"—a voluntary rejection of stable eternity for "unsiker" time (line 368). Yet by Chaucer's day, the severe Augustinian opposition between time and eternity had been modified, as had Augustinian ambivalence about time—in the twelfth century by Neoplatonic

---

[39]Derek Pearsall, *The Life of Geoffrey Chaucer: A Critical Biography* (Oxford, 1992), p. 182. On Chaucer's audience, see Strohm, *Social Chaucer*, pp. 47–83. On John Clanvowe, see Lawton, "Chaucer's Two Ways," pp. 38–40; Patterson, *Chaucer*, pp. 32–39.

influences, in the thirteenth by the reception of Aristotle.[40] Similarly discarded was Augustine's notion of time as interior, a function of mind or soul: during the renaissance of the twelfth century, time came to be viewed as an empirical aspect of the natural order, consistent, predictable, and quantifiable.[41] In Chaucer's day time was firmly associated with distance and space rather than mind and spiritual operation; and as Jacques Le Goff observes, this new "connection between the sense of time and the sense of space [represents] an innovation more revolutionary than is initially apparent."[42] Invented in the late thirteenth century, mechanical clocks began to measure the merchant's time of production and exchange, as well as the duration of journeys transporting commodities through space: exact accounting of time became part of orderly business. In later centuries the

---

[40]From Boethius and Calcidius, for example, the twelfth century received the Platonic and Neoplatonic notion that time is "the moving likeness of eternity" (*Tim.* 37d), imitating eternity as the sensible world imitates the intelligible archetype. Thus the relation of (Augustinian) opposition between time and eternity is replaced by one of (Platonic) imitation, effecting a new rapprochement between time *per successiones* and the divine *totum simul*. See, e.g., Boethius, *De consolatione*, Book V, pr. 6; and Calcidius, *Timaeus a Calcidio translatus commentarioque instructus*, ed. J. H. Waszink (London, 1962), pp. 30, 154; see also Charlotte Gross, "Twelfth-Century Concepts of Time," *Journal of the History of Philosophy* 23 (1985): 324–38. From Aristotle, the thirteenth century received the view that time is a matter of physics ("the number of motion in respect of 'before' and 'after'" [*Physics* 219b1]).

[41]On the "discovery of nature" that supported changing concepts of time in the twelfth century, see the classic study of M.-D. Chenu, *Nature, Man, and Society in the Twelfth Century: Essays on New Theological Perspectives in the Latin West*, trans. Jerome Taylor and Lester K. Little (Chicago, 1957), pp. 1–48.

[42]Jacques Le Goff, *Time, Work, and Culture in the Middle Ages*, trans. Arthur Goldhammer (Chicago, 1980), p. 34.

development of more accurate navigational instruments, dependent upon precise chronometers, would seem to confirm once and for all the Aristotelian association of time with motion and magnitude.[43] Thus, if Augustine saw space and time as distinct—the one exterior and a condition of body, the other interior and a condition of spirit— the later Middle Ages, for reasons both theoretical and practical, equated time with space or distance.[44] The two were indeed colloquially interchangeable; thus in The Reeve's Tale, the student John lies still in bed "a furlong wey" (about five minutes; I.4199).[45]

This paradigmatic shift in ways of looking at the world does not appear to affect theological concepts of time and eternity in religious treatises like The Parson's Tale, where the traditional association of temporality, materiality, and sin continues (so the Parson defines avarice as a "likerousnesse in herte" for temporal goods [X.741]).[46] Yet Chaucer's readers may well have experienced a tension between their everyday assumptions about time—a consistent feature of human activity and the natural order—and the older theological or Augustinian paradigm, in which the significance of time is largely spiritual. Indeed, the tag of the Parson's "newe Frenshe song, '*Jay tout perdu mon temps et mon labour*'" (line 248), itself a literary

---

[43]See Carlo Cipolla, *Clocks and Culture: 1300–1700* (1967; New York, 1978), pp. 37–75.

[44]Augustine, *The Literal Meaning of Genesis 8.20*, trans. John Hammond Taylor (New York, 1982), pp. 2, 20–21.

[45]On "furlong," see A. G. Rigg, "Clocks, Dials, and Other Terms," in *Middle English Studies Presented to Norman Davis*, ed. Douglas Gray and E. G. Stanley (Oxford, 1983), pp. 255–73.

[46]Although in Christian ontology all created things are good, Augustine often associates the material, temporal, and sinful. Since the change of will by which the soul turns away from God is necessarily temporal, Augustine writes of "the mutability of sin" (*Ennar. in Ps.* 147.5; cited by Marrou, *L'Ambivalence du temps*, p. 74).

commonplace, suggests, in the context of a penitential treatise, that time and temporal works are newly valued. Similarly—to turn to one of Chaucer's contemporaries—William Langland attempts to reclaim this newly measurable and profitable time for Christianity as an unambiguous medium of salvation. If for Augustine time distracts and fragments the soul seeking eternity, in *Piers Plowman* salvation is to be sought in time and by means of time. Thus, in an autobiographical passage of the C-text, Will compares himself to a merchant:

> . . . y haue ytynt tyme and tyme myspened;
> Ac ȝut, I hope, as he þat ofte hath ychaffared
> And ay loste and loste, and at þe laste hym happed
> A bouhte such a bargayn he was þe bet euere,
>
> . . . .
> So hope y to haue of hym þat is almyghty
> A gobet of his grace, and bigynne a tyme
> That alle tymes of my tyme to profit shal turne. (C.5.93–101).[47]

According to Langland's mercantile analogy, in which the right use of commodified time is figured as a business venture, the time redeemed by *grace* has the potential to become the time of spiritual *profit* and progress.

Given such changing religious attitudes towards time, it is perhaps not coincidental that Chaucer's elaborate computation of time at the beginning of the Parson's Prologue (involving the height of the sun, the measurement of his shadow, and the "moones exaltacioun") is

---

[47]Derek Pearsall, *Piers Plowman by William Langland: An Edition of the C-Text* (Berkeley, 1979), p. 102. As the Parson's "Frenshe song" and this quotation imply, the issue of dignifying time and temporal works leads to a discussion of Pelagianism, a topic beyond the scope of this essay. See Robert Adams, "Langland's Theology," in *A Companion to* Piers Plowman, ed. John Alford (Berkeley, 1988), pp. 95–98.

inaccurate in several respects (X.2–11).[48] Chaucer may wish less to express a traditional indifference to worldly time and temporal things, as has been suggested,[49] than to draw our attention to a growing disjunction between scientific and symbolic ways of looking at the world, and to the need to reconcile these perspectives. As both *The Canterbury Tales* and *Piers Plowman* suggest, in the later Middle Ages religious reform was concerned to resolve this disjunction, to reclaim for Christianity the time that according to traditional thought invariably "wasteth," "steleth," and "shendeth" (*CT* II.20–28).[50] For the Parson's goal is above all pragmatic. His treatise seeks to direct the individual Christian in temporal works—to clarify, regulate, and improve the "wey" of linear temporality or *expectatio futurorum*. Raised and then deferred in the Introduction to The Man of Law's Tale, the problem of Christian time, its nature and use, re-emerges in The Parson's Tale as a double construct, the "righte wey" (X.80) to "endelees blisse" (line 1076). In literary terms, the tale is rightly a deferral that celebrates itself, an ending that does not end.[51]

---

[48]See the Explanatory Notes to *The Riverside Chaucer*, p. 955; for example, the "exaltacioun" of the moon, or zodiacal sign, is Taurus rather than Libra.

[49]See the Explanatory Notes to *The Riverside Chaucer*, p. 955.

[50]On Intro to MLT and time, see V. A. Kolve, *Chaucer and the Imagery of Narrative* (Stanford, 1984), pp. 285–87; and David Raybin, "Custance and History: Woman as Outsider in Chaucer's *Man of Law's Tale*," *Studies in the Age of Chaucer* 12 (1990): 65–69. On Christian-Augustinian concepts of time as suffering, sin, and death, see Marrou, *L'Ambivalence du temps*, pp. 61–63, 71–74, and passim. For the later Middle Ages, the idea of destructive time is reinforced by classical antiquity: "For time," writes Aristotle, "is by its nature the cause of . . . decay, since it is the number of change, and change removes what is" (*Physics* 221b).

[51]A short version of this paper was read at the Ninth International Congress of the New Chaucer Society, Dublin, 1994.

Epilogue: Closing
the Eschatological Account

Linda Tarte Holley

Mapping out in rational terms the utter foolishness of sinning, the Parson shows us what the technical writer would call the "disincentives" for doing evil, flatly recording workaday sins and outlining reasonable steps for solution.

G. R. Owst furnishes a remarkable catalog of medieval sermons in the vernacular or Latin, in verse or prose. Because Chaucer had numbers of sermon types from which he might have chosen to knit up a great matter, we learn from what he rejects. For his Parson in this place at this moment, Chaucer passes up what is familiar to us in much of his poetry and familiar in many medieval sermons—the commonplace subjects of field sports, weather, marriage, riotous youths, misers, dreamers, frugal meals, home and hearth, dogs, boiling pots, chicken, rents, gossips. These sermon commonplaces attest to the power of the medieval pulpit. As Owst writes:

> Upon the same bookless adult society [of the Middle Ages], the pulpit bestowed also an entertaining Fiction, and the first smatterings of a knowledge of the world of nature, travel and antiquity that led to the demand for more. Its satire and complaint gave powerful ventilation to social wrongs, thus promoting the supply of popular "political" verse and helping to foster a national spirit. Finally, in its same shadow, we watched the emergence of a native school of vernacular comedy and tragedy, parent of our modern drama. All this, though not itself endowed with the qualities

of a great literature, is no mean achievement. It serves at least to remind us
that once the pulpit was a force to be reckoned with, alike in literature and
politics as religion.[1]

The exchange of influence between sermons and morality plays is
well attested, but Chaucer denies to the Parson anecdote and exemplum, satire and complaint, the "feudalization" of sacred texts, hell
mouth and Doomsday, allegory, proverbs. Rejecting the affective and
dramatic options for gaining audience response, the Parson catalogs
the qualities and manifestations of evil by means of technical information and explanation that have the force not of emotive response
but of persistent rational progress. Both rhetorical and moral pressures
intensify gradually under the cumulative significance of complex
intellectualized choices.

The subject matter in The Parson's Tale was not new: there were
plenty of manuals of vices and virtues, plenty of prescriptions for
effective penitence. Usually, allegory (that handy strategy for simultaneously teaching and delighting) provided an engaging narrative
impulse for setting out the vices and virtues, especially on the stage,
but visual and dramatic opportunities are mostly ignored by Chaucer's
Parson in favor of information that serves the rational and dialectical.
As a result of this decision, reason shapes content and method by
claiming deductions from observable information, and the compelling
dialectic is the call to act rather than pressure to participate in an
imagined or imaged field of activity as in the drama or narrative. In
fact, the reader/listener becomes the *site of activity*, the potentially
fruitful space of the mind. Harry wants the Parson to be fruitful in a
little space, but as usual Harry's observations mean one set of things
to him and quite other things to his audiences. Ultimately, the Parson's

---

[1]G. R. Owst, *Literature and Pulpit in Medieval England* (Oxford, 1966), p. 591.

contribution defines the uneasy space for the Middle Ages between the spiritual and the intellectual activities in the exercise of reason.

In fact, The Parson's Tale lays out the kind of rationalism we claim as modern. Alexander Murray points to language and mathematics, the matter of the medieval university curricula, as furnishing the base for the cultivation of an extraordinary paradigm shift toward the humanist view of reason as a way of knowing in the face of doctrines of faith.[2] The Parson's Tale lies in that uneasy space, narrow but fruitful, where the spiritual and the intellectual aspects of reason, as differentiated by medieval sensibilities, gain energy from each other. If, for example, we approach the natural world through reason—that is, as if we were reading a book for the purpose of understanding Nature at work as an ordered system rather than looking for miracles—a systematic belief in reason as distinct from faith may well lead to a clearer knowledge of God. Closely connected to this perception of systematic order and logic is the new work (new for the twelfth century) by which we *account* for experience so that we recognize events as part of a pattern available for our understanding and control. Mathematics furnishes the new paradigm for this systematic order and logic. Nature, now explainable by numbers and rational deduction, comes to include human nature with all its vices and virtues.

"It has always been clear that much is wrong with man," Murray writes:

> What has not been so clear is *what* is wrong. Two basic answers have been given in western tradition. One is that man's trouble lies ultimately in his mind. He would do what was right if he knew; if he had the right data or drew sounder conclusions from the data he had. The second view finds the

---

[2] Alexander Murray, *Reason and Society in the Middle Ages* (Oxford, 1991), pp. 1–13.

trouble in the will: men know what is right well enough (or could find out if they chose), but too often avoid doing it through perversity.[3]

The Parson operates under the assumption that there is a will and so furnishes the data for acting on good judgment and for taking and keeping proper account.

Systematizing complexities of good and evil furnished grist for classical as well as Christian thinkers. For Stoics like Seneca, Cicero, and Boethius, acting according to reason simultaneously brought knowledge and virtuous action since virtue exists in the presence of reason. But there were warnings against placing too much confidence in the intrinsic virtue of unevaluated knowledge, from Augustine, for example: "For, we do not call a man good because he knows what is good, but because he loves it";[4] or, more recently, from Aquinas:

Sciences are diversified according to the diverse nature of their knowable objects. For the astronomer and the physicist both prove the same conclusion—the earth, for instance, is round: the astronomer by means of mathematics (i.e., abstracting from matter), but the physicist by means of matter itself. Hence there is no reason why those things which are treated by the philosophical sciences, so far as they can be known by the light of natural reason, may not also be treated by another science so far as they are known by the light of the divine revelation.[5]

In terms of such thinking, the Parson is engaging in the risky operation of dialectic: he provides warrant and conclusions by means of rational

---

[3]Murray, *Reason and Society*, p. 2.

[4]Augustine, *The City of God* 11.28, ed. Vernon J. Bourke, trans. G. Walsh et al., with an introd. by Étienne Gilson (New York, 1958), p. 238.

[5]Thomas Aquinas, *The Summa Theologica*, question 1, article 1, in *Introduction to St. Thomas Aquinas*, ed. Anton C. Pegis (New York, 1948), p. 5.

argument in a tone and style that insist on action. He must be careful, however, not to fall into the error of reasoning to excess but, in his own act, must exercise reason so that it is "authorized, sustained, and confirmed at every point by an order of reality higher than itself."[6] Thus John of Salisbury, writing in the twelfth century, emphasizes the double obligation of reason, that guardian of body and soul:

> Reason, although divine, is as it were, set into motion by the winnowing fan of sensory perceptions and acts of the imagination. And since Prudence, in her inquiry into the truth, has need of reason's unvitiated examination, she [prudence] begets for reason "Philology." The latter is constantly attended by two handmaids, "Carefulness" [*periergia*, or extreme exactness] and "Vigilance" [*agrimnia*]. "Carefulness" concentrates on the labors of learning, while "Vigilance" diligently supervises these activities and moderates them lest anything become excessive.[7]

Reason defines the good and the bad and furnishes the guide to clear, reasonable choice. For the Parson, ignorance is the problem. And in a plain, workmanlike dialectic he maps out the solution for the truly contrite in terms of bookkeeping, a mathematical record of accounts:

> Wel may he be sory thanne, that oweth al his lif to God as longe as he hath lyved, and eek as longe as he shal lyve, that no goodnesse ne hath to paye with his dette to God to whom he oweth al his lyf./ For trust wel, "He shal yeven acountes," as seith Seint Bernard, "of alle the goodes that han be yeven hym in this present lyf, and how he hath hem despended,/ [in] so muche that ther shal nat perisse an heer of his heed, ne a moment of an houre ne shal nat perisse of his tyme, that he ne shal yeve of it a rekenyng."
> (X.252–54)

---

[6] Robert M. Hoopes, *Right Reason in the English Renaissance* (Oxford, 1993), p. 93.

[7] John of Salisbury, *Metalogicon* 4.17, trans. with Introduction and Notes by Daniel D. McGarry (Oxford, 1960), p. 59.

Reckoning, as metaphor, practice, and faith, provides the terms of the dialectic. This accountant's language and tone urge watchfulness and exactitude in the dense matters of human nature. The effect is a specialized genre, a manual of cognitive psychology or practical epistemology, an anatomy.

The Parson's pointed refusal to sow weeds on productive ground or clutter his information with fiction and rhyme demonstrates the practical work of keeping our accounts in good order, and in this context the precise guide for taking the measure of sloth furnishes an especially interesting example of the meticulous particularities of a sin and its remedies. The Parson's point is that the act of sinning is not dramatic, lacks the impulse of narrative to keep us in suspense, does not sing, will not surprise us. We know the bookkeeping system; we should be able to add up the accounts at any time. But the slothful one prefers not to act at all (like Melville's scrivener), so that *accidie* presents itself as the enemy to every estate of man, as a liability to innocence, prayer, grace; it lacks purveyance (that view of the future calling for action in the present). It so binds the slothful that he can neither think nor do well. Frankly, says St. Bernard, the slothful lacks strong arms and hard sinews. He hasn't the heart to take up a great enterprise like doing good works (lines 689–90).

Over time, this unreasonableness deepens into *wanhope* or, as we would say, despair, through which, the Parson says, the slothful "abaundoneth al his herte" (line 694); he is a coward who cries out "'*creant*' withoute nede" (line 698) because he fails to recognize God's mercy: "Allas, what nedeth man thanne to been despeired, sith that his mercy so redy is and large?" (line 705). It is reasonable to say that one who *dreads* God does not fail to do what he should. And, moreover, one who *loves* God will abandon himself, with all his might, to do well. But the idle man is "lyk to a place that hath no walles" (line 714), an image that gains significance in light of the way math was employed to assess the potential value, energy, or power of a space. One example of a specific mathematical strategic detail from a medieval military authority makes the point. Vegetius (admired by John of Salisbury and translated by Jean de Meun) reckons power by numbers: "When a general knows how many [men] a given area can hold, he cannot go wrong [since] an army of 10,000 men will cover 42 yards one way and 1,000 the other."[8] That is, a given space accommodates a specific number of soldiers so that power is quantified by the acre. But the slothful lacks the sharp edge of either the military strategist or the accountant; he tarries, thinking he will live long; he is lazy so that the result is poverty and destruction (his unattended sheep, in the Parson's potent image, "go renne to the wolf that is in the breres" [line 721]). His very heart is frozen. There is languor in the soul so that there is great sorrow that "werketh to the deeth of the soule and of the body also; for therof comth that a man is anoyed of his owene lif" (line 726).

Now comes the management plan: sloth makes a man feeble, but fortitude enforces the soul by means of great courage or magnanimity. Whereas sloth swallows the soul, courage makes folks undertake hard things by their own will, wisely and reasonably. Since the devil fights against man more "by queyntise and by sleighte than by strengthe, therfore men shal withstonden hym by wit and by resoun and by discrecioun" (line 733). Our souls, it seems, live by our wits. Then, as we would expect, come faith and hope but in practical, plainspoken, and applied terms, for the Parson uses words like *sikernesse* (security; line 735) and *magnificence* (the performance of good work and its rewards; line 736). There is *constaunce* (line 737) in courage apparent in heart, mouth, bearing, presence, and deed. And now the slothful man will have the might to perform his good intent: he will have the power to get the job done.

This reckoning, or setting out of accounts, characterizes the Parson's tale while it denies the narrative or dramatic movement of

---

[8]Quoted in Murray, *Reason and Society*, p. 129.

Chaucer's other tales and even those effects of sermons of Chaucer's day. But the language bears the potential of a rich field where, from energy of mind, fair fruit can be numbered. "Arithmetic," Murray writes, "was a skill in pure reason. In numbers, it was what the art of dialectic was in the less pure realm of words. . . . A consequence followed in psychology. If reason led to power, so also and especially must—arithmetic. . . . In a word, numerical skill could raise a man."[9] For all the limitations to the uses of mathematics in the medieval period, its rational character was proof of intellectual power—proof for Boethius, proof for John of Salisbury. John writes, "What mathematics concludes, in regard to such things as numbers, proportions, and figures is indubitably true and cannot be otherwise."[10] It is useful to recall that churchmen like Bacon and Pecham were mathematicians, that mathematician/theologians "helped government conduct its business—the business of economics, of politics, of war. Ascetic and Latin traditions might inhibit arithmetic in the church. But practice here pulled the other way."[11]

The slothful man, that place that has no walls, subverts Vegetius's military strategy where power is gauged by measuring space: there is no way to take measure, no accounting *by* this man or *for* this man. We are reminded of the opening of the Parson's ledger, where he cites St. Gregory on the condition of sinners:

> "To wrecche caytyves shal be deeth withoute deeth, and ende withouten ende, and defaute withoute failynge./ For hir deeth shal alwey lyven, and hir ende shal everemo bigynne, and hir defaute shal nat faille." (lines 214–15)

---

[9]Murray, *Reason and Society*, p. 206.

[10]John of Salisbury, *Metalogicon* 2.13.

[11]Murray, *Reason and Society*, p. 197.

There is no measure here. And the Parson goes on to cite Job, who says,

> in helle is noon ordre of rule./ And al be it so that God hath creat all thynges in right ordre, and no thyng withouten ordre, but alle thynges been ordeyned and nombred; yet, nathelees, they that been dampned been nothyng in ordre, ne holden noon ordre,/ for the erthe ne shal bere hem no fruyt. (lines 217–19)

Harry Bailly, a scrupulous accountant himself, speaks better than he knows when he asks the Parson to "[b]eth fructuous, and that in litel space" (line 71). For it is by our fruits that we give and take account. And the Parson is assured that, as reasonable folks, we would "understonde what is the fruyt of penaunce" (line 1076), where "every soule [is] replenyssed with the sighte of the parfit knowynge of God" (line 1079). This perfect knowing comes from God's reckoning in a created universe where the books balance: there is nothing in excess and nothing lacking.

> This blisful regne may men purchace by poverte espiritueel, and the glorie by lowenesse, the plentee of joye by hunger and thurst, and the reste by travaille, and the lyf by deeth and mortificacion of synne. (line 1080)

We can purchase this fruit with poverty, gain glory by humility, get our fill of joy by hunger and thirst, our rest by work, our life by death. The traditional Christian paradoxes draw the boundaries of the space where the Parson, having shown us how to keep our books, now shows us our earnings.

The Parson's Tale is a new genre designed to rationalize and quantify the complexities of human will and desire by laying out the options. It asserts the boundaries between faith and reason in order to effect a dialectic of the spirit. The essays of this collection carry out the promise offered from the beginning by characterizing the role of The Parson's Tale as closure in *The Canterbury Tales*. Striking as the tale is in its various implications of closure, it more clearly grants us a view from the edge, a site we can name either beginning or ending. The case is that The Parson's Tale teaches us a great deal about Chaucer's sense of ending in the same way that The Knight's Tale teaches us about his sense of beginning. The tales could open with the fruitful matter of the Parson's manual as reasonably as The Knight's Tale could effectively knit up the pilgrimage, for neither tale simply asserts beginning and ending as much as each solicitously puts the reader in the midst of *successioun*: what comes next? The same rich perplexity defines our own mood as we stand between end and beginning—at the millennium.

Bibliography of Scholarship
Treating The Parson's Tale

David Raybin

Aers, David. *Chaucer, Langland and the Creative Imagination*. London: Routledge & Kegan Paul, 1980. Pp. 106–16.

> Distinguishes Chaucer from the "one-dimensional and unself-conscious" Parson ("another official of the church"), contending that the Parson naively "assumes that he has direct access to a totally impersonal and timeless truth" and thus shows no awareness of "the complex mediations through which human beings come into contact with existence" (pp. 106–07). Among other things, the Parson misreads Jeremiah, evades distinctions between the Old and New Testaments, and displays an obsessive antipathy towards sexuality and marriage. Chaucer's strong interest in subjectivity makes it clear that he presents this "conventional 'objectivist' discourse" to give "readers the means to penetrate the disastrous limitations of such discourse" and encourage us "to supersede its style of thought and the attitudes to self, others and religion that it reflects" (p. 114).

Allen, Judson Boyce. "The Old Way and the Parson's Way: An Ironic Reading of the Parson's Tale." *Journal of Medieval and Renaissance Studies* 3 (1973): 255–71.

> Denies that "penitential religion is Chaucer's last word as well as the Parson's" (p. 255), arguing rather that (1) Chaucer's voice has not changed, so "that here, as elsewhere, meaning is communicated ironically," and (2) Chaucer's "aesthetic and moral attitudes are Boethian"

(p. 256). ParsT is part of "a kind of holiness group" incorporating the four closing tales (p. 269).

Ames, Ruth M. *God's Plenty: Chaucer's Christian Humanism*. Chicago: Loyola University Press, 1984.

Presents Chaucer as "an enlightened fourteenth-century gentleman who held dogma without being dogmatic, . . . a moral artist whose milieu was ironic humor, . . . a Catholic who did not find the justification of faith easy, but who believed that God so loved the world that he gave his only son for its redemption" (p. 2). ParsT is a "sermon" which "offers a convenient guide to the vices and virtues of the characters on the pilgrimage" (p. 77). It presents "the usual clerical view" (p. 105) on marriage and sex.

Ayres, Harry Morgan. "Chaucer and Seneca." *Romanic Review* 10 (1919): 1–15.

Though many of Chaucer's allusions to Seneca seem to be derived from Albertano of Brescia, a few allusions in ParsT and elsewhere suggest a greater familiarity, esp. X.144–45 and 759–62.

Baldwin, Ralph. *The Unity of the Canterbury Tales*. Anglistica, vol. 5. Copenhagen: Rosenkilde and Bagger, 1955; repr. New York: AMS Press, 1971. Pp. 83–110.

Examines the frame of *CT* to argue for an overall medieval Christian unity. *CT* as we know it represents Chaucer's intention. Chaucer's typically medieval Christianity informs *CT* from opening to closing lines. ParsPro indicates that *CT* will close in the voice of this carefully chosen speaker: "This very pilgrimage to Canterbury is to be the spiritual, that is, anagogical, figure for the pilgrimage to the heavenly Jerusalem" (p. 91), and the good Parson is the appropriate figure to show the way. ParsT "furnish[es] the ideal way of life" (p. 95), as his sermon insists that "[e]very one of the pilgrims must recognize his sins, secret and public" (p. 99). Retr offers Chaucer's own proper response.

Baumlin, Tita French. "Theology and Discourse in the *Pardoner's Tale*, the *Parson's Tale*, and the *Retraction*." *Renascence* 41/3 (1989): 127–42.

Searches for the "fruitfulness" (p. 127) in the *CT*, and especially in the sermons of Chaucer's preachers. Where the Pardoner is spiritually barren and his tale leads to chaos, the Parson "is the single pilgrim who is a living example of what he teaches" (p. 134), and his tale leads toward "true fruitfulness": the "fruyt of penaunce" and "a union of intention . . . and speech" (p. 136).

Bawcutt, Priscilla. "Dunbar's 'Tretis of the Tua Mariit Wemen and the Wedo' 185–187 and Chaucer's 'Parson's Tale'." *Notes and Queries*, n.s., 11 (1964): 332–33.

Dunbar's description of an impotent lover echoes ParsT [X.857–58].

Beer, Frances. "The Question of *Egrece*: The *Parson's Tale*, Line 118." *Notes and Queries*, n.s., 35 (1988): 298–301.

Argues on contextual grounds that "grace" in X.118 is a scribal misreading for "egrece," a presumed Middle English variant on the Anglo-Norman *egresce* (bitterness).

Benson, Larry D. "The Order of *The Canterbury Tales*." *Studies in the Age of Chaucer* 3 (1981): 77–120.

Examines closely and charts all manuscript orders to argue that "[t]he evidence for Chaucer's authorship of the Type *a* order as it appears in mss such as the Ellesmere is overwhelming" (p. 117).

Besserman, Lawrence. "*Glosynge is a Glorious Thyng*: Chaucer's Biblical Exegesis." In *Chaucer and Scriptural Tradition*. Edited by David Lyle Jeffrey. Ottawa: University of Ottawa Press, 1984. Pp. 65–73.

Among Chaucer's many attacks on *glosynge* as lying, that in X.31–36, 43–47 is the most reliable. Curiously, the Parson's argument lends credence to the Wife of Bath's similar usage.

Bestul, Thomas H. "Chaucer's Parson's Tale and the Late-Medieval Tradition of Religious Meditation." *Speculum* 64 (1989): 600–19.

> Argues for the relevance of the Parson and Harry Bailly calling the ParsT a "meditacioun" (p. 600; while acknowledging that the genre of the tale is that of a penitential handbook or treatise and not that of a sermon). Understanding of the tale is enhanced by recognizing the influence of a rich "tradition of meditative literature, in Latin and the vernacular" (p. 601). Meditations were often *compilatio* and frequently treated "the virtues and vices and self-examination as part of or prefatory to penitential discipline" (p. 603). The study of Chaucer's use of meditative literature and commonplaces in the ParsT supports "the likelihood that Chaucer himself made the compilation and that the treatment of sources is intelligent rather than merely mechanical" (p. 606), and shows the ostensibly "conservative" tale as "up-to-date in its employment of affective Passion themes from the meditative tradition" (p. 618).

Biggins, D. "*Canterbury Tales* X (I) 424: 'The Hyndre Part of a She-Ape in the Fulle of the Moone'." *Medium Aevum* 33 (1964): 200–03.

> Argues for Chaucer's originality and scientific awareness in the memorable simile characterizing the buttocks (and behavior) of those who dress immodestly.

———. "Chaucer: *CT* X (I) 42–46." *Philological Quarterly* 42/4 (1963): 558–62.

> Contends, against Skeat, that the Parson's condemnation of "rum, ram, ruf" offers a parodic literary judgment and, against Robinson, that Chaucer consciously chose "*these* particular nonsense words to represent alliteration" (p. 559).

Bloomfield, Morton W. *The Seven Deadly Sins: An Introduction to the History of a Religious Concept, with Special Reference to Medieval English Literature.* [East Lansing]: Michigan State College Press, 1952; repr. 1967.

> The ParsT discussion of sins and remedies is "badly joined" to the discussion of penance. This suggests that Chaucer intended the ParsT

combination of the different translations but at the time of his death had not yet provided the "proper links" (p. 192).

Boenig, Robert. *Chaucer and the Mystics:* The Canterbury Tales *and the Genre of Devotional Prose.* Lewisburg, Pa.: Bucknell University Press, 1995. Pp. 37–46.

The Parson, like Margery Kempe, exhibits a "Lollard-like tendency to judge others, particularly for cursing" (pp. 37–38), and a "tendency to see earthly pilgrimage in terms of an allegorical heavenly pilgrimage" (p. 38). This congruence reflects the place of ParsT "among the authoritative texts that make up the genre of Middle English devotional/ mystical literature" (p. 39). Indeed, if one might imagine "a Chaucer who wrote only devotional texts," one would grant his to be a worthy "fifth name among those of the Middle English mystics—Rolle, Hilton, Julian, Kempe, together with the anonymous *Cloud*-author" (p. 46).

Brown, Emerson, Jr. "The Poet's Last Words: Text and Meaning at the End of the *Parson's Prologue*." *Chaucer Review* 10 (1976): 236–42.

Argues against Manly's decision, followed by subsequent editors, to disregard the evidence of all known manuscripts regarding the close of ParsPro and move lines 69–70 below lines 71–74. The poetry of *CT* should end: "god sende yow his grace."

Cespedes, Frank V. "Chaucer's Pardoner and Preaching." *English Literary History* 44 (1977): 1–18.

ParsT is directly opposed to PardT in that whereas "the Pardoner is evil but eloquent, the Parson, beyond the ideal example of his charitable life, is severely limited in his ability to communicate the Christian message to a fallen world." *CT* investigates "the protean possibilities between these two positions" (p. 15).

Chapman, Coolidge O. "*The Parson's Tale*: A Mediaeval Sermon." *Modern Language Notes* 43 (1928): 229–34.

ParsT, composed in "strict accordance with the principles of mediaeval sermon writing" (p. 229), is one of the homilies to which Chaucer refers in Retr. Its discussion of the Seven Deadly Sins is justified and essential.

Clark, John W. "'This Litel Tretys' Again." *Chaucer Review* 6 (1971): 152–56.

> Argues, against Huppé and Robertson, that (1) the "litel tretys" referred to in Mel is an alternate version of the Melibee story and (2) the "litel tretys" referred to in Retr is ParsT.

Cooper, Helen. *Oxford Guides to Chaucer: The Canterbury Tales*. Oxford: Clarendon Press, 1989. Pp. 395–409.

> Discusses in a systematic way ParsPro and the date, text, genre and sources, structure and themes, context, and style of ParsT. Notes that while ParsT, like *CT*, is "encyclopaedic . . . concerned with the process of living in the world" (p. 405), its focus is both narrower ("in its condemnation of most human activity, its refusal to admit any aesthetic or literary values, its joylessness" [pp. 406–07]) and more general (as it turns away from the "individuality and social and professional distinctions" of GP to look "to the world" [p. 407]).

———. *The Structure of the Canterbury Tales*. Athens: University of Georgia Press, 1984. Pp. 200–07.

> Rejecting "the orthodox moralism that substitutes the Parson's Tale and Retractions for all the rest" as "not only inadequate but wrong" and an ironic reading as overly simple, notes that unlike Langland or Dante the Parson devotes almost all his attention to sin and largely ignores grace (pp. 202–04). Harry's final word is "grace"; the Parson's is "synne." His is a limited perspective that belies Chaucer's own observation of the myriad varieties of human behavior. In the end, ParsT "is a blind alley" (p. 207).

Correale, Robert M. "Nicholas of Clairvaux and the Quotation from 'Seint Bernard' in Chaucer's *The Parson's Tale*, 130–132." *American Notes and Queries* 20 (Sept./Oct. 1981): 2–3.

> Identifies a source for the quotation from "Saint Bernard" which Chaucer translates (from Pennaforte) in X.130–32.

————. "The Source of the Quotation from 'Crisostom' in 'The Parson's Tale'." *Notes and Queries* 225 (1980): 101–02.

Identifies a source for the quotation from "Crisostom" which Chaucer translates (from Pennaforte) in X.109–10.

————. "The Sources of Some Patristic Quotations in Chaucer's The Parson's Tale." *English Language Notes* 19 (1981): 95–98.

Identifies sources for five quotations which Chaucer translates (from Pennaforte and Peraldus) in X.85, 89, 237–40, 470, and 1047.

Corsa, Helen Storm. *Chaucer: Poet of Mirth and Morality*. Notre Dame, Ind.: University of Notre Dame Press, 1964. Pp. 234–41.

ParsT knits up *CT* in a close examination of human nature that sees diverse individuals as enabled through penance to achieve the common goal of "eternal happiness in God's infinite mercy and love" (p. 235). The Parson's message is severe but nonetheless "divinely myrie" (p. 236), pointing indirectly to the failings (and virtues) of the pilgrims not as unrealistic types but simply as "members of the human race" (p. 238).

Cowgill, Jane. "Patterns of Feminine and Masculine Persuasion in the *Melibee* and the *Parson's Tale*." In *Chaucer's Religious Tales*. Edited by C. David Benson and Elizabeth Robertson. Cambridge: D. S. Brewer, 1990. Pp. 171–83.

Mel presents a pattern of effective feminine suasive discourse characteristic of strong women in *CT*. ParsT illustrates a patriarchal discourse that is generally assigned to unsuccessful authoritarian persuaders.

Dean, James. "Chaucer's Repentance: A Likely Story." *Chaucer Review* 24 (1989): 64–76.

Describes a fourteenth-century and "especially Ricardian" (p. 67) pattern of works with a journey/pilgrimage frame, an episodes/storytelling body, and an old age/sickness and/or penitence conclusion.

———. "Dismantling the Canterbury Book." *PMLA* 100 (1985): 746–62.

Examines SNT, CYT, MancT, and ParsT "to demonstrate the thematic coherence of these tales as a closure group." Chaucer closes his book in a way designed to expose its structure and art and thus "to reintegrate himself into his community as an act of penance" (p. 746). In four steps, he presents a "fictional ideal," "questions ... the fictional steps of story and of pilgrims," "defies our sense of story," and offers "a tale that is no tale." The process concludes in Retr, where Chaucer "dismantles his fictional persona" (p. 747).

Delasanta, Rodney. "The Horsemen of the *Canterbury Tales*." *Chaucer Review* 3 (1968): 29–36.

The horses and horsemanship of the pilgrims are to be evaluated in light of the discussion of horses in X.430ff., with its reference to Christ's entry into Jerusalem. The pilgrims' clothing may be similarly evaluated in light of the discussion in X.415ff.

———. "Penance and Poetry in the *Canterbury Tales*." *PMLA* 93 (1978): 240–47.

Rejects ironical readings of ParsT and Retr, insisting that "the penitential earnestness of the ending is *dignum et justum*" (p. 240). ParsT, as Pfander noted, is "a confessional manual designed for the priest to use with the layman in performing the rubric of the sacrament" (p. 242). Those who criticize the form of ParsT miss the point that penance is inherently formulaic.

———. "The Theme of Judgment in *The Canterbury Tales*." *Modern Language Quarterly* 31(1970): 298–307.

The judgment and supper proposed by Harry Bailly parody the Last Judgment and eschatological supper offered by Christ, such that GP leads to ParsPro and the tales serve as a "necessary prelude" both "to the judgment of the Host" and "to the absolution of the Parson and to the greater Judgment beyond" (p. 302). The reference to the ascendancy of Libra in X.11 suggests the "coming of eternal Judgment" (p. 303) as a central theme in ParsPro and ParsT.

Dempster, Germaine. *"The Parson's Tale."* In *Sources and Analogues of Chaucer's Canterbury Tales*. Edited by W. F. Bryan and Germaine Dempster. Chicago: University of Chicago Press, 1941; repr. New York: Humanities Press, 1958. Pp. 723–60.

> Notes very distant relationship of ParsT to Peraldus as opposed to a closer relationship to Pennaforte. Neither work is likely to have been Chaucer's direct source. Presents analogous selections from Pennaforte, Peraldus, an Anglo-Norman *Compileison*, and Frère Laurent's *Le Livre de vices et de vertus* or *Somme le roy*.

Dickson, Arthur. *"Canterbury Tales*, I, 355ff." *Modern Language Notes* 62 (1947): 562.

> X.355–56 is drawn from Exodus 15.

Donaldson, E. Talbot. *Chaucer's Poetry: An Anthology for the Modern Reader*. New York: Ronald Press Company, 1958. Pp. 947–50.

> Sugggests that ParsT was written early in Chaucer's career, ParsPro and "heartfelt" (p. 949) Retr in Chaucer's leased house in the garden of Westminster Abbey in the final months of his life.

———. "Medieval Poetry and Medieval Sin." In *Speaking of Chaucer*. New York: W. W. Norton & Company, 1970. Pp. 164–74.

> Examines "all Chaucer's uses of the word *sin* as well as of the words for the individual members of the deadly septet," concluding that these words "occur mostly in sinless contexts" (p. 164), and mostly in ParsT. Pays special attention to the one use of *sin* in the MilT, read in the context of the discussion of marital intercourse in the ParsT and contemporary treatises. Concludes that ParsT "seems a most inappropriate gloss for many of Chaucer's best poetic writings" (p. 173).

Dunning, T. P. "Chaucer's Icarus-Complex: Some Notes on His Adventures in Theology." In *English Studies Today*. Edited by G. I. Duthie. 3rd series. Edinburgh: Edinburgh University Press, 1964. Pp. 89–106.

> Addresses the difficulty in X.920, where Chaucer assesses the sinfulness in marital sex, by examining the opinions of thirteenth- and

fourteenth-century theologians, most especially St. Thomas, Nicholas Oresme, Friar Lorens, and Peraldus. All hold that marital sex may be without sin, and that even lustful sexual behavior may in the marital context be not deadly sin but venial. Though Chaucer's fear of mis-peaking on a matter of doctrine seems to have caused him to obfuscate his language, this seems to be his position, too.

Eade, J. C. *The Forgotten Sky: A Guide to Astrology in English Literature.* Oxford: Clarendon Press, 1984. Pp. 137–41.

Explains astronomical and especially astrological systems as a basis for examining planetary references in literature from the fourteenth century to the eighteenth century. The allusions in ParsPro X.1–12 indicate that Chaucer drew his information directly from astronomical tables (presumably those of Nicholas of Lynn) and that the scene takes place on April 14–17.

Ebin, Lois. "Chaucer, Lydgate, and the 'Myrie Tale'." *Chaucer Review* 13 (1979): 316–36, esp. 325–30.

ParsPro transforms the meaning of "myrie tale" from one that promises amusement or diversion to one that is "fructuous" or edifying.

Eilers, Wilhelm. "Dissertation on *The Parson's Tale* and the *Somme de Vices et de Vertus* of Frere Lorens." *Essays on Chaucer* Part 5. Chaucer Society, 2nd series, no. 19; London 1884. Pp. 501–610.

ParsT is a composite work. Chaucer did not write the section on sins and remedies.

Eliason, Norman E. *The Language of Chaucer's Poetry: An Appraisal of the Verse, Style, and Structure.* Anglistica, vol. 17. Copenhagen: Rosenkilde and Bagger, 1972. Pp. 75–80.

Asserts that "Chaucer's good ear, manifest in all his verse, is rarely manifest in his prose," which is dull and schematic, and lacks the "rhythm of speech" (p. 75).

Elliott, Ralph W. V. "Chaucer's Clerical Voices." In *Medieval English Religious and Ethical Literature: Essays in Honour of G. H. Russell*. Edited by Gregory Kratzmann and James Simpson. Cambridge: D. S. Brewer, 1986. Pp. 146–55.

> Against the "homely diction" and "powerful emotional appeal" of the rhyme-royal tales and the ironic spiritual voice of the "mature master-pieces" in decasyllabic couplets (p. 155), the prose ParsT "stands deliberately and conspicuously by itself" (p. 147).

———. *Chaucer's English*. London: [André Deutsch], 1974. Pp. 143–53.

> That ParsT, like Mel, had a French source is indicated by certain unusual word choices and by French adjectival endings and syntactical patterns. It is "a very even work" and its "language and style are carefully controlled" (p. 146). Abundant syntactic variation and striking rhetorical figures indicate that "Chaucer was not translating mechanically" but striving for "life and artistic character" (p. 148). Overall, ParsT is easy to understand, with many characteristically light Chaucerian touches.

Emmerson, Richard K., and Ronald B. Herzman. *The Apocalyptic Imagination in Medieval Literature*. Philadelphia: University of Pennsylvania Press, 1992.

> ParsT is informed by a Dantesque "conjunction of the universal and the individual, the apocalyp[t]ic and the contemporary" (p. 152). Pilgrimage is a central image for the medieval Christian, figuring both the "life of the individual Christian journeying through the world's wilderness toward the celestial Jerusalem" and the course of Christian history (p. 156). Such is the movement in *CT* from the spring morning of GP to the approaching darkness of ParsPro. As KnT is "the poem of the Earthly City," ParsT is "the treatise of the Heavenly City," the movement signaling "that this world is to be judged from the perspective of the next" (pp. 158–60).

————. *"The Canterbury Tales* in Eschatological Perspective." In *The Use and Abuse of Eschatology in the Middle Ages.* Edited by Werner Verbeke, Daniel Verhelst, and Andries Welkenhuysen. Leuven: Leuven University Press, 1988. Pp. 404–24.

> It was a medieval "commonplace" that "a great pilgrimage poem should conclude with an explicitly eschatological perspective" (p. 411); thus one is not surprised when ParsPro adopts an apocalyptic setting and imagery to signal the imminent closing of *CT.* That pilgrimage figures the essential Christian journey, an understanding stressed also in Chaucer's short poem "Truth," is made "explicit" in "the Parson's introductory comments and sermon" (p. 416).

Finke, Laurie A. "'To Knytte Up Al this Feeste': The Parson's Rhetoric and the Ending of the *Canterbury Tales." Leeds Studies in English*, n.s., 15 (1984): 95–107.

> Argues that *CT* presents a "pluralistic world" in which ParsT "represents just one possible view of life and man's nature." The contrasting rhetorical stances of Harry Bailly (playful use of language, an enjoyment "more aesthetic than moral") and the Parson (familiar, self-congratulatory, ethical), constitute "two poles between which Chaucer can manipulate almost infinite possibilities of response" (p. 97). Close examination of the rhetoric of ParsT suggests that, paradoxically, the tale's moral force is limited by its "orthodoxy" (p. 98), which precludes its saying anything new, and by "the Parson's un-Chaucerian intolerance" (p. 102).

Finlayson, John. "The Satiric Mode and the *Parson's Tale." Chaucer Review* 6 (1971): 94–116.

> Contends that "the events and created values of the *whole* of *The Canterbury Tales* ... decide the significance of the *Parson's Tale*," and that "the *manner* of presentation" controls a reader's moral response (pp. 97–98). The pilgrimage is no more than a frame, "the excuse for the tales" (p. 103), so that in the absence of a strong narrator's voice, no "one part of, or element in, *The Canterbury Tales* can unequivocally be

taken as the center of values" (p. 100). ParsT, as the closing tale, reestablishes the implicit moral norm in the context of which Chaucer's satire operates. The "key" to *CT* "lies in the dominant comic-satiric mode of the presentation" (p. 111).

Fleming, John. "The 'Figure' of Chaucer's Good Parson and a Reprimand by Grosseteste." *Notes and Queries* 209 (1964): 167.

Grosseteste may provide a link between Gregory and the rusted gold image in the GP description of the Parson, I.498–500.

Fox, Robert C. "Chaucer and Aristotle." *Notes and Queries* 203 (1958): 523–24.

Identifies the "philosophre" who defines envy in X.484 as Aristotle, in his *Rhetoric* II.10.

———. "The Philosophre of Chaucer's Parson." *Modern Language Notes* 75 (1960): 101–02.

Identifies the philosopher who defines *ire* in X.[5]36 as Seneca, in his *De ira* II.19.3.

Friend, Albert C. "Sampson, David, and Salomon in the Parson's Tale." *Modern Philology* 46 (1948–49): 117–21.

Argues from the reference in X.955 that Chaucer's immediate source for ParsT "resembled . . . the verses of Roger of Caen" (p. 120).

Georgianna, Linda. "Love So Dearly Bought: The Terms of Redemption in *The Canterbury Tales*." *Studies in the Age of Chaucer* 12 (1990): 85–116.

Examines the use of the language of commercial exchange in articulating "the essential spiritual transaction which informs the Christian life as a whole" (p. 87), the exchange of Christ's blood for people's sins and concomitant offer of penitence to one who hopes to reap the rewards of this exchange. Such language appears throughout *CT*, beginning with GP, but is especially prevalent in ParsT, where it signals the hope of redemption that is crucial to the notion of pilgrimage.

Gillmeister, Heiner. *Chaucer's Conversion: Allegorical Thought in Medieval Literature*. Frankfurt: Verlag Peter Lang, 1984. Pp. 129–34.

> In line with the message of his poem "Truth," Chaucer matched virtues and vices drawn from a variety of sources to show "the way by which conversion could be achieved." Indeed, in applying the important medieval concept of "the cure of sins by their very contraries," ParsT "marks the beginning of Chaucer's attempt to turn the *Tales* into something like an allegory of his own life, and of his conversion," such that Chaucer's life and art "become almost inseparably linked" (p. 133).

Glowka, Arthur W. "Chaucer's Parson and the Devil's Other Hand." *Interpretations* 14/2 (1983): 15–19.

> Examines Chaucer's rearrangement in X.852–62 of the five steps used in alluring women. The reordering offers indications of the poet's attitude toward sex.

Green, Donald C. "The Semantics of Power: *Maistrie* and *Soveraynetee* in The Canterbury Tales." *Modern Philology* 84 (1986): 18–23.

> Reads X.772–73 as confirming Chaucer's view "that sovereignty is inherent in certain roles," reflecting "the divine order" (p. 21), while in X.924–26 *maistrie* is confirmed as "individually defined" (p. 23).

Grennan, Eamon. "Dual Characterization: A Note on Chaucer's Use of 'But' in the Portrait of the Parson." *Chaucer Review* 16 (1982): 195–200.

> Sees the repeated use of *but* in the portrait of the Parson as defining the principled, morally discriminating character both of the Parson and of the Narrator himself.

Guinagh, Kevin. "Source of the Quotation from Augustine in *The Parson's Tale*, 985." *Modern Language Notes* 55 (1940): 211–12.

> Passage is drawn from *Liber de vera et falsa poenitentia* X.25.

Hammond, Eleanor P. *Chaucer: A Bibliographical Manual*. New York: MacMillan, 1908; repr. Peter Smith, 1933. Pp. 318–20.

> Provides helpful bibliographical material for late-nineteenth-century studies.

Hartung, Albert E. "'The Parson's Tale' and Chaucer's Penance." In *Literature and Religion in the Later Middle Ages: Philological Studies in Honor of Siegfried Wenzel.* Edited by Richard G. Newhauser and John A. Alford. Binghamton, N.Y.: Medieval & Renaissance Texts & Studies, 1995. Pp. 61–80.

> Chaucer's varied styles in ParsT pose a "problem in critical analysis" that is "considerably lessened if one considers the work as a separate, personal penitential statement" (p. 70) attached only later (perhaps by Chaucer himself) to *CT*. His "disturbed response to sexuality and women" (p. 70) in ParsT is especially curious in that Chaucer's revisions of source material consistently associate the sexual with the excremental.

Harwood, Britton J. "Language and the Real: Chaucer's Manciple." *Chaucer Review* 6 (1972): 268–79, esp. 276–79.

> The Manciple and the Parson are similar in their self-presentation but opposite in their sincerity and accuracy. Thus the Manciple's emphasis on the relation of "word" and "dede" serves to prepare the pilgrims "for the Word become flesh" (p. 279) of ParsT.

Hazelton, Richard. "Chaucer and Cato." *Speculum* 35 (1960): 357–80.

> Chaucer knew of Cato from his earliest schoolboy training in Latin and ethics. Where Langland, Gower, and other fourteenth-century writers treat Cato with "sober respect," Chaucer's extensive use of Cato is "openly irreverent and at times even mocking," suggesting a parodic intent reminiscent of twelfth-century French and Latin poets (pp. 370–71).

———. "Chaucer's Parson's Tale and the 'Moralium Dogma Philosophorum'." *Traditio* 16 (1960): 255–74.

> Argues that in composing the remedies against the Seven Deadly Sins, Chaucer was indebted to the *Moralium dogma philosophorum*, an influential and much-translated twelfth-century adaptation of Cicero's *De officiis*, relying "on both a Latin text and a French translation of that text" (p. 255). Disputes the derivation of ParsT from Peraldus.

Hill, John M. *Chaucerian Belief: The Poetics of Reverence and Delight.* New Haven: Yale University Press, 1991.

> ParsT is not the "meditacioun" promised in ParsPro but a "predicacioun" of the kind rejected by the Host in Epi to MLT (p. 49). Where ParsPro speaks of the path to the celestial Jerusalem, ParsT shows not "the Way" but "right correction." The resultant implication is that ParsT "is not properly part of the tales of Canterbury" (p. 50).

Homans, George C. "Free Bull." *Review of English Studies* 14 (1938): 447–49.

> The comparison of an incontinent priest to a "free bole" in X.897–99 recalls a privilege possessed by medieval lords of the manor.

Howard, Donald R. *The Idea of the Canterbury Tales.* Berkeley: University of California Press, 1976. Pp. 376–87.

> ParsT is above all *"practical"*: as a treatise it is "mercifully short," "easy to follow," "clear and forthright," and "filled with specific details and examples," and it "embodies the natural rhythms of speech" (p. 377). Its power is that "it is so different from everything else that . . . it tells us something about the whole book that has gone before" (p. 380). *CT* feels "unfinished" because Chaucer "created a literary form and structure, a literary idea, whose possibilities were inexhaustable" (p. 385). In so doing he gave English literature "its ability to put the reader in touch with a reality he could not know in any other way" (p. 386).

Hudson, Anne. *The Premature Reformation: Wycliffite Texts and Lollard History.* Oxford: Clarendon Press, 1988. Pp. 390–94.

> Though the orthodox ParsT confirms that the Host is mistaken in calling the Parson a Lollard, Chaucer's general treatment of the Parson suggests an awareness of characteristic Wycliffite language and perhaps a measure of sympathy for Wycliffite concerns.

Huppé, Bernard F. *A Reading of the* Canterbury Tales. Albany: State University of New York, 1964. Pp. 231–41.

In Retr, as in Mel, "this litel tretys" refers to *CT*, the "sentence" of which accords completely with the doctrine of both prose tales (pp. 235–36). ParsT is "the end 'for oure doctrine' toward which all the tales have been moving" (p. 239).

Ives, Doris V. "'A Man of Religion'." *Modern Language Review* 27 (1932): 144–48.

Speculates that Wyclif was the model for the Parson's portrait.

Johnson, Dudley R. "'Homicide' in the *Parson's Tale*." *PMLA* 57 (1942): 51–56.

Argues that Chaucer's source for the discussion of homicide in X.564–79 is Raymund of Pennaforte, "Summa Casuum Conscientiae," Liber II, Titulus I, "De Homicidio."

Jordan, Robert M. *Chaucer and the Shape of Creation: The Aesthetic Possibilities of Inorganic Structure.* Cambridge, Mass.: Harvard University Press, 1967. Pp. 227–41.

Argues for the "supremely important role" of ParsT "within the total strategy of the *Canterbury Tales*"; it "is the pinnacle, reaching heavenward, upon which the diverse earthly tales converge" (pp. 227–28). Modern readers are blinded to this by a shift in the understanding of the role of *art* as a servant of *Truth*. Close examination of the gothic structure of ParsT exposes the tale's typicality in that "[i]n Chaucer's inorganic aesthetic, exhaustiveness of treatment and clarity of display are primary standards" (p. 237).

———. *Chaucer's Poetics and the Modern Reader.* Berkeley: University of California Press, 1987. Pp. 162–70.

While accepting that "Chaucer's destination" in ParsT "is the celestial Jerusalem, the truth that is not made by art or artifice but simply *is*" (p. 163), argues against Baldwin that the unity of *CT* is "an interpretive construct" and "not a demonstrable feature of the text" (pp. 164–65).

Chaucer's work illustrates both "the will for coherence and striving for design" and "the resistance of its matter" (p. 167).

Joseph, Gerhard. "The Gifts of Nature, Fortune, and Grace in the *Physician's, Pardoner's*, and *Parson's Tales.*" *Chaucer Review* 9 (1975): 237–45.

The gifts in PhyT and PardT may be better understood in light of the discussion of "goodes" in X.450–55.

Josipovici, G. D. "Fiction and Game in *The Canterbury Tales.*" *Critical Quarterly* 7 (1965): 185–97.

Chaucer's insistence on the reportorial status of his narrator serves to emphasize the fictional quality of the narrative, hence its inherent irony. ParsT is "to be listened to as morality by the pilgrims, but read as fiction by the reader" (p. 192).

Jost, Jean E. "The Parson's Tale: Ending 'Thilke Parfit Glorious Pilgrymage that Highte Jerusalem Celestial." *Proceedings of the Medieval Association of the Midwest* 3 (1995): 94–109.

ParsT and the rest of *CT* form a "problem-solution relationship" wherein ParsT critiques the "multivalent vowing and foreswearing" characteristic of the tales as its distinctive discourse offers "the means for exonerating betrayal in actual life through penance" (p. 94).

Kaske, Carol V. "Getting Around the Parson's Tale: An Alternative to Allegory and Irony." In *Chaucer at Albany*. Edited by Rossell Hope Robbins. New York: Burt Franklin, 1975. Pp. 147–77.

Seeking to bridge the chasm between Robertson and his opponents regarding the centrality of ParsT, attempts to find in medieval literature a "mode" of expression which "tells literal truth so far as it goes, but which deliberately gives only the first round of a debate" (p. 149). Chaucer, like Dante, distinguishes between the Beatrice-Parson figure, whose knowledge is based on Christian truth, and the Virgil-Knight/Franklin figure, whose knowledge is based solely on reason and experience.

Kellogg, Alfred L. "Seith Moyses by the Devel: A Problem in the 'Parson's Tale'." *Revue Belge de Philologie et d'Histoire* 31 (1953): 61–64; repr. in *Chaucer, Langland, Arthur: Essays in Middle English Literature*. New Brunswick, N.J.: Rutgers University Press, 1972. Pp. 339–42.

Suggests a distant biblical source for X.355–56.

―――. "St. Augustine and the 'Parson's Tale'." *Traditio* 8 (1952): 424–30; repr. in *Chaucer, Langland, Arthur: Essays in Middle English Literature*. New Brunswick, N.J.: Rutgers University Press, 1972. Pp. 343–52.

Disputes Petersen's conclusion that the ultimate sources of ParsT are Pennaforte and Peraldus; suggests also an "immense indebtedness" (p. 345) to Augustine.

Knapp, Peggy. *Chaucer and the Social Contest*. New York: Routledge, 1990. Pp. 90–94.

Sees the Parson as Wycliffite and ParsT as sharing "some notable congruences with Lollard discourse" (p. 92). The question of the moral authority of ParsT is problematic.

Knight, Stephen. "Chaucer's Religious Canterbury Tales." In *Medieval English Religious and Ethical Literature: Essays in Honour of G. H. Russell*. Edited by Gregory Kratzmann and James Simpson. Cambridge: D. S. Brewer, 1986. Pp. 156–66.

As Canterbury Cathedral's western front "suddenly comes into view" and "the Caen stone catches the late afternoon spring sunshine," ParsT "fulfils the religious impulse" of *CT* as it "rejects all poetry" and "develops wisdom beyond secular limits" (p. 165).

―――. *Geoffrey Chaucer*. Oxford: Basil Blackwell, 1986. Pp. 153–57.

Imagines ParsT recited in view of Canterbury Cathedral. Chaucer's placement of the Christian position in this closing space is the natural response of one "who could see the poverty of the feudal and aristocratic viewpoint, could trace the new world of mercantile and individual values being formed," but could not conceptualize "the whole structure of bourgeois individualism and its complex cultural ideology" (p. 154).

Koch, J[ohn]. "Über die neuesten veröffentlichungen der 'Chaucer Society'." *Anglia* 2 (1879): 532–45, esp. 540–44.

> Counters Simon's conclusion that Chaucer did not write ParsT.

Koeppel, Emil. "Über das Verhältniss von Chaucers Prosawerken zu seinen Dichtungen und die Echtheit der 'Parson's Tale'." *Archiv für das Studium der neueren Sprachen und Literaturen* 87 (1891): 33–54.

> Affirms Chaucer's authorship of ParsT, dating the tale to the poet's final years.

Koff, Leonard Michael. *Chaucer and the Art of Storytelling*. Berkeley: University of California Press, 1988. Pp. 222–36.

> Distinguishes modern reader-based (author-evaluative) and medieval author-based (reader-evaluative) interpretation, arguing against "authoritarian" (p. 226) readings of *CT* and especially its conclusion. Chaucer expects his readers not "to decide the morality or immorality of the Parson's Tale" but "to read it in the light of their personal preferences" (p. 227). Chaucer's withdrawal at the close of *CT* shows faith and modesty, even as it opens up a space for readers to make our own decisions about the nature of truth. Thus "Chaucer's 'leave-taking'" offers "closure that encourages us to begin again, Chaucerian closure that renews" (p. 236).

Landrum, Grace W. "Chaucer's Use of the Vulgate." *PMLA* 39 (1924): 75–100.

> Chaucer's "independent borrowings" in *CT* from 48 of the 74 books of the Vulgate show "275 cases of direct dependence upon the Vulgate" (pp. 98–99), thus indicating that he knew the Vulgate well.

Langhans, Victor. "Die Datierung der Prosastücke Chaucers." *Anglia* 53 (1929): 235–68, esp. 243–68.

> ParsT was an early work, perhaps written as early as 1358.

Laskaya, Anne. *Chaucer's Approach to Gender in the* Canterbury Tales.
Cambridge: D. S. Brewer, 1995. Pp. 127–140.

> Unlike the other males in *CT*, whose approach even to spirituality is
> competitive, the Parson rejects conflict, pointing out the extent to which
> sin promotes "disruptive competition" (p. 132). Paradoxically, though,
> insofar as ParsT's call to non-competitive introspection is heeded,
> readers will approach the other tales from its perspective; thus ParsT
> "'wins' the game" (p. 134). The conservativism of ParsT is highlighted
> in its treatment of gender. Where patriarchic gender discourse is
> challenged elsewhere in *CT*, ParsT "discusses divinity in almost ex-
> clusively masculine terms" (p. 135), positing traditional (misogynist)
> gender-based hierarchies and assumptions as inscribed by the Fall and
> thus essential.

Lawler, Traugott. "Chaucer." In *Middle English Prose: A Critical Guide to
Major Authors and Genres.* Edited by A. S. G. Edwards. New Brunswick,
N.J.: Rutgers University Press, 1984. Pp. 291–313.

> Comprehensive survey of scholarship treating Chaucer's prose. The
> history of ParsT criticism is discussed on pp. 296–99.

———. *The One and the Many in the Canterbury Tales.* Hamden, Conn.:
Archon Books, 1980. Pp. 147–72.

> ParsT balances KnT as it privileges the one over the many, "knit[ting]
> up the feast with fine decorum" (p. 147). Particular focus is placed on
> the tale's valuing of community, order, and patient sufferance.

Lawton, David. "Chaucer's Two Ways: The Pilgrimage Frame of *The Canterbury Tales.*" *Studies in the Age of Chaucer* 9 (1987): 3–40.

> Conflicting reactions to ParsT are "conditioned by" four types of "ha-
> bitual and shared responses" to *CT* (p. 3): "absolute," which assumes
> that ParsT "offers a set of absolute standards that should be accepted as
> absolutely serious" (p. 4); "ironic," which expresses a "dislike" for
> ParsT morality and a "reluctance to see it as Chaucer's" (p. 5);
> "dualistic," which finds "heremeneutic unity" by acknowledging the
> fundamental paradox that what underlies *CT* is not an absolute or its

negation, but a "displaced absolute" that marks Chaucer's voice (p. 7); "textual," which challenges the "prominence" of ParsT and Retr as an accident of textual transmission (p. 9). Opts for a combination of the "dualistic" and "textual" insofar as the "textual position" of ParsT "shows that it is conceived—either by Chaucer himself or . . . by [h]is [fifteenth-century] editors"—as a "suitable ending to the Canterbury pilgrimage" (p. 12). Juxtaposing ParsT and GP supports this reading.

Leyerle, John. "Thematic Interlace in 'The Canterbury Tales'." *Essays and Studies* 29 (1976): 107–21.

> *CT* possesses "interior coherence," a function of "several thematic threads woven together to form the string that connects the tales together" (p. 108). ParsT "contributes to the total design by tying up the threads," not necessarily "resolv[ing] the issues" (p. 109).

Liddell, Mark H. "A New Source of *The Parson's Tale.*" In *An English Miscellany Presented to Dr. Furnivall in Honour of His Seventy-Fifth Birthday.* Oxford: Clarendon Press, 1901; reissued 1969. Pp. 255–77.

> ParsT is unfinished material that Chaucer "proposed to make use of for a sermon to be put into the Parson's mouth" (p. 257). The hitherto unedited *The Clensying of Mannes Sowle* offers "an interesting analogue of Chaucer's tract" (p. 258).

Lowes, John Livingston. "Chaucer and the Seven Deadly Sins." *PMLA* 30 (1915): 237–371.

> Counters Tupper's hypothesis that ParsT offers "the crowning argument for Chaucer's deliberate use of the Sins *motif*" throughout *CT* (pp. 240–41). Tales do not exemplify sins. ParsT does not present rigid categories. Chaucer's use of sins and exempla is subject to his "unsurpassed and unsurpassable *irony*" (p. 369) and glorious art.

Luengo, Anthony E. "Synthesis and Orthodoxy in Chaucer's Parson's Tale." *University of Ottawa Quarterly* 50 (1980): 223–32.

> The Parson's "lucid and logical methodology employed in handling *sententiae*" (p. 232) contrasts sharply with the sloppy presentations of the Pardoner and Wife of Bath to which he responds. The method

governing the Parson's careful systematization is particularly elucidated by comparison to the English Dominican Thomas Walleys' fourteenth-century sermon manual, *De modo componendi sermones*.

Madeleva, Sister Mary. *A Lost Language and Other Essays on Chaucer*. Boston: Sheed & Ward, 1951; repr. New York: Russell & Russell, 1967. Pp. 61–79.

ParsT displays the spiritual philosophy and ethics central to Chaucer's prose translations. It indicates an intense interest in penance typical of fourteenth-century England but lost to most readers today. Carefully ordered and plainly written, ParsT is both profound and "deliciously funny" (p. 77), filled with the sharp-minded wit of one who has composed his final treatise "in the spirit of love" (p. 75).

Makarewicz, Sister Mary Raynelda. *The Patristic Influence on Chaucer*. Washington, D.C.: Catholic University of America Press, 1953. Pp. 147–84.

Argues for Chaucer's dependence on the Church Fathers, juxtaposing passages from ParsT treating the causes of sin, the Seven Deadly Sins, and the remedies against sin with related passages drawn from the writings of Alcuin, Ambrose, Aquinas, Bonaventure, Gregory the Great, Hugh of St.-Victor, Jerome, Peter the Lombard, and, most especially, Augustine.

Manly, John Matthews. "Tales of the Homeward Journey." *Studies in Philology* 28 (1931): 613–17.

The "thropes ende" in X.12 refers to a village near London. Spatial and temporal allusions in Fragments VIII, IX, and X indicate that MancT was to be the first tale of the homeward journey, ParsT the last.

Mann, Jill. *Geoffrey Chaucer*. Atlantic Highlands, N.J.: Humanities Press International, 1991.

If there is a "non-fictional 'core'" to the *CT* it is not ParsT but Mel. Whereas ParsT is another tale told by a pilgrim, Mel "is given special authority by being told by Chaucer himself" (p. 121).

Mariella, Sister. "The Head, the Foot, and the Rib of Adam." *Notes and Queries* 171 (1936): 119.

> Notes historical usage of the head, foot, and rib of Adam analogy.

———. "The Parson's Tale and the Marriage Group." *Modern Language Notes* 53 (1938): 251–56.

> The Parson's analogy that God made Eve from neither Adam's head nor foot but from his rib is not in Peraldus but has been in general spiritual use from the late twelfth century to the present day. Chaucer's added speculation as to what would result if head or foot were tried out suggests that the passage should be considered in direct relation to the marriage group.

Maxfield, Ezra Kempton. "Chaucer and Religious Reform." *PMLA* 39 (1924): 64–74.

> Though Wyclif was generally orthodox, opposing not institutions but corrupt individuals, his doctrines included "a denial of transubstantiation, a protest against tithing, and a disbelief in excommunication" (p. 68). Chaucer's Parson is similarly orthodox, but he shows no particular signs of Lollardry in either his portrait or his sermon.

McDonald, William C. "The Nobility of Soul: Uncharted Echoes of the Peraldean Tradition in Late Medieval German Literature." *Deutsche Vierteljahrsschrift für Literaturwissenschaft und Geistesgeschichte* 60 (1986): 543–71.

> Examining the "pervasive influence of Peraldus" (p. 549), "traces the concept of the 'nobility of the soul' in the late Middle Ages, with special reference to Geoffrey Chaucer, Heinrich von Langenstein and Michel Beheim" (p. 543).

McGerr, Rosemarie Potz. "Retraction and Memory: Retrospective Structure in the *Canterbury Tales*." *Comparative Literature* 37 (1985): 97–113.

> Retr follows Augustine in stressing the reader's "responsibility for judging the value of the material," implicitly asking the reader "to review his experience of the *Canterbury Tales* from the vantage point

of the end . . . of the work" (p. 102). This stress on subjectivity causes us to question even the self-asserted finality of ParsT as we "wonder whether truly objective narration is possible at all" (p. 108).

Mehl, Dieter. "Chaucer's Narrator: *Troilus and Criseyde* and the *Canterbury Tales*. In *The Cambridge Chaucer Companion*. Edited by Piero Boitani and Jill Mann. Cambridge: Cambridge University Press, 1986. Pp. 213–26.

Retr is designed so as to demand a reader's response; Chaucer offers not "a wholesale repudiation of his poetry or an attempt to cancel what he had written, but a final appeal to the reader to make the proper use of the author's labours and to reflect on the powerful vitality of literature for good or evil" (p. 222). ParsT is similarly not a "definitive and authoritative answer . . . but an offer we may accept or reject" (p. 224).

Minnis, A. J. *Medieval Theory of Authorship: Scholastic Literary Attitudes in the Later Middle Ages*. 2nd ed. Philadephia: University of Pennsylvania Press, 1988. Pp. 207–10.

The "litel tretys" mentioned in Retr is ParsT (p. 207); indeed, Retr seems "to be linked to the Parson's Tale but not to the *Canterbury Tales* as a whole." Chaucer (or possibly someone else) apparently added these to *CT* "in keeping with the usual practice of *compilatio*" (p. 208).

Mogan, Joseph J., Jr. "Chaucer and the *Bona Matrimonii*." *Chaucer Review* 4 (1970): 123–41.

Chaucer was intensely interested in the theology governing marital sexual relations, a central issue in the Marriage Group. A partial summary of the theological material is offered in ParsT.

Mroczkowski, Przemyslaw. "Faith and the Critical Spirit in Chaucer and His Time." In *Religion in the Poetry and Drama of the Late Middle Ages in England*. Edited by Piero Boitani and Anna Torti. J. A. W. Bennett Memorial Lectures, Perugia 1988. Cambridge: D. S. Brewer, 1990. Pp. 83–100.

ParsT "presupposes in the reader a certain number of dogmatic [doctrinal] assumptions as unchanged near the end of the fourteenth century as they had been in the thirteenth" (p. 89). To grant these assumptions is to see the Parson as winning the game.

Muscatine, Charles. "Chaucer's Religion and the Chaucer Religion." In *Chaucer Traditions: Studies in Honour of Derek Brewer*. Edited by Ruth Morse and Barry Windeatt. Cambridge: Cambridge University Press, 1990. Pp. 249–62.

> Questions why the "almost puritanical Chaucer" (p. 250) who emerged in the mid-twentieth century has survived even though he is inimical to the late twentieth-century sensibility. Sees Baldwin, with his focus on ParsT, as offering the "ur-text" (p. 251) reflected in Howard, David, Kolve, Patterson, etc. This is curious, given that ParsT is "not poetry," has long been an object of "derision," is doubtful in its textual authenticity (pp. 255–56), and is in any case an "endless, narrow, small-minded, inveterately enumerative, circumstantially punitive list of sinful acts" (p. 258).

Myers, D. E. "Justesse rationnelle: le 'Myrie Tale in Prose' de Chaucer." *Moyen Âge* 78 (1972): 267–86.

> Viewed as a sermon, ParsT is well-constructed, aesthetically satisfying, and perfectly suited to the character of its narrator.

North, J. D. "Kalenderes Enlumyned Ben They, Part III." *Review of English Studies*, n. s., 20 (1969): 418–44, esp. 422–26.

> The calendar of Nicholas of Lynn (which one may be "virtually certain" [p. 423] Chaucer consulted) indicates that Intro to MLT is set on 18 April and ParsPro is set on 14 or 15 April. Both texts were written after 1387.

Norton-Smith, John. *Geoffrey Chaucer*. London: Routledge and Kegan Paul, 1974. Pp. 101–03, pp. 154–59.

> The "'end-of-day' *topos*" in ParsPro reflects Chaucer's intention to construct *CT* "in two major divisions, each ending with a prose tale" (pp. 101–02). ParsT itself offers "a closely interconnected, logical and analytic account of man's nature" unlike anything else in *CT*. Chaucer's goal seems to be to encourage a "certain kind of remembering in order to forget properly in obedience to man's reason and our proper spiritual nature" (p. 157).

Olmert, Michael. "The Parson's Ludic Formula for Winning on the Road (to Canterbury)." *Chaucer Review* 20 (1985): 158–68.

> ParsT knits up the feast in ludic terms as well as physical and spiritual. Pilgrimage is inherently ludic; ParsT "is steeped in play and presents the rules for playing the game of life" (p. 159). The three parts of ParsT respectively offer accounts of the pains of hell; the Garden of Eden, locus for proper and improper human behavior; and the endless joy of heaven.

Olson, Paul A. *The* Canterbury Tales *and the Good Society*. Princeton: Princeton University Press, 1986. Pp. 276–93.

> ParsT is neither "an 'anti-tale' which implicitly rejects tale-telling," nor "a tale fundamentally different in *kind* from the other tales" (p. 276). Rather, ParsT offers a spiritual ideal against which the other tales (and pilgrims) are to be measured much as ClT "interprets the pilgrimage's false learning" and KnT "places all of the narration's temporal rulers in perspective" (p. 278). Following Paul, Parson "does not despise fables but fables-and-wretchedness" (p. 279). He argues for a "Christian commonwealth" that will reverse the inversion of order introduced by sin and aid in "restoring God's law and man's nature" (p. 282). Thus Chaucer balances his analysis of sin in relation to both temporal and spiritual power, paying special attention to the sins of spiritual and secular lords of the status of those who would know the tales and those who would later possess *CT* manuscripts. The model is that "a good this-worldly society moves toward the condition of the Parson's good other-worldly one" (p. 292).

Owen, Charles A., Jr. *The Manuscripts of the Canterbury Tales*. Cambridge: D. S. Brewer, 1991.

> ParsT was not composed as part of *CT*. Hengwrt represents "the first attempt to bring all the tales into one manuscript" (p. 123). The scribe worked from a variety of copytexts, including individual tales and small groups, with no clear ordering. Recognizing the role of the "Hengwrt-Ellesmere supervisor" in organizing the tales so as to give "the impression of completeness or near-completeness" allows us to read *CT* as

Chaucer wrote it, perhaps even offering us "the courage to reject . . . that final piece of prose which the author himself calls 'this litel tretys' from any of the plans Chaucer made for his unfinished masterpiece" (p. 125).

————. *Pilgrimage and Storytelling in the Canterbury Tales: The Dialectic of "Ernest" and "Game."* Norman, Okla.: University of Oklahoma Press, 1977. Pp. 25–33, 210.

An early plan for *CT* involved opening with MLT and closing with ParsPro and a tale assigned to the Parson. In this spirit, Chaucer wrote the dialogue between the Host and Parson that enlivens Epi to MLT and ParsPro. Fragment I, apparently written subsequently, reflects "late changes in Chaucer's plan" (p. 33).

————. "Relationship between the *Physician's Tale* and the *Parson's Tale*." *Modern Language Notes* 71 (1956): 84–87.

The passage on sloth in ParsT (X.[720–]22) indicates an indebtedness to a lengthy digression in PhyT (closing III.102), an indebtedness shared by X.678 and X.484. Chaucer wrote PhyT ca. 1388 and ParsT in early 1390s, sometime before PardPro&T and MerT.

————. "What the Manuscripts Tell Us about the Parson's Tale." *Medium Aevum* 63 (1994): 239–49.

While most *CT* manuscripts include ParsT (always as the closing tale), close examination of some of the manuscripts suggests an "uneasiness" with the tale and "the possibility that Chaucer intended it as an independent work, the *Treatise on Penitence*, with the Retraction as a fitting conclusion" (p. 239).

Patterson, Lee W. *Chaucer and the Subject of History*. Madison: University of Wisconsin Press, 1991.

WBPro&T's displacement of ParsT early in *CT* is necessary; when ParsT finally is told, its rejection of the form and content of *CT* will preempt "all discourse that is not conducted in the authorized language of penance" (p. 316).

————. "The 'Parson's Tale' and the Quitting of the 'Canterbury Tales'."
Traditio 34 (1978): 331–80.

> Treats the tale in light of other works in its genre and in relation to its
> sources to demonstrate its ambition and achievement. ParsT is a
> "manual for penitents" (p. 338), of a type most similar to *The Clensyng
> of Mannes Sowle*, *The Weye to Paradys*, and *The Boke of Penance*. Each
> has a three-part structure, discussing contrition, confession and the
> Seven Deadly Sins, and satisfaction. Nonetheless, ParsT is distinctive
> in its tight intellectual and theoretical focus: "in both his choice of
> sources and in his revisions Chaucer has elected to use just those
> elements from the paradigms of religious writing that will enforce a
> sense of theoretical cohesion" (p. 340). Sin is presented "as the central
> fact of the human situation," with a carefully patterned presentation of
> the many types of sin (a methodology peculiar to Chaucer) playing
> against "an apparently limitless enumeration of specific sinful acts"
> (p. 342). In this orderly and logical presentation exempla and other
> "vivifying images and comparisons" (p. 345) are pointedly omitted from
> the discussions of "individual instances of sin," focusing attention on
> "the larger structure from which these instances must derive their
> significance" (p. 346). The second section of the essay examines thirty-
> five passages in ParsT "that echo passages in the preceding tales"
> (p. 357), arguing that while most are insignificant, the four more sub-
> stantial allusions suggest a late date for the tale ("there seems no reason
> not to accept the obvious biographical implication that it was his last
> work" [p. 380]) without implying that the tale is to be read "retro-
> spectively" (p. 369). In ParsT, as in *Troilus*, "Chaucer forces us to look
> beyond the specific world that has so far occupied our attention . . . to
> a higher, more inclusive perspective" (p. 370).

Pearsall, Derek. *The Canterbury Tales*. London: George Allen & Unwin,
1985. Pp. 288–93.

> ParsT is "a treatise on penitence" (and not a sermon) which "expresses
> a deep and orthodox piety." It "is not a tale at all . . . for it contains no

narrative" and "is not, itself, 'literature'" (p. 289). As regards related passages in other parts of *CT*, "the significant direction of change is all *from*" ParsT to the given tale (p. 291). In denying "the validity of fiction" ParsT closes with the "deliberate denial of art" that is Retr (p. 292).

———. "Chaucer's Religious Tales: A Question of Genre." In *Chaucer's Religious Tales*. Edited by C. David Benson and Elizabeth Robertson. Cambridge: D. S. Brewer, 1990. Pp. 11–19.

Not a tale, ParsT is rather "a lengthy statement, in merciless prose, of the system of conduct that may win salvation" (p. 13).

Peck, Russell A. "Biblical Interpretation: St. Paul and *The Canterbury Tales*." In *Chaucer and Scriptural Tradition*. Edited by David Lyle Jeffrey. Ottawa: University of Ottawa Press, 1984. Pp. 143–70, esp. pp. 143–44, pp. 150–52.

The contrasting citations of Paul in NPT and ParsT suggest alternate attitudes toward fiction, each appropriate to its position in the *CT* narrative.

———. "Number Symbolism in the Prologue to Chaucer's *Parson's Tale*." *English Studies* 48 (1967): 205–15.

Uses medieval number symbolism to explain X.1–12. *Twenty-nine*, standing between the perfect numbers *thirty* and *twenty-eight*, represents spiritual deficiency; *four*, a number associated with Fortune, suggests potential perfection; *six*, "the number of the soul," and *eleven*, a sign of transgression between the perfection of *ten* and *twelve*, "relate . . . to the measuring of the pilgrim Chaucer himself" (pp. 212–13), which will be completed in Retr.

———. "St. Paul and the Canterbury Tales." *Mediaevalia* 7 (1981): 91–131.

Considers the many and various references to Paul (the model for a Christian pilgrim) and Pauline doctrine as they (1) emphasize every pilgrim's need to exercise "critical judgment"; (2) define the pilgrimage journey "as a spiritual rather than a social" one; (3) develop important themes such as "the proper use of time and the making of a good ending"; (4) explore "the dilemma of old men"; and (5) determine "complex attitudes toward the human body as a vehicle in life's journey" (p. 92).

Petersen, Kate Oelzner. *The Sources of The Parson's Tale*. Radcliffe College Monographs No. 12. Boston: Ginn and Company, 1901. Reprint, New York: [?], 1973.

> Basic early source study argues that the ultimate sources of ParsT are Raymund of Pennaforte's *Summa casuum poenitentiae*, "affording not only the general structure of the *P.T.*, but also a considerable part of its phraseology," and Guilielmus Peraldus's *Summa seu tractatus de viciis*, adapted for "the digression on the Seven Deadly Sins" (p. 2). Extended annotated comparisons of ParsT to these two texts lead to the conclusions that "both tracts must have suffered many changes . . . before they came into Chaucer's hands" and that Chaucer's direct source was probably "a single treatise" (p. 80).

Pfander, Homer G. "Some Medieval Manuals of Religious Instruction in England and Observations on Chaucer's Parson's Tale." *Journal of English and Germanic Philology* 35 (1936): 243–58.

> Lists and classifies manuals of religious instruction written in England from the thirteenth century through the fifteenth century in Latin, French, and English prose and verse. ParsT is such a manual (of the confessional type), most likely translated from an unknown French original. Its particular correspondences with Peraldus and Pennaforte are minor.

Portnoy, Phyllis. "Beyond the Gothic Cathedral: Post-Modern Reflections on the *Canterbury Tales*." *Chaucer Review* 28 (1994): 279–92.

> Structural gaps in *CT* result from metonymy as well as metaphor. As only "the metaphoric configuration . . . provides any sense of unity, totality, and closure," metaphor informs the suggestion in the narrative frame of a kind of "perfect hierarchic order" (p. 281). Displacement, however, and thus metonymy, enters *CT* from the opening of GP, and remains as various "interrelated sub-themes of domestic power,

dominance, and subjection . . . gather and disperse" at key moments, "centers of varied and contradictory interpretations" (p. 287). Some readers see ParsT and Retr as restoring order, but the wide range in readers' responses confirms the ultimate textual gap.

Regan, Charles Lionel. "Chaucer's 'Parson's Tale' 1025: A Probable Source." *Notes & Queries* 209 (1964): 210.

Identifies as likely source a Pseudo-Augustinian treatise, *De vera et falsa poenitentia, liber unus.*

Robertson, D. W., Jr. *A Preface to Chaucer: Studies in Medieval Perspectives.* Princeton: Princeton University Press, 1962. Pp. 335–36.

Characterizes ParsT as "an excellent specimen of the series of penitential manuals which developed as a result of the decree concerning penance issued by the Fourth Lateran Council" (p. 335). The Parson offers his sermon "as a preacher or expositor and not as a poet" (p. 336).

Rogers, William E. *Upon The Ways: The Structure of* The Canterbury Tales. Victoria, B.C.: English Literary Studies, 1986. Pp. 120–21.

Balancing the secular KnT, ParsT is the "spiritual pole" of the pilgrimage, presenting sin as the "all-encompassing category for the understanding of human experience." Following on CYT and MancT, ParsT offers "*the* orthodox answer . . . to the deep questionings of the validity of language" in those tales, "redeem[ing] language" as the product of God's Word that enables us to understand sin (pp. 120–21).

Root, Robert K. "The Manciple's Prologue." *Modern Language Notes* 44 (1929): 493–96.

"Bobbe-up-and-doun" refers to Harbledown, a town about one mile west of Canterbury. This identification supports Manly's view that MancT was meant to begin the return journey and ParsT to close it.

Rowland, Beryl. "Chaucer's She-Ape (*The Parson's Tale*, 424)." *Chaucer Review* 2 (1968): 159–65.

> The simile "may derive from zoological fact." It is of interest both for its use of color and for the implication of unrestrained sexuality in its "moral and psychological assessments" (p. 159).

———. "Sermon and Penitential in *The Parson's Tale* and Their Effect on Style." *Florilegium* 9 (1987): 125–45.

> Style in ParsT is marked by a "lack of consistency" (p. 131) and "inappropriate" and "remote" comparisons (p. 136). "[S]everal redactors may have been involved" in its composition (p. 142).

Rudat, Wolfgang E. H. "Chaucer's *The Parson's Tale*." *Explicator* 42/1 (1983): 6–8.

> The reference to Augustine in X.269 is a misattribution suggestive of the Parson's hesitancy about mentioning Augustine in connection with sexuality.

———. "Pope's *Rape of the Lock* and Chaucer's *Parson's Tale*." *American Notes and Queries* 21 (1982): 7–8.

> Ariel's advice to Belinda to reject Mankind in favor of a Sylph (I, 67–70) alludes parodically to the ParsT discussion of chastity in X.944–50.

———. *Earnest Exuberance in Chaucer's Poetics*. Lewiston, N.Y.: Edwin Mellen Press, 1993. Pp. 68–78, pp. 241–44.

> Chaucer mocks the Parson's unsuccessful struggle to express Augustinian views of sexuality as indicative of the Parson's inability to control his own sexual impulses.

Ruggiers, Paul G. "Serious Chaucer: The *Tale of Melibeus* and the Parson's Tale." In *Chaucerian Problems and Perspectives: Essays Presented to Paul E. Beichner, C.S.C.* Edited by Edward Vasta and Zacharias P. Thundy. Notre Dame, Ind.: University of Notre Dame Press, 1979. Pp. 83–94.

> Sees a Dantesque Chaucer who makes "materials generally inimical to poetry . . . the foundation stones on which the whole poem is built" (p. 93). Functioning in relation to *CT* the way smaller moral statements

work in relation to individual tales, Mel and ParsT are "peak statements in the more overtly serious and didactic aspects of the 'plot' of the *Canterbury Tales*," indicating the medieval norms "against which to view the tales" (p. 85). Mel deals "with the correction of the intelligence and the use of counsels in this world" (p. 86). ParsT treats "the corrections of the will" (p. 86) and announces salvation as the theme of *CT* (p. 89), demanding in the priest "a range of knowledge encompassing the whole of life" (p. 92).

Sadlek, Gregory M. "The Image of the Devil's Five Fingers in the *South English Legendary*'s 'St. Michael' and in Chaucer's Parson's Tale." In *The South English Legendary: A Critical Assessment*. Edited by Klaus P. Janofsky. Tübingen: Francke Verlag, 1992. Pp. 49–64.

In contrast to the usual association of the hand and fingers with God, Chaucer (drawing on Peraldus) and the author of the *SEL* refer to the devil's fingers. Chaucer's "sophisticated and dramatic" association of "the devil's fingers with the *gradus amoris*," further enhanced by "enlivening metaphor" (pp. 54–56), is not in Peraldus.

Sanderlin, George. "Quotations from St. Bernard in 'The Parson's Tale'." *Modern Language Notes* 54 (1939): 447–48.

X.256–59 is drawn from Bernard's "In Feria IV Hebdomadae Sanctae, Sermo," para. 11; X.690 from "Epistola seu Tractatus ad Fratres de Monte Dei," chap. VIII, para. 23, formerly attributed to Bernard.

Scanlon, Larry. *Narrative, Authority, and Power: The Medieval Exemplum and the Chaucerian Tradition*. Cambridge: Cambridge University Press, 1994. Pp. 3–26.

ParsT represents an "authorization" of Chaucer's voice "so implicit it has gone unnoticed" (p. 13), offering "a systematic exposition of doctrine which at once rounds out the Parson as a moral ideal and asserts Chaucer's own right as a lay poet to establish such ideals" (pp. 13–14). The closure of the ParsT is produced within the narratives of the *CT* and not imposed by external authority; thus this overtly exemplary tale— "the first extant penitential manual in English to be compiled by a non-cleric" (p. 14)—is a lay writer's "appropriation of clerical authority rather than a capitulation to it" (p. 7).

Schlauch, Margaret. "Chaucer's Prose Rhythms." *PMLA* 65 (1950): 568–89.

Examines the theory of medieval prose style as it relates to Chaucer, considering the idea of *cursus*, the relation of Latin rules to English practice, Chaucer's own awareness of such rules, and specific differences between Middle English and Latin. Analysis of the metrics of selected passages from Chaucer's prose texts indicates that Chaucer adapted traditional forms to English usage.

———. "The Art of Chaucer's Prose." In *Chaucer and Chaucerians: Critical Studies in Middle English Literature.* Edited by D. S. Brewer. London: Nelson, 1966. Pp. 140–63.

Examines the levels of diction in Chaucer's prose compositions, distinguishing "the plain style of scientific exposition" (p. 143) in Astr, "the heightened style of homiletic discourse" (p. 148) in ParsT, "eloquent style" (p. 153) in Mel, and "rhythmical prose" (p. 156) in Bo.

Schmidt, A. V. C. "Chaucer's 'Philosophre': A Note on 'The Parson's Tale', 534–7." *Notes and Queries* 213 (1968): 327–28.

A possible source for the reference to ire in X.534–37 is Aristotle's *De anima*, Book 1, chap. 1, lines 24–29.

Shain, Charles E. "Pulpit Rhetoric in Three Canterbury Tales." *Modern Language Notes* 70 (1955): 235–45.

ParsT "cannot be called a sermon" (p. 236). Its "true genre . . . is the religious manual" (p. 237).

Shaw, Judith. "Corporeal and Spiritual Homicide, the Sin of Wrath, and the 'Parson's Tale'." *Traditio* 38 (1982): 281–300.

Examines treatments of corporeal homicide, spiritual homicide, and wrath in the writing of canonists and in vernacular penitential and catechetical manuals. The confused lines X.564–79 reflect both traditions.

————. "Wrath in the Canterbury Pilgrims." *English Language Notes* 21/3 (1984): 7–10.

> Ire, as displayed by the Reeve and Friar John and discussed in X.537–43, is akin to spiritual homicide.

Shimagosa, Tokuji. "Chaucer's Colloquial Style in *The Parson's Tale*." *Era*, n.s., 2 (1981): 46–61.

> Unavailable.

————. "Chaucer's Parallelism in *The Parson's Tale*." *Bulletin of Yamaguchi Women's University* (1982): 11–27.

> Unavailable.

Simon, Hugo. "Chaucer a Wicliffite: An Essay on Chaucer's Parson and *Parson's Tale*." *Essays on Chaucer*, Part 3. Chaucer Society, 2nd series, no. 16 (London, 1876). Pp. 227–92.

> A Wycliffite, Chaucer wrote only those parts of ParsT congenial with Lollardry. More Catholic sections later were interpolated into his treatise on penitence.

Slaughter, Eugene Edward. *Love and the Virtues and Vices in Chaucer*. Nashville: The Joint University Libraries, 1946.

> Condensed dissertation classifies different views on the virtues and vices, then notes their appearance in Chaucer's works. The full-page listing for ParsT is the book's longest (pp. 27–28).

Smith, Esther M. G. "'And Was a Povre Persoun of a Toun'." In *Chaucer's Pilgrims: An Historical Guide to the Pilgrims in* The Canterbury Tales. Edited by Laura C. Lambdin and Robert T. Lambdin. Westport, Conn.: Greenwood Press, 1996. Pp. 256–62.

> Parson reflects various ideals of Wycliffite reformers. ParsT is a treatise in the manner of William of Pagula's *Oculus sacerdotis*.

Spies, Heinrich. "Chaucer's religiöse Grundstimmung und die Echtheit der Parson's Tale: Eine textkritische Untersuchung." *Festschrift für Lorenz Morsbach*. Edited by F. Holthausen and H. Spies. Studien zur Englischen Philologie, vol. 50. Halle, 1913. Pp. 626–721.

> Affirms Chaucer's authorship of ParsT, with the discussion of the sins and remedies antedating the framing discussion of penance.

Stone, Brian. *Chaucer: A Critical Study*. Harmondsworth: Penguin, 1987. 118–20.

> ParsT responds to the question implied in the passage from Jeremiah 6.16 with which it opens, with "Thou shalt not" the principal motto of this "forbidding reading" (p. 119).

Strohm, Paul. *Social Chaucer*. Cambridge, Mass.: Harvard University Press, 1989. Pp. 174–81.

> ParsT upholds traditional church authority, promoting a vertical clerical and lay hierarchical model very much opposed to "the horizontal world of new social arrangements" (p. 178) characteristic of *CT*. A self-contained monologue and as such opposed to the polyphony of a multi-voiced, unfinished *CT*, ParsT asserts finality, but its monovocality cannot close the "discursive space within which various conceptions of social reality can coexist" (p. 181).

Swanson, Robert N. "Chaucer's Parson and Other Priests." *Studies in the Age of Chaucer* 13 (1991): 41–80.

> Examines what is known about fourteenth-century parsons and their parishes, duties, education, election, income, and patronage, measuring this (in a necessarily limited way as a consequence of the paucity of information offered in *CT*) against Chaucer's Parson.

Taylor, Paul Beekman. *Chaucer's Chain of Love*. Madison, N.J.: Fairleigh Dickinson University Press, 1996. Pp. 138–44.

> Balancing the springtime "*reverdie*" of GP (p. 139), ParsT "is a *tertium quid* between the jesting seasonal entertainment along the road and the

earnest spiritual feast at its end," rehabilitating the "word as reflector of thought and informer of deed" (p. 141).

————. "The Parson's Amyable Tongue." *English Studies* 64 (1983): 401–09.

Examines Parson's statements regarding language, most especially the relationship between sins of the tongue and repentance. Parson argues for "the rejoining of intent, word, and deed" (p. 402) in the service of a generous, forgiving God.

Thundy, Zacharias. "Chaucer's Quest for Wisdom in *The Canterbury Tales.*" *Neuphilologische Mitteilungen* 77 (1976): 582–98.

CT exhibits "a progressive movement from the tragic rational wisdom of *The Knight's Tale* to the complementary function of revelation emphasized in *The Parson's Tale*" (p. 582). Thus a key structuring principle in *CT* is that, viewed allegorically, pilgrimage offers a medium for a quest for wisdom that "begins with reason and philosophy and ends in revelation and religion" (p. 585).

Tupper, Frederick. "Chaucer and the Seven Deadly Sins." *PMLA* 29 (1914): 93–128.

Contends that Chaucer reflects Gower in that certain of the *CT* were intended as exempla of the Seven Deadly Sins: PhysT-Lechery; PardT-Avarice & Gluttony; SNT-Idleness; WBT-Pride; MancT-Wrath; MLT-Envy. This view in confirmed by "the close connection between these [tales] and Chaucer's own detailed discussion of the Sins in . . . the Parson's sermon" (p. 114).

————. "Chaucer's Bed's Head." *Modern Language Notes* 30 (1915): 5–12.

Dan Jon Gaytringe's fourteenth-century "Sermon on Shrift" offers an interesting parallel to ParsT. Both sermons voice to a lay audience "the commonplaces of the fourteenth-century Confessional" (pp. 11–12).

————. "Chaucer's Sinners and Sins." *Journal of English and Germanic Philology* 15 (1916): 56–106.

Reaffirms his thesis in the face of Lowes's attack, noting that "Interpretation is largely a study of emphasis" and that it is in their understanding of where "the artist lay[s] his stress" that he and Lowes "are hopelessly at odds" (p. 57).

Volk-Birke, Sabine. *Chaucer and Medieval Preaching: Rhetoric for Listeners in Sermons and Poetry*. Tübingen: Gunter Narr Verlag, 1991. Pp. 193–227.

Close examination of ParsT and contemporary sermon literature in terms of (1) the interaction of speaker with audience, (2) use of formulas, (3) structural organization (presented in skeletal form in a chart on p. 208), (4) narrativity, (5) characteristic syntactic patterns, and (6) use of rhetorical figures indicate that "there is no fundamental difference or contradiction between preaching techniques in late fourteenth century England and the Parson's way of teaching penance" (pp. 221–22). The form of ParsT is not that of a manual for confessors (Pfander and Donaldson), nor is the tale more obviously a manual for penitents (Patterson and Pantin) than it is a sermon. While it is obvious that Chaucer relied on penitential manuals and treatises in composing ParsT, "it is equally obvious that the sermons which his contemporaries heard could also deal with similar material in similar ways and that the preaching techniques of his time left their mark on the *Parson's Tale*" (p. 227).

Wall, John. "Penance as Poetry in the Late Fourteenth Century." In *Medieval English Religious and Ethical Literature: Essays in Honour of G. H. Russell*. Edited by Gregory Kratzmann and James Simpson. Cambridge: D. S. Brewer, 1986. Pp. 179–91.

Penance is a crucial theme in the work of the three principal poets of late-fourteenth-century England: the *Pearl*-poet, Langland, and Chaucer. Like *Piers Plowman*, *CT* "begins with the vision of the field and ends with the shout after Conscience." Standing at the end of *CT*, ParsT figures the world of the poem as one "where, although (as in Langland's work) Redemption has definitively taken place already in Christ's death and resurrection, salvation has yet to be worked out in successive ages and individuals." The placement of ParsT thus encourages the distinctly penitential task of shaping and judging the tales "so that the inherent integrity of God's creation announced in the General Prologue may be realised" (p. 189).

Wenzel, Siegfried. "Chaucer and the Language of Contemporary Preaching." *Studies in Philology* 73 (1976): 138–61.

Questions whether Chaucer drew on the language of contemporary preaching to create a sermon-like structure for his own preachers' tales, arguing instead that Chaucer shared story plots, certain images, and the terminology of "techniques and devices commonly used in late medieval popular preaching" (p. 151). Considers in particular the meaning of the noun *knot* and the verb *to knit* as they relate to contemporary sermon literature (pp. 155–61).

———. "Chaucer's Parson's Tale: 'Every Tales Strengthe'." In *Europäische Lehrdichtung: Festschrift für Walter Naumann zum 70. Geburtstag*. Edited by Hans Gerd Rötzer and Herbert Walz. Darmstadt: Wissenschaftliche Buchgesellschaft, 1981. Pp. 86–98.

Argues that ParsPro carefully introduces a tale set apart from those which have preceded it and will present "not just another aspect of reality and human behavior, but a higher one" (p. 97). Marking this change are Chaucer's insistence that the ensuing tale "is to be the last and will conclude the poem" (p. 91); his repeated use of the image of "knitting up," a key term in contemporary preaching discourse; the deliberate rhetorical weighting in the use of astronomical language at the opening of ParsPro; and the "remarkable" scene in which the role of guide is transferred from Harry Bailly to the Parson (pp. 93–94).

———. "Notes on the *Parson's Tale*." *Chaucer Review* 16 (1982): 237–56.

Observes individual words, passages and topics, and the larger matters of ParsT genre and tone to show that these units "carry ideas, images, or expressions that were current" in contemporary penitential literature of the type of ParsT (p. 237). Notes that in his choice of a key image "Chaucer replaces Pennaforte's three-day journeys with the Tree of Penance," an image he may have found in the Anglo-Norman *Compileison* (p. 241). Argues that "the opening of [ParsT] is patently different from that of a formal sermon; rather, it follows exactly the patterns utilized in a large number of contemporary penitential handbooks" (p. 249).

————. "The Source for the 'Remedia' of the Parson's Tale." *Traditio* 27 (1971): 433–53.

Juxtaposes passages from ParsT and sections from a newly examined text, *Postquam*, which "furnish precise parallels to the *Remedia* of the the Parson's Tale" (p. 436).

————. "The Source of Chaucer's Seven Deadly Sins." *Traditio* 30 (1974): 351–78.

Juxtaposes passages from ParsT, passages from Peraldus's *Summa de vitiis*, and passages from two closely related treatises on the vices, *Primo* and *Quoniam* (both derived from Peraldus), which "are certainly the closest models [to Chaucer's discussion of the Seven Deadly Sins] we have so far discovered" (p. 378). The deviation of ParsT from *Quoniam/Primo* may indicate a still closer source or may indicate that "Chaucer himself took a modest part in the process of adapting Peraldus" (p. 377).

Whittock, Trevor. *A Reading of the Canterbury Tales*. Cambridge: Cambridge University Press, 1968. Pp. 280–99.

Argues for the appropriateness of ending the pilgrimage with the Parson's spiritual voice. All the tales are meant to be read "against a divine background," as insights into each pilgrim's "spiritual condition." Distinguishing Chaucer are his extraordinary "compassion and wisdom": the "infinite sympathy, undeceived patience, rigour of judgement, and . . . benign forgiveness" of his stance (p. 293). This does not necessarily privilege ParsT, however: ParsT presents "the received guidance of the Church" (p. 296), but like the other tales, it should be read in the context of "Chaucer's own multidimensional ambiguity" (p. 295). Includes a full outline of "the main branches and sub-divisions" of ParsT (pp. 286–90).

Windeatt, Barry. "Literary Structures in Chaucer." In *The Cambridge Chaucer Companion*. Edited by Piero Boitani and Jill Mann. Cambridge: Cambridge University Press, 1986. Pp. 195–212.

> Examines the larger structures of *CT* and Chaucer's other poems: lengthy prologues, framed stories, interpolated commentaries, paired tales, closed and unclosed tales. The spiritually directed closure of ParsT is distinctive: "the placing of the *Parson's Tale* at the conclusion of the *Canterbury Tales* must be an ending to all endings, an absolute ending, for it ends with the absolute, with that truth which is our ultimate end" (p. 209).

Witlieb, Bernard L. "Chaucer and the 'Ovide Moralisé'." *Notes and Queries* 215 (1970): 202–07.

> Parallels to the discussion of reason and sensuality in X.261–62 and X.275 are found in the story of Orpheus in the *Ovide moralisé*.

Wood, Chauncey. "Artistic Intention and Chaucer's Uses of Scriptural Allusion." In *Chaucer and Scriptural Tradition*. Edited by David Lyle Jeffrey. Ottawa: University of Ottawa Press, 1984. Pp. 35–46.

> The reference to Jeremiah that opens ParsT is Chaucer's most explicit scriptural allusion, glossed with his own "clearly typological exegesis" (p. 36). Chaucer's less overt and explicit scriptural allusions elsewhere in *CT* put more strain on a reader.

———. *Chaucer and the Country of the Stars: Poetic Uses of Astrological Imagery*. Princeton: Princeton University Press, 1970. Pp. 272–97.

> The astronomical image in ParsPro recalls those in Intro to MLT and NPT, and the reference to Libra balances the reference to Aries in GP. Libra suggests divine judgment tempered by mercy, as "made possible by Christ's sacrifice on the cross" (p. 286).

————. "Chaucer's Most 'Gowerian' Tale." In *Chaucer and Gower: Difference, Mutuality, Exchange*. Edited by R. F. Yeager. Victoria, B. C.: University of Victoria, 1991. Pp. 75–84.

> The role of ParsT is to render the entire *CT* Gowerian, such that the tale's presence "is in one sense a continuation of the homage Chaucer had already paid to Gower by dedicating the *Troilus* to him" (p. 77). Yet ParsT is also non-Gowerian in its emphasis on penance, which Gower neglects in favor of self-change.

————. "Speech, the Principle of Contraries, and Chaucer's Tales of the Manciple and the Parson." *Mediaevalia* 6 (1980): 209–29.

> The medieval principle of contraries found in Augustine, Boethius, and Jean de Meun is adopted by Chaucer in his juxtaposition of opposing tales. ParsT and MancT are paired as examples of the proper and improper uses of speech.

Work, James A. "Chaucer's Sermon and Retractations." *Modern Language Notes* 47 (1932): 257–59.

> The casualness of the reference to *CT* in Retr along with Retr's verbal linkage to ParsT would support Manly's contention that these works were not intended by Chaucer to be included in *CT*.

————. "The Position of the Tales of the Manciple and the Parson on Chaucer's Canterbury Pilgrimage." *Journal of English and Germanic Philology* 35 (1936): 62–65.

> Argues, against Root and ten Brink, that MancT and ParsT are the closing tales of a one-way journey to Canterbury, not the opening and closing tales of a return trip to Southwark.

Wurtele, Douglas J. "The Anti-Lollardry of Chaucer's Parson." *Mediaevalia* 11 (1985): 151–68.

> A close look at the doctrinal independence of the language in ParsT suggests, against Simon and others who call the Parson a Wycliffite, that the "Parson is meant to stand as the best of the zealous, orthodox

priests" (p. 161), whose standards, were they followed, would render Wycliff's criticism irrelevant.

————. "The Penitence of Geoffrey Chaucer." *Viator* 11 (1980): 335–59. Retr as it appears in the manuscripts contains an interpolation, apparently added by Chaucer himself or at his request. Lines X.1081–84 and 1090b–92 originally concluded ParsT. Lines 1085–90a were interposed along with the rubric separating line 1081 from ParsT to form a retraction on the order of Augustine, namely an effort to note the writer's errors so as to avoid misleading others. This reading lends credence to Gascoigne's fifteenth-century report of Chaucer's deathbed repentance.

CONTRIBUTORS

JUDITH FERSTER (Ph.D., Brown University) is Professor of English at North Carolina State University. Her first book was *Chaucer on Medieval Interpretation* (1985); her second, *Fictions of Advice: The Literature and Politics of Counsel in Late Medieval England* (1996), contains a chapter on Chaucer's Tale of Melibee.

CHARLOTTE GROSS (Ph.D., Columbia University) is Associate Professor of English at North Carolina State University. She has published essays on medieval philosophy, troubadour lyric, and the *Pearl*-poet and is currently working on a study of time in medieval thought.

LINDA TARTE HOLLEY (Ph.D., Tulane University) is Professor of English at North Carolina State University. She is the author of *Chaucer's Measuring Eye* (1990) and has published articles on Chaucer in *The Chaucer Review* and *Parergon*.

PEGGY KNAPP (Ph.D., University of Pittsburgh) is Professor of English at Carnegie Mellon University. She founded and edited *Assays: Critical Approaches to Medieval and Renaissance Texts* and has written for such journals as *PMLA, ELH, College English*, and *The Chaucer Review*. Her books include *Chaucer and the Social Contest* (1990) and *Time Bound Words: Semantic and Social Economies from Chaucer's England to Shakespeare's* (forthcoming).

RICHARD NEWHAUSER (Ph.D., University of Pennsylvania) is Professor of English and Chair of the Medieval Studies Program, Trinity University, San Antonio, Texas. He is co-editor of *Literature and Religion in the Later Middle Ages: Philological Studies in Honor of Siegfried Wenzel* (1951), a field editor for *The Chaucer Encyclopedia*, and a member of the editorial board of *Arthuriana*. His most recent publications include *A Catalogue of Latin Texts with Material on the Vices and Virtues in Manuscripts in Hungary* (1996), *The Treatise on Vices and Virtues in Latin and the Vernacular* (1993), and articles in *Companion to the Gawain-Poet*, *Lexikon des Mittelalters*, and *Studies in Philology*.

DANIEL J. RANSOM (Ph.D., Cornell University) is Associate Professor of English at the University of Oklahoma and Director of *The Variorum Chaucer*. His published work includes *Poets at Play: Irony and Parody in the Harley Lyrics* (1985) and the Textual Commentary and Notes in the Variorum edition of Chaucer's General Prologue (1993). Currently he is editing the *Chaucer Encyclopedia*, a work undertaken with Paul G. Ruggiers.

DAVID RAYBIN (Ph.D., Columbia University) is Professor of English at Eastern Illinois University. He is co-editor of *Rebels and Rivals: The Contestive Spirit in The Canterbury Tales* (1991). His publications on Chaucer include articles in *The Chaucer Review*, *JEGP*, and *Studies in the Age of Chaucer*.

GREGORY ROPER (Ph.D., University of Virginia) is Associate Professor of English at Northwest Missouri State University. He has had articles published in *The Chaucer Review* and *Poetica* dealing with medieval penance, *Pearl*, and the Middle English lyrics. He is currently working on a textbook that combines insights in composition studies with medieval notions of *imitatio*.

SIEGFRIED WENZEL (Ph.D., Ohio State University) has taught at the University of North Carolina and at the University of Pennsylvania. He has contributed materials on The Parson's Tale for *The Riverside Chaucer*. His scholarly works on The Parson's Tale have been published in *Studies in Philology*, *The Chaucer Review*, *Traditio*, and *Europäische Lehrdichtung: Festschrift für Walter Naumann zum 70. Geburtstag*.

INDEX